Praise
To End a Presidency

"Mr. Tribe and Mr. Matz have written a powerful, clear and even-handed guide to the legal and political aspects of impeachment . . . [an] enlightening book. It is the definitive treatment of a vital subject and will remain so long after this presidency."

—*Economist*

"A learned, judicious, and surprisingly cautious study of the impeachment power. . . . The clear-eyed and clear-thinking message of *To End a Presidency* deserves the widest audience. It is an aspirin to cool a political fever, and a hopeful summons to defend an imperiled democracy with a renewed and enlarged commitment to democratic action."

—*Atlantic*

"Brilliant. . . . In their terrific, accessible, and thoughtful new book, *To End a Presidency: The Power of Impeachment,* the Harvard law professor Laurence Tribe and the constitutional lawyer Joshua Matz do better than offering a simple yes or no: they give us a framework for thinking about the question. . . . To their great credit, Tribe and Matz didn't write a legal brief or a political strategy memo. They instead make clear to anyone even contemplating impeachment that the decision to end a presidency isn't simple or straightforward."

—*Guardian*

"Impeachment is a fearsome power. This bracing, restrained, and fiercely judicious account of the process's origins and purpose explains why no U.S. president has ever been removed from office by impeachment, and what it might mean if one were."

—Jill Lepore, author of *These Truths: A History of the United States*

"'Impeachment is neither a magic wand nor a doomsday device.' So write Laurence Tribe and Joshua Matz in this deeply informed, even-handed look at how a president can be impeached and what the consequences would be. This book is essential reading for anyone who cares about the future of our democracy in the Age of Trump."

—Max Boot, senior fellow, Council on Foreign Relations, and bestselling author of *The Road Not Taken*

"The most important book on impeachment in decades."

—Jennifer Rubin, *Washington Post* "Right Turn"

"Very few books are accessible to a wide audience of lay people and experts, written compellingly and reading easily, while also having depth, insight, and deep scholarship. *To End a Presidency* is one of the rare ones. Laurence Tribe and Joshua Matz have given us a thorough, lively history of presidential impeachment, enriched with strong legal and political analysis, fair-minded and thoughtful without being bland. This is an important, timely, and extraordinarily useful book at a critical time in American politics."

—Norman Ornstein, resident scholar, American Enterprise Institute and coauthor of *One Nation after Trump: A Guide for the Perplexed, the Disillusioned, the Desperate, and the Not-Yet-Deported*

"Laurence Tribe and Joshua Matz have produced the single best overview ever written of the impeachment process. At a time when Americans both in the public and in government are hungry for a comprehensive and deep analysis of the subject, they have provided it. It is indispensable for our generation and for future ones to come."

—Norman L. Eisen, chair and cofounder, Citizens for Responsibility and Ethics in Washington

"This is the definitive book on how to end a national nightmare. No dubious constitutional theories, just real law, real procedures, and real ideas for moving forward. Where Special Counsel Robert Mueller leaves off this book will pick up. The real deal."

—Richard W. Painter, S. Walter Richey Professor of Corporate Law, University of Minnesota Law School, and chief ethics counsel for President George W. Bush

"This is a spectacular book. It is essential, riveting reading for anyone trying to make sense of the impeachment question as citizens—or as members of Congress. Laurence Tribe and Joshua Matz have a special knack for logical and historical clarity, and *To End a Presidency* left me not only knowing more, but also thinking better."

—Zephyr Teachout, author of *Corruption in America*

"Their intelligent and informative book insists that impeachment is an awkward weapon, one that can't be 'readily fired twice during a single presidency,' and that holds no magic bullet for the problems of American democracy—useful reminders for #Resistance enthusiasts and Never Trumpers alike." —*Weekly Standard*

"A comprehensive, restrained, and indispensable resource on the powers and limits of impeachment . . . an eminently comprehensible, thorough legal, historical, and political text, a *must-read* guide for navigating the choppy and turbulent waters facing President Trump and the country in the days ahead."

—*Jewish Week*

"With wisdom and lucidity, they explain the origins of impeachment in the U.S. Constitution, exactly how it works, and what criteria should be used in evaluating whether impeachment is called for." —*Washington Times*

"[A] sobering dive into the reality of the process, as dictated by the framers and as executed by lawmakers. It is thorough, intriguing, often entertaining, and unfortunately necessary."

—WhoWhatWhy

"Tribe and Matz provide a fair, balanced, and relevant examination of an often misunderstood function of our national government."

—*Booklist*

TO END A
PRESIDENCY

THE POWER OF IMPEACHMENT

LAURENCE TRIBE
and JOSHUA MATZ

BASIC BOOKS
New York

Basic Books
Hachette Book Group
1290 Avenue of the Americas, New York, NY 10104
www.basicbooks.com

Printed in the United States of America

Originally published in hardcover and ebook by Basic Books in May 2018
First Trade Paperback Edition: March 2019

Published by Basic Books, an imprint of Perseus Books, LLC, a subsidiary of Hachette Book Group, Inc. The Basic Books name and logo is a trademark of the Hachette Book Group.

The Hachette Speakers Bureau provides a wide range of authors for speaking events. To find out more, go to www.hachettespeakersbureau.com or call (866) 376-6591.

The publisher is not responsible for websites (or their content) that are not owned by the publisher.

Library of Congress Cataloging-in-Publication Data

Names: Tribe, Laurence H., author. | Matz, Joshua, author.
Title: To end a presidency : the power of impeachment / Laurence Tribe,
    Joshua Matz.
Description: New York, NY : Basic Books, 2018.
Identifiers: LCCN 2018010873 (print) | LCCN 2018011754 (ebook) | ISBN
    9781541644878 (ebook) | ISBN 9781541644885 (hardback)
Subjects: LCSH: Impeachments—United States. | President—Legal status, laws,
    etc.—United States. | United States—Politics and government—1989- |
    BISAC: LAW / Constitutional. | POLITICAL SCIENCE / Constitutions. |
    POLITICAL SCIENCE / Government / Legislative Branch. | POLITICAL SCIENCE /
    Government / Executive Branch. | LAW / Government / Federal.
Classification: LCC KF5075 (ebook) | LCC KF5075 .T75 2018 (print) | DDC
    342.73/062—dc23
LC record available at https://lccn.loc.gov/2018010873

ISBNs: 978-1-5416-4488-5 (hardcover), 978-1-5416-4487-8 (ebook),
978-1-5416-4489-2 (paperback)

LSC-C

10 9 8 7 6 5 4 3 2 1

For our partners, Elizabeth and Hillel

CONTENTS

PREFACE

Impeachment haunts Trumpland. Never before has an American leader so quickly faced such credible, widespread calls for his removal. By early 2018, the list of alleged "high Crimes and Misdemeanors" included abuse of the pardon power, obstruction of justice, assaults on the free press, promotion of violence against racial and religious minorities, receipt of unlawful emoluments, deliberate refusal to protect the nation from cyberattacks, and corrupt dealings relating to Russia. President Donald J. Trump fueled these fires by rejecting bipartisan norms of presidential conduct and by ferociously attacking anyone who dared to challenge him. Reeling from this onslaught, the American public has fractured. Some warn that Trump is moving us inexorably toward tyranny and global war. Others have circled their wagons, convinced that Trump is uniquely capable of saving the United States—if only political elites will let him. A dwindling group of fence-sitters finds itself besieged on all sides. Calls for Trump's impeachment, and indignant rebukes of those calls, echo everywhere from TV screens and editorials to Facebook comments and Twitter feeds.

It's now clear that as long as Trump holds the nation's highest office, Americans will actively debate his impeachment. Indeed, as we write this book, over 40 percent of the US electorate supports action to force Trump from power. Roughly 30 percent of voters, in contrast, would view impeachment proceedings as a coup in disguise. In these stormy waters, it is entirely possible that impeachment investigations will already have begun when this book is published. That's an extraordinary disclaimer to include less than halfway through a presidential term. But since Trump took office in January 2017, "extraordinary" has become the new normal.

Of course, that story is much larger than events in the Oval Office. These are angry, anxious times. Tempers run high on TV and social media, fueled by the chattering class and a booming outrage industry. Sharp partisan divisions poison US politics, and the government frequently struggles to govern. We've seen a sharp rise in hate crimes, economic inequality, drug addiction, and social conflict. We've also witnessed steps toward the unraveling of a liberal international order, including triumphs by right-wing extremists abroad. An unyielding sense of crisis has gripped much of the nation, centered on Trump but swirling outward into every corner of the polity. Democracy itself feels threatened by enemies foreign and domestic. Many now count Trump among those enemies, though millions still view him as the nation's long-awaited savior.

This combination of political polarization, incendiary rhetoric, and widespread anxiety has yielded a highly unstable climate in which to debate impeachment. It's therefore important that the American people develop a shared, well-grounded understanding of impeachment's role in the US constitutional order. We need a baseline for reasoned discussion and disagreement. That calls for cool and evenhanded reflection, informed by the Constitution and lessons from history. It also requires nuance, rather than absolutes, and the capacity to look beyond reflexive partisan loyalties. Impeachment is not just another form of political combat; it's an emergency measure meant to save the democratic foundation on which all other politics unfold.

In approaching this issue, we must aim to strike a balance. Intense disagreements and the pressures of partisan hostility can lead people who lose an election to view the victor as an existential threat. Over the past twenty years, the switch from "electoral loser" to "impeachment supporter" has occurred faster—and on a larger scale—than at any previous point in US history. But sore losers are often matched by self-righteous winners. Especially when the other side has cried wolf many times before, a president's base can too quickly ignore well-founded fears of tyranny and corruption. A premise of the impeachment power is that leaders may disappoint our expectations in the most tragic and destructive ways. It's therefore essential to resist both of these attitudes toward impeachment. The specter of a banana republic lurks at either extreme.

While casual calls for #impeachment now litter the Internet, ending a presidency this way remains a *very big deal*. It's easy to forget that the United States has never actually impeached and removed a president. Although that was the likely outcome had Richard Nixon remained in office, he resigned before the House of Representatives formally approved articles of impeachment against him. On the two occasions that the House did impeach a president—Andrew Johnson and Bill Clinton—the Senate ultimately acquitted, albeit in Johnson's case by only a single vote. We therefore have no historical experience with the full consequences of pushing that red button. Instead, we've generally relied on presidential term limits, the forces of civil society, federalism, and checks and balances to mitigate the damage inflicted by terrible leaders.

There can be little doubt that a successful impeachment campaign would inflict enduring national trauma. For months or years, politics would shift from ordinary governance toward a grand inquest into the president's alleged evil deeds. With the highest conceivable stakes, political interests and factions on every side would hold nothing back. The resulting enmities, cynicism, and disenchantment with democracy could persist for generations. Throughout the impeachment struggle, moreover, the United States would appear vulnerable to its enemies and unreliable to its allies. An embattled president—or his opponents—might engage in acts of desperation that shatter norms, institutions, and the rule of law. And once removed, the ex-president may not go quietly into the night. The would-be tyrant and his remaining supporters, estranged from our national community, might disavow or seek to destroy American democracy.

That's not to say we should never end a presidency through the impeachment power. Faced with a disastrously corrupt or abusive executive, doing nothing may be far riskier than attempting to oust him. As journalist Ezra Klein notes, we must not be "too afraid of the consequences of impeachment and too complacent about the consequences of leaving an unfit president in office."[1] Especially in this era of a powerful chief executive and decreasingly effective checks on his power, thwarting a tyrant may be worth almost any price. Even then, however, the country would face a terrible choice and a rocky path forward. While an impeachment campaign might rally the public against a threat to liberty, it could also promote division and disunion.

Accordingly, in responsible discussions about ending a presidency, there are three vital questions to ask. First, has the president engaged in conduct that authorizes his removal under the standard set forth in the Constitution? Second, as a matter of political reality, is the effort to remove the president likely to succeed in the House and then in the Senate? And third, is it genuinely necessary to resort to the impeachment power, recognizing that the resulting collateral damage will likely be significant?

Put differently: (1) Is removal *permissible*, (2) Is removal *likely to succeed*, and (3) Is removal *worth the price the nation will pay*?

Anybody who favors impeaching a president should be able to explain why all three of these considerations support that decision. Unfortunately, much writing on impeachment comes up short. More often than not, writers adopt what we call the "Roman Coliseum" style of impeachment analysis. In ancient Rome, crowds passed judgment on defeated gladiators by voting thumbs-up (spare him) or thumbs-down (kill him). This was a yes-or-no determination that occurred in a single moment and in response to a single event. In pronouncing its sentence, the crowd didn't have to reckon with any continuing consequences in the wider world.

We're willing to wager that you have seen a few hundred articles that fit the Roman Coliseum formula: an account of some specific misdeed allegedly committed by the president; a sprinkling of nonspecific quotes by Framers of the Constitution; and then a solemn thumbs-up or -down on whether the president must immediately be impeached. On a rare occasion, the author might glancingly concede the wisdom of awaiting further investigation. And that's it. The president has (or has not) committed alleged "high Crimes and Misdemeanors," and therefore he must (or must not) be removed. Arguments about expelling the most powerful leader in the world from office are presented in a simple, one-step analysis.

As you can probably tell, we're not fans of the Roman Coliseum style. You shouldn't be, either. It's quick and easy—and totally inadequate. Often it treats as the *only* question what should really be the first of *many* questions: whether the president may have committed an impeachable offense.

We've written this book to offer a more comprehensive, realistic, and pragmatic view of ending a presidency. Rising above the daily clamor, we map out and address the big questions presented by any impeachment. Along the way, we explore how the impeachment power has shaped (and been shaped by) the broader architecture of our legal and political systems. Many of the issues that we cover have previously received shockingly little attention. And when we arrive at more familiar terrain, such as the definition of impeachable offenses, we show that there's more to the story than conventional wisdom suggests.

Our approach has been heavily influenced by the recognition that an impeachment is a dynamic undertaking that unfolds over months or years. Unlike a verdict in the Roman Coliseum, ending a presidency can't be reduced to a flash-frozen judgment in which Congress votes yea or nay on particular "high Crimes" and then Americans all get on with their lives. We take seriously the fraught political path toward impeachment; the intricacies of prosecuting, defending, and adjudicating an impeachment case;

and the importance of anticipating and seeking to minimize disruptive consequences that may follow. We also highlight the many decision makers involved and the many decision points they face. With these issues in mind, suspicion of "high Crimes and Misdemeanors" is revealed as just the tip of the iceberg. The public must therefore think panoramically to determine whether impeaching a president would be wise—and to decide how best to pursue or oppose an impeachment campaign.

That perspective underlies this book. It led us to divide our inquiry into six parts.

In Chapter 1, we begin at the beginning: Why have an impeachment process at all? When the Framers assembled in Philadelphia over the summer of 1787, it was hardly a foregone conclusion that they would embrace the obscure English practice of impeachment. We recount their deliberations to illuminate the original purposes of the impeachment power. We also show how the Framers structured impeachment to harmonize it with rest of their constitutional design. Building on that foundation, we identify several lessons of history concerning the use and abuse of impeachment. That discussion leads us through the contemptible efforts to remove John Tyler (1842) and Bill Clinton (1998) from office, and it concludes with Nixon and the infamous Watergate scandal.

In Chapter 2, we venture into the Roman Coliseum and explain what kind of conduct justifies impeachment. The short answer is easy: "Treason, Bribery, or other high Crimes and Misdemeanors." But unpacking what that means—if it means anything at all—requires a deeper analysis. We give substance to this famously vague phrase by drawing on original understanding, constitutional text and structure, centuries of historical practice, and a dash of common sense. We then explain why it is wrong and harmful to think that only criminal offenses may qualify as "high Crimes and Misdemeanors." We also show why it is appropriate to account for patterns of tyrannical conduct in formulating articles of impeachment. With a working definition in place, we then address several of President Trump's alleged impeachable offenses.

In Chapter 3, we explore a frequently overlooked subject: Congress's discretion in deciding whether to impeach the president when faced with credible evidence that he may have committed "high Crimes and Misdemeanors." There can be no doubt that such discretion exists. The House of Representatives holds the *power* to impeach, not the *duty* to do so. And on many occasions—including the Iran–Contra scandal—Congress has decided against seeking the president's removal when that was a plausible option. After situating this discretion in the Constitution, we discuss the nature and scope of Congress's formidable power *not* to impeach. First, we describe other powers that Congress may invoke to address a rogue president, including censure. Next, we explain how legislators' discretion operates at every step of the impeachment process, from the first hints of wrongdoing to a final vote in the Senate. Finally, we develop a general framework to guide exercises of the impeachment power, identifying a broad array of factors that should inform decisions about whether, when, and how to pursue presidential impeachment.

In Chapter 4, we go deeper into the halls of Congress. We begin by exploring why the Framers vested the impeachment power in the legislature, rather than in the judiciary, and why they split this power between the House and the Senate. We then consider the many implications of that fateful decision. To start, we describe what actually happens in the House and Senate during an impeachment proceeding. Because the Constitution says almost nothing on this topic, Congress's chosen procedures illuminate how it has interpreted its own role. They also demarcate the strange, haphazard, and intensely political minefield that lawyers must navigate when advancing or opposing a case against the president. Based on this discussion of process, we consider the values and principles that *should* guide Congress in making impeachment decisions. With that idealized account in hand, we then discuss the wide array of partisan, political, institutional, and other factors that have historically increased the odds that Congress will support impeachment.

In Chapter 5, we offer a broad history of "impeachment talk" throughout the life of the Republic. Beginning with Thomas Jefferson and ending with Donald Trump, this colorful tale covers every impeachment resolution submitted in the House of Representatives. It also captures selected moments in which the American people aggressively debated ending a presidency but nobody initiated formal impeachment proceedings. These stories show the many and creative purposes for which impeachment has been invoked. Viewed together, they also reveal just how unusual our own era is. Impeachment talk has historically been infrequent and marginal in US politics. That held true until late in the twentieth century, notwithstanding spikes under Woodrow Wilson, Harry Truman, and Richard Nixon. But everything changed after the failed attempt to remove Bill Clinton from office. Under George W. Bush, Barack Obama, and Trump, impeachment talk has become a far more significant aspect of US political discourse and strategy. We discuss that development and conclude with a warning: over the long haul, this saturation of our politics with impeachment talk is likely to do more harm than good.

Finally, in Chapter 6, we move from the past to the present and examine impeachment in a world of broken politics. By requiring that a majority of the House of Representatives and two-thirds of the Senate agree, the US Constitution ensures that no impeachment will succeed without durable, bipartisan support. But what happens when polarization, hyperpartisanship, "alternative facts," and other forces of democratic decline make it almost impossible to achieve consensus? We conclude by asking whether the impeachment power can still achieve its underlying purpose in this strange new reality. We also consider calls to invoke the Twenty-Fifth Amendment, which provides a complex process for sidelining the president when he is "unable to discharge the powers and duties of his office." Ultimately, we warn against recent trends toward fantastical, apocalyptic thinking about impeachment. This historical moment calls for a realistic and savvy defense of democracy. Maybe that involves ending a presidency; maybe it doesn't. Either way, in the heat of partisan strife, the public must not lose sight of what is truly at stake: our democracy.

Through all six chapters, we emphasize the constant importance of exercising good judgment in the here and now. That may sound obvious, but a great deal of writing about impeachment implies that the Framers, the Constitution, the criminal code, Congress, or someone else has already made the judgment calls that truly matter. For example, in a generally excellent book about impeachment, Professor Cass Sunstein writes: "[The Framers] knew what they were doing. They threaded a needle. They accomplished a miracle. There's no reason to depart from their understanding of their framework. We can't do better than they did, and if we tried, we would probably do worse."[2] Language like this comes awfully close to misty-eyed Framer worship. It can also be read to suggest—falsely—that our role in the impeachment process amounts to little more than faithfully executing a vision set to holy parchment more than two centuries ago.

Those who wrote the US Constitution were blessed with great insight, but it blinks reality to think that their intent or understanding can answer all of our questions. Since 1789, the world and the Constitution have changed in innumerable ways, and any useful account of impeachment must reckon with those changes. They affect the scope of impeachable offenses, the odds that any impeachment campaign will succeed, and the likely consequences of pursuing (or deciding against) an impeachment. Moreover, any individual impeachment involves innumerable discrete decisions made by many different actors. On most of these issues, the Constitution speaks only in majestic generalities—if it speaks at all. We most faithfully fulfill the Framers' vision when we respect the decisions they made, recognize the decisions they declined to make, and carefully exercise the responsibility they entrusted to us.

Acting responsibly here means recognizing that impeachment is a fearsome power. In principle, ending a presidency this way carries the potential to save or destroy the constitutional system. Because of its extraordinary danger, impeachment should be invoked only under dire circumstances. And even then, it must be handled with care. Every effort should be made to carry out the impeachment process in a manner that brings the country together rather than rending it apart. To be sure, there are times when impeachment is the last, best hope for democracy; faced with abuse and corruption of the highest order, our duty is to act. But striking at the president in a fit of passion—and without a plan for the future—risks exploding all that we're trying to preserve. A well-intentioned effort to save democracy through impeachment could thus tragically backfire—unleashing outrage and aftershocks that exacerbate our system's underlying dysfunctions.

As we'll see, that is one of many paradoxes that afflict discussions of impeachment. This subject is rife with surprising and counter-intuitive dynamics that often pass unnoticed:

- In some cases, well-justified calls to impeach the president can simultaneously empower him, harm his political opponents, and make his removal from office *less* likely.
- When a demagogue gains power by sowing division and confusion, the importance of impeaching him may increase even as the possibility of mustering a consensus to do so diminishes.
- Because removing a truly determined tyrant may unleash havoc, the risks of impeaching a president are apt to be most extreme precisely when ending his tenure is most necessary.
- As a matter of political reality, an impeachment may be most likely to succeed in Congress when other, less extreme measures are also most viable.

To avoid these sand traps, the American people must think strategically about their response to abuse and corruption. Democracy requires vigilant protection against presidential tyranny.

If you're reading this book in 2018, you're probably thinking about Trump. So are we. It's impossible to write about impeachment without confronting a president whom millions regard as a menace to liberty, but whom many others view as their hope for a better life. Our own views on Trump are no secret. We're among the lawyers suing him for accepting illegal emoluments. We've opposed him on many other legal and political fronts, too. It will suffice to say that we both think Trump is an abysmal president and that we're appalled by his conduct in office. When we discuss Trump in relation to impeachment—at the end of Chapters 2 and 5, and in Chapter 6—we pull no punches in our assessment of the damage that he has done to American democracy.

But this book is *not* a brief for removing Trump. It does not reflect partisan talking points, and it does not rely on "liberal" or "conservative" methodologies. Rather, we've undertaken a wide-ranging exploration of law, history, and politics bearing on exercise of the impeachment power. We have sought to identify general principles and frameworks that should govern any impeachment analysis. It is our hope that these ideas serve as a basis for bipartisan discussion in this divisive era. We are confident that our constitutional study will stand the test of time and will remain useful for many years to come. Whether you support or oppose removing Trump from office, we promise that this book will challenge your views and deepen your insight.

* * *

When we began this project, we ordered a copy of the House Judiciary Committee report on the impeachment of Richard M. Nixon. To our surprise, Amazon sent us a copy signed by civil rights legend John Doar, who served as special counsel to the committee.

His signature was dated August 1974, the month Nixon resigned from office, and it was accompanied by an inscription: "The Constitution is well worth fighting for."

This is a book about ending presidencies through the power of impeachment. It's also a book about fighting for the Constitution and the democracy it protects. Whether those are the same thing—or are instead diametrically opposed—is for each of us to decide in our own time.

1
WHY IMPEACHMENT?

If we don't allow presidential impeachment, warned Benjamin Franklin, then the only recourse for abuse of power will be assassination. In Franklin's view, that's what history taught about "cases where the chief Magistrate rendered himself obnoxious." Yet assassination is a deeply flawed and unjust remedy. The victim is "not only deprived of his life but of the opportunity of vindicating his character." Surely it would be better "to provide in the Constitution for the regular punishment of the Executive when his misconduct should deserve it, and for his honorable acquittal when he should be unjustly accused."[1]

Franklin made this plea to the Constitutional Convention on July 20, 1787. By then, the Framers had already begun designing the office of the presidency. Although we now take many features of that office for granted, nearly everything was up for grabs at the Convention. Disagreements ran deep. What powers should be vested in the executive branch? Should the chief executive be one person or several? How should the chief executive be selected, how long should his term in office last, and should there be limits on running for reelection? Also, what should we call this newfangled position? (It wasn't until August that the Convention's Committee of Detail settled on the title "president.")

In the thick of these debates, the Framers started to worry. They were creating a powerful chief executive to preside over a powerful federal government. Despite all the safeguards they had layered in the Constitution, including the Electoral College, evil or incompetent leaders might someday hold that position. The results of tyranny or corruption at the highest level could be devastating. Clearly, something had to be done. But what? The scope of the president's power—and his independence of the other branches—would partly depend on who could remove him from office (and on what basis). Unless carefully bounded, the mighty power to end a presidency could too easily become the power to control a president.

As Franklin reminded his colleagues, world history offered little guidance. For millennia, nations had struggled and failed to deal with powerful leaders who jumped the rails. Ancient Athenians briefly experimented with formal ostracism, allowing the Assembly to exile any citizen, for any reason, for a period of ten years. The Romans, in turn, empowered magistrates called "censors" to expel members of the Senate for illegal or corrupt conduct—though this right of removal did not reach emperors (many of whom instead fell to usurpers' blades). Neither the Greek nor the Roman examples came highly recommended. Indeed, virtually without exception, the history of bad rulers known to Franklin and company was a brutal, bloody, and tragic tale.

But Franklin saw a way to break that cycle. In his telling, the English doctrine of impeachment offered a civilized answer to problems once solved by assassins and revolutions. Dating to 1376, impeachment had been forged in the crucible of contests between Crown and Parliament. To curb abuse and protect its prerogatives, the House of Commons prosecuted powerful offenders before the House of Lords. This practice quickly fell into disuse after it was first invented, but a newly assertive Parliament revitalized it in the mid-seventeenth century (following the English Civil War). At that point, the political theory of rule by divine right made it inconceivable that Parliament could lawfully remove the king from power. As a workaround, Parliament instead began impeaching royal ministers—not only for personal misconduct, but also to express disapproval of royal policies. In these cases, Parliament relied on the threadbare fiction that faulty advisors must have led the king astray. Ultimately, as Professor Raoul Berger explains, Parliament used impeachment to make "ministers chosen by the King accountable to it rather than the Crown, replacing absolutist pretensions [with] parliamentary supremacy."[2]

Impeachment thus had a long pedigree in England. But that wasn't true in the New World. American colonial assemblies never enjoyed a formal right to impeach anyone for anything. The colonists, though, were nothing if not precocious when it came to thwarting tyranny. As two leading historians recount, "American men of affairs, concerned with the safety of their communities and with their own political advantage . . . often ignored or refashioned rules of law to fit exigency and interest."[3] By the early 1700s, many colonists had come to view the impeachment power as a birthright. During the years leading up to the Revolution, some legislatures refused to stop impeaching even when ordered to stand down by panicked royal councilors.

When Franklin spoke of assassins and alternatives at the Constitutional Convention, he invoked this rich history. Revised into an American vocabulary, the impeachment power would allow "We the People" to inflict political death—but nothing more—on tyrannical leaders who posed a grave threat to the Republic.

In principle, this was an elegant solution. Yet as was often true that hot summer in Philadelphia, the details were devil-ridden. To understand the place of impeachment in our democracy today, we must first reckon with a series of trade-offs made by the Framers in the eighteenth century. Those decisions shed light on the impeachment power as structured by the Constitution. They also provide a useful frame of reference for ending presidencies in the modern world.

* * *

Franklin's remarks on impeachment were part of a long-running debate that had finally neared its end. That same day, the Convention would vote on a resolution making the president "removable on impeachment and conviction of malpractice or neglect of duty."[4]

By this point, everyone knew the deck was heavily stacked in favor of allowing presidential impeachment. Indeed, the Convention had passed an identical, preliminary resolution nearly two months earlier. Since then, many delegates had set forth plans of government that included a mechanism for removing the chief executive from office. An assumption that presidents could be impeached thus pervaded the underlying harmony of the Constitution as it took shape in June and July 1787. In debating judicial appointments, for instance, George Mason cautioned that "if the Judges were to form a tribunal for [impeachment], they surely ought not to be appointed by the Executive."[5] Although Mason's concern was ultimately rendered moot, it reflected his expectations about the existence of an impeachment power.

On July 20, however, the Framers began with first principles: whether they should allow *any* form of presidential impeachment. When that question reached the floor, Charles Pinckney and Gouverneur Morris raised immediate objections. In their view, impeachment would destroy the separation of powers and defeat a core purpose of the Constitution. They added that other checks and balances in the federal system would suffice to address any instances of presidential wrongdoing.

This opening volley of criticism was met straightaway by a devastating series of responses from Mason, Franklin, James Madison, William Davie, Elbridge Gerry, and Edmund Randolph. (We shiver at the thought of finding ourselves on the wrong side of an argument with that group.) These statements illuminate the specific anxieties and general principles that led some Framers to conclude that the Constitution must authorize impeachment.

Their first concern involved electoral integrity. After months of debate, the Framers had established the Electoral College. They were satisfied with it as a tool for picking presidents but feared that individual electors might be intimidated or corrupted. In

Mason's view, the risk of election fraud "furnished a peculiar reason in favor of impeachments." He asked, "Shall the man who has practised corruption & by that means procured his appointment in the first instance, be suffered to escape punishment, by repeating his guilt?"[6] Without an impeachment process, presidents could obtain office corruptly and then enjoy the poisonous fruit of their own electoral treachery. Democracy itself might be destroyed.

Davie worried about elections, too, but he didn't limit his concern to manipulation of the Electoral College. If a president couldn't be impeached, then he might commit abuses and seek to escape punishment by sparing "no efforts or means whatever to get himself re-elected."[7] Including an impeachment power in the Constitution would prevent corrupt and criminal presidents from seeking victory at any cost. Even if returned to office by loyal supporters, they could still face justice for their wrongdoing.

Many Constitutional Convention delegates also worried that presidents might be tempted to accept foreign bribes and conspire with enemy powers. These fears of betrayal weren't hypothetical. The Framers knew that King Louis XIV of France had used lavish pensions to corrupt King Charles II of England. Based on this experience, they appreciated that powerful leaders could be vulnerable to foreign influence. That is why they separately forbade federal office holders from accepting "any present, Emolument, Office, or Title, of any kind whatever, from any King, Prince, or foreign state." And it was one reason why Madison argued in favor of allowing impeachment. An American president, he observed, might someday "betray his trust to foreign powers."

In Madison's view, the threat of foreign bribery related to a more general risk that presidents could seek to improperly enrich themselves. The Constitution, he concluded, had to address the possibility that a president "might pervert his administration into a scheme of peculation or oppression."[8] (No longer a common term, *peculation* refers to embezzling public monies.) Randolph echoed and expanded upon Madison's point: "The Executive will have great opportunitys of abusing his power; particularly in time of war when the military force, and in some respects the public money will be in his hands."[9]

Finally, with characteristic foresight, Madison identified a distinct imperative: "defending the Community [against] the incapacity . . . of the chief Magistrate." Here, he warned against the danger posed by a president who has "lo[st] his capacity after his appointment." In Madison's view, quadrennial elections alone were "not a sufficient security" against this nightmare scenario.[10] (As we explain in Chapter 6, it was not until ratification of the Twenty-Fifth Amendment in 1967 that the Constitution explicitly addressed presidential incapacity.)

Electoral corruption, foreign bribery, treason, and abuse of the fisc and army anchored the case for an impeachment power. But arguments in favor of this position flowed from deeper principles. For Mason, impeachment was about vindicating the rule of law: "Shall any man be above Justice? Above all shall that man be above it, who can commit the most extensive injustice?" Randolph voiced a similar view: "Guilt wherever found ought to be punished." Gerry, for his part, sought to bury the maxim "that the chief Magistrate could do [no] wrong." Urging the necessity of impeachments, he emphasized: "A good magistrate will not fear them. A bad one ought to be kept in fear of them."[11]

Other delegates highlighted the risk of *not* allowing presidential impeachment. Randolph, for example, echoed Franklin's concern about domestic strife: "Should no regular punishment be provided, it will be irregularly inflicted by tumults & insurrections."[12] Franklin, in turn, warned against condemning the nation to disruptive uncertainty in cases of suspected presidential misconduct. Here he referenced "the case of the Prince of Orange," who had broken a promise to deploy the Dutch fleet to rendezvous with French forces. Suspicion of the prince spread like wildfire. "Yet as he could not be impeached and no regular examination took place, he remained in his office . . . [giving] birth to the most violent animosities & contentions." In Franklin's view, "had [the prince] been impeachable, a regular & peaceable inquiry would have taken place and he would if guilty have been duly punished, if innocent restored to the confidence of the public."[13]

These observations nicely captured the political zeitgeist. The American people had only recently endured decades of royal abuse. They had risked their lives combating tyranny and corruption. Many of the Framers had signed the Declaration of Independence, whose bill of particulars against King George III modeled what we'd now view as articles of impeachment. In that context, the Constitutional Convention was not about to create a more robust federal government—presided over by an energetic chief executive—and then deny the nation an escape hatch. As Mason noted early in the deliberations, "Some mode of displacing an unfit magistrate is rendered indispensable by the fallibility of those who choose, as well as by the corruptibility of the man chosen."[14] This was not mere political theory. To the Framers, it was hard-won wisdom.

Of course, arguments in favor of impeachment were not invented out of whole cloth at the Convention. Every delegate who addressed the subject in Philadelphia had personal experience with colonial or state impeachment practice. That background familiarized them with a distinctly American conception of this parliamentary power. It also led them to reject the English notion that a head of state could never be impeached. Indeed, Alexander Hamilton later invoked this point while defending the Constitution from its critics. The president, Hamilton argued in *Federalist* No. 69, would have no more resemblance to the British king than to "the Grand Seignior, to the khan of Tartary, to the Man of the Seven Mountains, or to the governor of New York." Whereas "the person of the king of Great Britain is sacred and inviolable," the American president could be "impeached, tried, and upon conviction . . . removed from office."[15]

Eventually, the case for including an impeachment power in the Constitution achieved something that happens all too rarely in politics: it persuaded someone. By the end of the debate, Morris came around, declaring that "he was now sensible of the necessity of impeachments."[16] Just days later, Morris defended his new position with a convert's zeal. "No man," he emphasized, would say "an Executive known to be in the pay of an Enemy, should not be removable in some way or other."[17]

This may seem self-evident. But originally Morris had believed that a combination of term limits, electoral accountability, and criminal punishments for their co-conspirators would keep wayward presidents in line. As he explained, reelection "will be sufficient proof [of] innocence." On reflection, however, Morris saw that this logic didn't hold up. If monarchs with lifelong thrones and hereditary fortunes could be bribed, then presidents— who were given only a brief taste of power—would surely be vulnerable to foreign influence. Further, as Madison pointed out, even temporary presidential corruption could be "fatal to the Republic."[18] Waiting until the next election might not be an option.

That risk loomed large because the president was vested with formidable authority. Although colonists had come to despise strong centralized control, the failure of the Articles of Confederation had convinced many Framers that the legislature could not govern alone. Americans needed a robust chief executive who could stand his ground against Congress. As Professor Michael Klarman has observed, this belief led the Framers to create an "extraordinarily powerful" presidency.[19]

The Framers' obsession with calibrating power between Congress and the executive branch explains why some delegates never came around on impeachment. In their view, if Congress were given the power to end presidencies, a finely wrought balance would be destroyed. Pinckney thus insisted that impeachments "ought not to issue from the Legislature," which would "hold them as a rod over the Executive and by that means effectually destroy his independence."[20]

This fear was understandable. As Chief Justice John G. Roberts Jr. has observed, "in a system of checks and balances, power abhors a vacuum."[21] Constitutional powers must always be understood with an eye to who can exercise them—and with what constraints. It was not unreasonable in 1787 to believe that giving the impeachment power to Congress would sabotage the presidency. But in the Framers' considered opinion, nobody other than Congress could properly wield this authority. The Convention thus faced a choice: include a presidential impeachment power and risk its misuse by Congress, or deny the nation any lawful means of swiftly removing a disastrous leader. Either path could threaten the constitutional plan. Still, a decision had to be made.

When caught between Scylla and Charybdis, sometimes the only path is to pick your monster and hope for the best. Here, the Framers concluded that they would not leave the nation defenseless against leaders who betrayed all that they sought to build. With that historic decision behind them, the Framers turned to a much more difficult question: How should they structure and limit the impeachment power?

*　*　*

In 1831, an ambitious French aristocrat arrived in Rhode Island to study prisons and penitentiaries. Sensing transformation on the horizon, Alexis de Tocqueville took a broad view of his mandate, traveling the young nation and examining its social and political order. He grew convinced that "a great democratic revolution is taking place among us."[22] Keen to understand the promise and perils of that revolution, he wrote *Democracy in America*—a book so deservedly famous that it's still required reading for political science undergraduates.

Tocqueville devoted a whole chapter to the impeachment power. He built his analysis around an apparent paradox. Americans had made impeachment "the most formidable weapon that has ever been placed in the grasp of a majority."[23] However, they had done so by rendering impeachment "an imperfect weapon," bounded by limits that he had never seen before.[24] Intrigued by these innovations,

Tocqueville undertook an exploration of how American-style impeachment fit within the broader constitutional plan.

This study probed an uneasy balance struck at the Convention. The Framers resolved to include a power to remove out-of-control presidents. But they also wanted an executive capable of resisting pressure from Congress when disagreements emerged in the ordinary course. After extensive deliberations, they sought to achieve both goals at once through clever constitutional design. In that effort, the Framers had access to a helpful tool kit: state constitutions that had been adopted since the American Revolution. As Professor Michael Gerhardt has noted, although there were "vast differences" across the states, the Convention ultimately adopted "the basic features of the most popular state impeachment systems."[25]

Drawing on this background and their own creativity, the Framers imposed four main limitations on the impeachment power. The first was a rule of wrongdoing. The president can be removed from office only upon proof of "Treason, Bribery, or other high Crimes and Misdemeanors." The Constitution thus requires proof of conduct so terrible that it makes the president unviable as a national leader. Presidents can't be removed from office on the sole basis of poor judgment, general inadequacy, perceived incapacity, or strong policy disagreements.

Second, the Constitution limits who can be impeached. By its terms, the impeachment power extends only to "the President, Vice President and all civil Officers of the United States." As Tocqueville emphasized, the Framers thus departed from European custom, which allowed legislatures to impeach any "great offenders, whatever may be their birth, their rank, or their power in the state."[26] In America, unlike in Europe, private citizens could *never* be impeached or otherwise prosecuted by the legislature. To fortify this limit, the Framers also forbade bills of attainder, which single out private individuals for trial and punishment without judicial protection. As a result of these categorical restrictions, the impeachment power is limited in scope to officers of the United States.

In the early years of the Republic, there was some confusion about whether legislators also could be impeached. But that issue was practically resolved in the 1790s, when the House impeached Senator William Blount for violating US neutrality laws by urging Native Americans to attack Spanish territories. Instead of holding an impeachment trial, the Senate expelled Blount under Article I, Section 5 of the Constitution, which allows each house to "punish its Members for disorderly Behaviour, and, with the Concurrence of two thirds, expel a Member." Yet even after Blount's expulsion, the articles of impeachment against him lingered in the Senate. Mounting a constitutional defense, Blount argued with great force that he was not a "civil officer." In 1799, a majority of the Senate apparently agreed and dismissed the impeachment charges for lack of jurisdiction. This precedent suggests that legislators can't be impeached. Accordingly, the impeachment power likely reaches only principal *executive* and *judicial* officers, including the president.

Third, the Constitution divides impeachment between the two houses of Congress. The House of Representatives is given "the sole Power of Impeachment." The Senate, in turn, enjoys "the sole Power to try all Impeachments." Whereas the House can impeach by majority vote, the Senate cannot convict on articles of impeachment "without the Concurrence of two thirds of the Members present." This plan generally ensures a president will not be removed absent a strong national consensus in favor of that result.

Finally, the consequences of a conviction are strictly limited. The Constitution is unusually explicit on this point: "Judgement in Cases of impeachment shall not extend further than to removal from Office, and disqualification to hold and enjoy any Office of honor, Trust or Profit under the United States." If the Senate convicts on articles of impeachment, it *must* remove the official from his position of power. If it wishes, the Senate may further disqualify him from future office holding. But unlike in England and France, where legislatures could impose capital punishment in cases of impeachment, Congress can do nothing more. Only the criminal justice system can impose fines, imprisonment, or a death sentence as punishment for misdeeds committed while in office.

* * *

The limited consequences of an impeachment are rarely discussed in modern accounts. They seem obvious to us. Nowadays, nobody thinks that Congress should have the power to mete out a death sentence if it finds that the president abused his power or betrayed the nation. We recognize that those kinds of criminal judgments are properly reserved for the courts.

To contemporaries, though, this rule was seen as central to the underlying theory of American impeachment. Justice Joseph Story therefore discussed it at length in his *Commentaries on the Constitution of the United States* (1833). Story began by observing that impeachment often will be applied to "political" offenses that may be "exaggerated by party spirit." As a result of the surrounding political drama, Congress might be tempted to impose punishment "wholly out of proportion to the offence." In the criminal code—which is enforced in courts—we can seek to prevent such unfairness by attaching specific sentences to specific crimes. But with impeachment, that's not an option. Impeachable conduct is so diverse that it is not possible to "define the offenses" or fix their "appropriate measure of punishment" in advance. The impeachment power is therefore "peculiarly subject to abuse."[27]

The Framers solved that problem by drawing a sharp line between political and criminal penalties. As Story explained, "the power of the senate to inflict punishment should merely reach the right and qualifications to office." This limit removes the "temptation in factious times to sacrifice good and great men upon the altar of party." Once a president has been removed from our highest office, he cannot use its power to cause harm and thus there's no need for Congress to stay involved. At that point, Story emphasized, it's best to let the judiciary take control. Otherwise a president might be unjustly jailed or killed by overzealous legislators.

In Story's view, this wasn't merely wise policy. Rather, it spoke to the very essence of impeachment as political rather than criminal in character. From that premise, Story developed an elaborate theory of which offenses are impeachable and why politicians rather than judges hold the impeachment power. Story also celebrated impeachment as carefully, prudently limited by the Constitution.

Story's work was well known to Tocqueville. In fact, during the Frenchman's nine-month tour, they met for an interview. Tocqueville was impressed. When *Democracy in America* appeared four years later, it generously cited Story's *Commentaries*. But the admiration was not mutual. In 1840, Story bitterly complained: "The work of De Tocqueville has a great reputation abroad, partly founded on their ignorance that he has borrowed the greater part of his reflections from American works, and little from his own observation. The main body of his materials will be found in the *Federalist* and in Story's [*Commentaries*], *sic vos non vobis*."[28] This Latin conclusion was lifted straight from Virgil. Translated as "thus we [labor] but not for ourselves," it unsubtly signaled that Story saw Tocqueville as a second-rate plagiarist.

Tocqueville indeed echoed Story in assigning great significance to the limited consequences of impeachment in America. However, Tocqueville took a very different lesson. In Europe, he wrote, impeachment tribunals were "invested with terrible powers which they are afraid to use."[29] The risk of a "horrible assassination"[30] was too great. Americans, in contrast, didn't allow impeachment to "menace the lives of the citizens."[31] Instead, it served only to remove political authority from "him who would make a bad use of it."[32] Thus, the "less formidable" American impeachment power could more easily evolve into an "ordinary means of government."[33] On this basis, Tocqueville anticipated that impeachment would become a "regular influence," which was "at all times available."[34] And even in its milder form, impeachment would still deter official misconduct: "Ordinary offenders will dread it as a condemnation that destroys their position in the world, casts a blight upon their honor, and condemns them to a shameful inactivity worse than death."[35] Ultimately, Tocqueville worried that it was *too* easy to invoke impeachment, and that our ship of state would list toward popular tyranny rather than effective administration.

In Tocqueville's telling, the irony is exquisite. The Framers feared that Congress would aggrandize its authority—and terrorize presidents—through abuse of the impeachment power. So they wove a tangled web of limits meant to preserve the president's independence and restrain congressional excess. Yet it turns out that the very limits they carefully placed on impeachment would actually make Congress *more* willing to exercise this power at the president's expense.

Irony, however, isn't the end of this story. Tocqueville's theory was brilliant and devious, but it was also wrong. Nearly two centuries later, while there are many things to say about impeachment, "at all times available" isn't among them. The casual use of impeachment that Tocqueville foresaw has never materialized. To the contrary, Americans convinced of executive tyranny have long agonized over the political and practical difficulties of ending a presidency. And apart from Richard Nixon, who resigned before the process had run its course, we have never actually removed a sitting president. The exceptionally steep path to impeachment, in turn, has allowed most American officials to ignore the fear of "blight" that Tocqueville thought would pervade our society.

This analysis brings us to an important point. Constitutional design is more art than science, and its implications are not easy to predict—even for a genius like Tocqueville. Savvy students of government thus heed Justice Stephen Breyer's warning that power is not always "susceptible to the equations of elementary arithmetic."[36] The dynamics of power in the federal system are fluid, contested, and ever-changing; rules meant to restrain may empower, or cripple, or send the whole edifice spinning in an unforeseen direction. Words on a page can describe structures of government, but the actual operation of that system—especially with the passage of time—can surprise even the most cautious of prophets. That's why history books are littered with the broken remains of clever political theories. And it's why even the best intentions can backfire when the ground rules for government are being written.

This perspective must guide our assessment of the Constitution. The Framers possessed great foresight. But the task they faced was daunting: to define, map, and balance the many powers and incentives of a form of government that nobody in human history had ever experienced. Amazingly, they got a lot right. We have enjoyed extraordinary progress under the Constitution they established. Many of the Framers' basic structural choices remain central to American governance. However, the Framers also got important things wrong. It's no damning criticism to say they couldn't anticipate *every* respect in which the world—and the Constitution—would change, sometimes in ways that overturned premises of their original plan.

That's true of impeachment. The United States retains the basic structure hammered out by the Framers. Some dynamics have worked as they imagined in 1787. But others haven't. The Framers' design was closely linked to many factual and legal assumptions that no longer hold true. For example, they did not anticipate the birth of political parties, changes in how the vice president is selected, a switch to direct popular election of senators, the escalation of partisan gerrymandering, the creation of a standing army that can instantly be deployed anywhere in the world, or the vast twentieth-century expansion of federal authority. Today, however, it would be strange *not* to account for these developments in an assessment of the impeachment power. By the same token, it would be irresponsible to ignore lessons that we have learned from centuries of historical experience and multiple impeachment proceedings. Thus, although we've discussed the Framers at length and will later return to their debates, that should not be mistaken for a suggestion that their word is final. Now and always, the Constitution belongs to the living.

*　*　*

Broad claims about exercising good judgment in the modern world can be intimidating and unhelpful when stated abstractly. The rest of this book is devoted to clarifying and framing the judgments that must be made about impeachment. As a first cut, we can distill some high-level principles—based in history and the Constitution—to guide our analysis. We'll approach that task by considering three points: (1) all presidents use power in controversial ways; (2) it is improper to impeach based on mere partisan disagreement; and (3) there are many kinds of misconduct that can justify impeachment.

Let's start with some wisdom from Spider-Man creators Stan Lee and Steve Ditko: "With great power there must also come—great responsibility."[37] That was true for the young superhero Peter Parker, and it's true for the president of the United States. Yet this principle is easier stated than applied. Presidents must quickly judge the best course in extraordinary circumstances and with limited information. They must consider the whole country—often the whole world—all at once and make decisions that shape the path of human history. In perilous times, their action (or inaction) can define how millions live and millions die.

Responding to this heavy burden, nearly every president has used power in ways denounced at the time as tyrannical—sometimes for good reason, sometimes not. George Washington ignited a national firestorm when he signed a deeply unpopular treaty with Britain. Thomas Jefferson approved the Louisiana Purchase in apparent defiance of his views of the Constitution. Abraham Lincoln suspended key civil liberties, including free speech and habeas corpus, during the Civil War. Andrew Johnson pardoned former Confederates who had fought against the Union. Woodrow Wilson jailed pacifists who opposed entry into World War I. The list goes on: Franklin D. Roosevelt approved the internment of innocent Japanese American citizens. Harry Truman unila⸳⸳ ally ordered racial integration of the armed services. Dwight Eisenhower deployed troops on his own authority to keep peace in Little Rock, Arkansas. Many important developments in American history involved uses of presidential authority that sparked intense debate.

It's also safe to say that nearly every president has used power in *illegal* ways. At one point or another, presidents inevitably support or approve unlawful exercises of federal authority. This is so common as to be unremarkable. The Supreme Court rules against the executive branch on a regular basis. Usually it does so in minor cases arising from criminal, immigration, or regulatory disputes, but occasionally it strikes down major presidential programs. And if we look beyond issues subject to judicial review, most presidents have made military, national security, or foreign affairs judgments that drift past the letter of the law. Although some of these decisions caused a public outcry, many of them have been accepted or even celebrated. Illegality should be rare in the upper echelons of the executive branch, but it can never be avoided completely.

Since the mid-1970s, disputes over presidential power have only become more common. Responding to partisan breakdowns and congressional paralysis, presidents from both parties have made increasingly aggressive use of their authority. Today, almost no issue of national significance remains untouched by the chief executive and his vast bureaucracy. Under crushing political pressure, presidents have laid claim to new and expanded powers— and have also used existing powers in ways that strike many as offensive or unnerving. As a result of these developments, accusations of executive tyranny and lawlessness are now standard fare in American political discourse. The public has been immersed for decades in unrelenting, outraged, and often hyperbolic claims that the president is a dictator who will destroy our freedom.

This poses a challenge for clear thinking about impeachment. On the one hand, all presidents act in ways that trigger alarm bells.

And those alarms are important. When we sense abuse of power in the White House, it's our duty as a free people to identify, resist, and remedy the breach. On the other hand, it's essential to maintain a sense of proportion. The vast majority of presidential abuses are properly addressed through normal legal and political checks. Despite the heated rhetoric that now engulfs society, not every scandal requires torches and pitchforks.

The Impeachment Clause thus expects that we will recognize shades of gray in concerns about the presidency. Most of the time this is easy. But in the fog of battle—and when crisis looms—we run the risk of allowing an all-consuming grayness to obscure our moral vision. It's in those tense circumstances that deciding whether to impeach is most difficult.

Of course, not every democracy makes this demand of its citizens. In countries with parliamentary systems, there's no need for legislators to establish whether the leader has become an existential threat before removing him from office. Nor is it necessary to hold a trial and convict him of anything. Rather, when a legislature loses faith in the prime minister, it can hold a vote of no confidence and thereby express its determination that he is unfit to remain in office. When that occurs, the prime minister resigns and a new election usually occurs in short order. A parliamentary motion of no confidence may be approved for any reason, ranging from proof of criminal acts to a simple conclusion that the prime minister's leadership isn't right for the nation.

Whatever the virtues of parliamentary democracy, however, it is not our system of government. Indeed, it's become a cliché in scholarly circles to distinguish the American impeachment power from parliamentary no-confidence votes—and to suggest that the Framers had this very distinction in mind. Strictly speaking, that isn't true: in 1789, there weren't yet full-fledged parliamentary systems for the Framers to reject. But the comparison is helpful as a guide to how impeachment *shouldn't* be used.

Unlike parliamentary systems, ours doesn't remove leaders whenever a majority of the legislature loses faith in them. That practice would be squarely at odds with the basic framework of the Constitution. When a president is elected, the nation is entitled to expect that he will serve a full four-year term—barring proof of incapacity or dastardly conduct that reveals him as a menace to the political order. American democracy deals with unpopular or unwise presidents by checking them, balancing them, and running out the clock on their four-year term. In the event that an awful president is somehow reelected, the Twenty-Second Amendment imposes term limits and thereby forces turnover. (This amendment was ratified in 1951 as a response to FDR, who breached a precedent first set by George Washington when he served in office for more than two consecutive terms.)

Accordingly, even when many Americans view a presidency as catastrophic, impeachment should not be pursued solely on the basis of strong policy differences or deep personal revulsion. Indeed, only the most cynical and faithless observer, wholly unconcerned with core premises of our constitutional plan, would treat impeachment as little more than partisan warfare by other means. Impeachment is not an extension of ordinary political debate; rather, it is reserved for conduct that threatens the very terrain on which such debates occur. Historically, attempts to use the impeachment power in ways that violate this principle have failed—and have been roundly condemned by later generations.

Consider, for example, the abortive effort to impeach President John Tyler in 1842. One year earlier, when President William Henry Harrison died a mere month after inauguration, Tyler became the first vice president to ascend to the presidency. Harrison and Tyler had run on the Whig ticket, but Tyler wasn't a true Whig. In fact, he disagreed with major parts of their banking, tariff, and infrastructure programs. In the 1840s, that was a *very* big deal. Political warfare soon erupted between Tyler and the Whig-controlled Congress. Wielding his veto pen with abandon, Tyler stymied major bills at every turn. Finally, congressional Whigs decided to rush the gate. Their leader, Henry Clay, told his allies "the more vetoes the better," since "the inevitable tendency of events is toward impeachment."[38] By August 1842, all but one member of Tyler's cabinet had resigned in protest. Worse, a House committee led by John Quincy Adams had issued a report suggesting impeachment for supposed abuses of the veto power.

Tyler was stunned: "The high crime of . . . daring to have an opinion of my own, Congress to the contrary notwithstanding, I plead guilty also to that, and if these be impeachable matters, why then I ought to be impeached."[39] Ultimately, though, Tyler was saved by a political tidal wave. In late 1842, Democrats swept the midterm congressional elections. When the lame-duck Whig leadership later forced a vote on whether to open an impeachment inquiry, their proposal went down in flames (127 to 83). Tyler remained in office and served out his term, though with few achievements and no base of political support.

This is a prime example of how impeachment should *not* be used. The impeachment power is not a tool for Congress to eject a president solely because of disagreement with his policies. It's to the credit of the lame-duck House majority that it defeated this misguided, partisan effort to end Tyler's presidency. The right way for Congress to handle Tyler was to override his vetoes, block his nominations, and otherwise invoke the full panoply of ordinary legislative powers. And that's exactly what happened in Tyler's final years. As Professor Gerhardt reports, in that period, "the Senate blocked a majority of his nominations (including four cabinet and two minister nominations), and the Senate rejected eight of his nine Supreme Court nominations—the largest number of unsuccessful Supreme Court nominations ever made by a single president."[40]

Unfortunately, lessons of history often pass unlearned. Just over 156 years after Tyler's struggle, the House approved articles of impeachment against President Bill Clinton. Almost entirely along partisan lines, the House accused Clinton of perjuring himself and obstructing justice during an investigation led by Independent Counsel Kenneth Starr. That investigation hadn't uncovered any abuses of executive power. Rather, it had been launched by evidence of questionable land deals and had quickly sidetracked into a merciless examination of Clinton's extramarital affairs.

There's no doubt that perjury and obstruction can be removable offenses in certain circumstances. But the case for impeaching Clinton was a weak one, for four reasons. First, although Clinton grossly and unforgivably used his position to seduce an intern, he did not abuse the formal powers of his office while doing so. Second, while Clinton's conduct was faithless to his marriage and to the court in which he testified, it hardly broke faith with the nation as a whole or foreshadowed grave peril if he remained in office. Third, there was no sign that Clinton had so lost the confidence of the citizenry that he could not govern effectively until the end of his four-year term. Finally, ordinary checks and balances seemed fully capable of addressing any further objections to how Clinton conducted himself while in office.

Given these substantial vulnerabilities in the articles of impeachment against Clinton, most Americans correctly perceived that House Republicans sought his removal on the basis of political (and personal) animus. Although Clinton's acts were contemptible, they did not provide compelling grounds for impeachment and conviction. Here, as in Tyler's case, impeachment was misused by partisans opposed to the president but unable to identify a great offense against the nation. This decision exemplifies bad judgment in the realm of impeachment.

* * *

If these cases suggest ways in which the impeachment power shouldn't be used, that leaves the question: When *should* it be invoked?

To many, Watergate is the classic example—so much so that we now append -*gate* to our most unsavory scandals. The story began on June 17, 1972, when a group of burglars was arrested at the Democratic National Committee office, then located at the Watergate complex in Washington, DC. It soon became clear that these burglars were somehow connected to Richard Nixon's reelection campaign. Over the following years, as journalists and prosecutors hustled around the capital, irrefutable evidence emerged of shocking conduct by Nixon and his senior staff. Their misconduct included surveillance and sabotage of political opponents, illegal campaign financing, and an elaborate cover-up led by Nixon himself. Revelation of this jaw-dropping criminal conspiracy made Nixon's continuation in office unthinkable. The House Judiciary Committee prepared numerous articles of impeachment, but Nixon ultimately resigned before they could be considered by the full House.

Once the key facts came to light, Watergate was an easy case on the merits. Our constitutional system could not abide a president who used executive power to corrupt the democratic process, enrich his political allies, sabotage his political enemies, commit outrageous felonies, and cover up his own wrongdoing.

We must be careful, though, not to treat Watergate as an exclusive model of when to impeach. Presidential abuses come in many shapes and sizes. Although the events constituting Watergate justified removal, so could many other terrible but very different courses of conduct. As the Framers knew, democracy can fall to charismatic demagogues, would-be monarchs, self-interested kleptocrats, sophisticated criminals, and high-functioning morons. Because threats from the presidency can be so diverse, our vision of the impeachment power must be equally capacious.

That vision must also account for the persistence throughout US history of deep disagreements over constitutional meaning. As we've noted, all presidents use power in new, questionable, and possibly threatening ways. Often those invocations of executive power trigger robust dissent. But as urgent as they may feel in the moment, few such disagreements truly strain the constitutional system's legitimacy—or its viability as a means of keeping political clashes from ripping the nation apart. By and large, we have tacitly agreed to live in a state of perpetual unsettlement regarding the outermost boundaries of many executive powers. Most limits on acceptable presidential conduct are thus defined by evolving norms and culture, not law. These fragile restraints are at least as important for American democracy as the formal rules hardwired into the Constitution. And they usually function well enough for government work.

At times, though, a president might engage in a pattern of conduct that shatters norms and formal constraints accepted by most of us as vital limits on the office. When that happens—and when less extreme measures will not suffice—we must consider taking drastic measures to eject the renegade president.

Simply put, impeachment is our system's last resort for avoiding genuine catastrophe at the hands of the president. This power is designed for moments when the nation faces clear peril and the constitutional scheme offers no other plausible exit. Impeachment should occur when a president's prior misdeeds are so awful in their own right, and so disturbing a signal of future conduct, that allowing the president to remain in office poses a clear danger of grave harm to the constitutional order. When circumstances like these arise, *failing* to impeach can pose a threat even greater than the inherent risks of impeachment. And that decision is left, in the first instance, to the House of Representatives, acting for the nation as a whole.

This may all sound a bit vague. Fair enough. Impeachment requires good judgment amid uncertainty, not a preprinted checklist of relevant considerations. In the coming chapters, we will explore the contours of that judgment and identify general principles that should guide decisions to end a presidency.

* * *

Franklin saw impeachment as a decent substitute for assassination. In truth, it's so much more.

Assassins strike alone in the shadows, moved by motives high and low to end a ruler's life. They can speak for everyone or no one, for a traitorous cabal or a silent majority. They land a single blow and the world is instantly, unexpectedly transformed. They have only one tool—death—and they wield it at risk of their own life. Even the most celebrated assassination in world history—that of Julius Caesar—was so morally fraught that to this day, we contest whether Brutus was "an honorable man."[41]

Impeachment shouldn't be understood as merely a cleaner and more orderly form of political assassination. Rather, it's a democratic process by which the American people, speaking through Congress, decide that for the constitutional system to live, a presidency must die. This is a great power, and a terrible one. But it's a power that befits any nation in which the people are truly sovereign. And it's a power that might someday save us all.

2
IMPEACHABLE OFFENSES

Richard Nixon hated the Warren Court. He hated its protection of criminal defendants, its sympathy for civil rights, and its muscular vision of judicial power. Most of all, he hated Justice William O. Douglas, the brilliant and erratic arch-liberal appointed decades earlier by Franklin D. Roosevelt. In 1969, Nixon unleashed the full power of his office to crush Douglas. Aided and abetted by FBI director J. Edgar Hoover, the president's minions sowed rumors of corruption and impropriety. But if they thought the justice would cave under pressure, they were badly mistaken. When Attorney General John Mitchell phoned Douglas to informally accuse him of wrongdoing, the wily and combative Westerner replied, "Well, Mr. Attorney General, saddle up your horses."[1]

Mitchell's agents ultimately fell far short of proving serious misconduct. The best they could muster was a few sketchy deals and some scandalous gossip. Nonetheless, on April 15, 1970, Nixon's closest ally in the House called for Douglas's impeachment. Ticking off a list of half-baked claims, Representative Gerald Ford emphasized that his colleagues had the raw power to impeach Douglas for any reason. "An impeachable offense," he insisted, "is whatever a majority of the House of Representatives considers it to be at a given moment in history."[2] Conviction by the Senate, he added, depended only on "whatever offense or offenses two-thirds of the other body considers to be sufficiently serious to require removal of the accused from office." In Ford's telling, there were "few fixed principles" to restrain Congress from giving an expansive interpretation to the phrase "high Crimes and Misdemeanors."[3]

Within a year, the campaign to impeach Douglas died a well-deserved death. But Ford's cynical view of impeachment lives on. Despite extensive criticism, some politicians still find it irresistible. In September 2017, for instance, Representative Maxine Waters echoed Ford while advocating the impeachment of Donald Trump: "Impeachment is about whatever the Congress says it is. There is no law that dictates impeachment. What the Constitution says is 'high crimes and misdemeanors,' and we define that."[4]

In a miserly sense—one that treats principle as mere window dressing on real politics—Ford wasn't wrong. The Supreme Court does not review impeachment decisions. Indeed, when it was asked by an impeached federal judge to second-guess the Senate's trial procedures, the Court dismissed his case as presenting a "political question" reserved only to the Senate.[5] Because Congress enjoys the final word on matters of impeachment, it has the raw power to remove officials for whatever arbitrary reasons strike its fancy.

So why did the Framers even bother including a standard such as "high Crimes and Misdemeanors"? Given that Congress can so easily warp this language, what was it meant to achieve?

To put the question in context, many constitutions with an impeachment process don't follow the American approach. Some jurisdictions, including twelve US states, say nothing at all. In Georgia, for example, the House wields "the sole power to vote impeachment charges," but isn't told by its constitution when impeachment is proper.[6] This manner of writing a constitution embraces the political judgment that must be made and doesn't try to constrain it. A radically different approach—uncommon in the US, but popular abroad—is to declare that all criminal violations or unconstitutional acts are grounds for impeachment. That strategy has been embraced by Argentina, Germany, India, South Africa, and Poland, among others. A third option, seen by some as a middle ground, is to enumerate specific acts that qualify as impeachable. Like many constitutions worldwide, the US Constitution takes this approach to "Treason" and "Bribery."

Finally, a constitution can define impeachable offenses using an open-ended standard. The US Constitution employs the phrase "high Crimes and Misdemeanors." Many American state constitutions follow a similar approach in their impeachment clauses, though with different standards of wrongdoing. For example, Pennsylvania targets "misbehavior," New Jersey aims at "misdemeanor[s]," and Massachusetts forbids "misconduct and mal-administration."[7] These terms, and their synonyms, can also be found in a fistful of foreign constitutions—often modified by adjectives such as *grave* and *high*. Nations that have adopted this constitutional strategy include Nigeria, Palau, Sierra Leone, and Russia.

As a matter of constitutional design, choosing an impeachment standard from among these options involves delicate trade-offs. Looking to the language used in our Constitution, there's no denying that the phrase "high Crimes and Misdemeanors" is vague. While not quite a Rorschach test, these words are pliable. Under the right circumstances, politicians could credibly contend that they mean all sorts of things that shouldn't actually be accepted as grounds for undoing the results of an election.

Yet in writing a constitution meant for the ages, there are compelling reasons to favor an adaptable, flexible standard. To start, it would be impossible to anticipate every act that might someday require impeachment—particularly given that the Impeachment Clause applies not only to the president and federal judges, but also to many other senior executive branch officials. And even if creating such a list were somehow possible, it wouldn't be desirable to write a constitution that way. As Chief Justice John Marshall explained in 1819, a well-written constitution cannot "partake of the prolixity of a legal code." Rather, its nature "requires only that its great outlines should be marked, its important objects designated, and the minor ingredients which compose those objects be deduced from the nature of the objects themselves."[8]

In practice, moreover, the decision to specify "high Crimes and Misdemeanors" *wasn't* an empty choice. This formulation inevitably frames our national discussion of impeachment. It guides, though it doesn't always resolve, investigations and political assessments of alleged misconduct. For generations, those words have shaped popular expectations about removing a president. And those expectations have disciplined politicians. As Representative Brad Sherman explained in December 2017, "We're more or less a democracy. There are 320 million people out there. When they hear the term 'high crimes and misdemeanors,' their reaction is, 'Show me the crime.'"[9] Sherman added, "The legal theoreticians will tell you that impeachment is just a matter of politics. I'm a politician, and I'm here to tell you that it's a matter of legal analysis."

In truth, impeachment blends legal, political, and many other kinds of judgment. But as Sherman's remarks indicate, a broad cross-section of the public has grasped that the Constitution demands wrongdoing of a very high order to justify impeachment. With centuries of experience under our belt, it's safe to say that a requirement of truly bad acts has generally been taken seriously. We don't live in a system where political differences alone bring an end to four-year presidential terms.

By and large, that's a good thing. The Impeachment Clause is one of the Constitution's architectural cornerstones. Because it identifies a key feature of US governmental structure, its stability and predictability are important. To raise or lower the impeachment bar is to move the nation closer to an imperial presidency or a parliamentary system. Especially now that Americans' daily lives can be affected so directly by the president and his relationship to Congress, tinkering with the impeachment standard is serious business. Tossing it up for grabs would risk significant political instability.

In a narrow sense, Gerald Ford was correct: Congress's word on impeachments is final. Although he found that idea liberating, exactly the opposite is true. If Congress errs here, the American people must live forever with the consequences. No *deus ex machina* will magically appear to set the system straight. That makes it more important, not less, that Congress interpret the requirement of "high Crimes and Misdemeanors" in good faith. Doing otherwise would involve a severe betrayal of trust and could have disturbing consequences for the future of the Republic.

*   *   *

Article II, Section 4 of the Constitution provides: "The President, Vice President, and all civil Officers of the United States, shall be removed from Office on Impeachment for, and Conviction of, Treason, Bribery, or other high Crimes and Misdemeanors." Most Americans are at least roughly familiar with this language. Like few other lines in the Constitution, it has penetrated and shaped public consciousness.

Let's start by considering the definition of "Treason." Even a cursory glance at the Constitution reveals that the Framers took this term *very* seriously: it's the first impeachable offense listed in Article II, and it's the only criminal offense defined in the Constitution itself. Specifically, while establishing federal judicial power, Article III declares that "treason against the United States, shall consist only in levying War against them, or in adhering to their Enemies, giving them Aid and Comfort." The Constitution then proceeds to create a special rule of evidence for this offense: "No Person shall be convicted of Treason unless on the Testimony of two Witnesses to the same overt Act, or on Confession in open Court." As if that's not enough, the Constitution then limits the sentences that can be imposed: "Congress shall have Power to declare the Punishment of Treason, but no Attainder of Treason shall work Corruption of Blood, or Forfeiture except during the Life of the Person attainted." Put simply, Congress can't punish a traitor by disabling his successors from claiming their inheritance. In the United States, treason doesn't corrupt the bloodline.

These elaborate rules reflect lessons that the Framers had learned from English history. To protect political dissent, they devoted considerable energy to carefully limiting the law of treason. This Americanized doctrine outlaws just two forms of perfidy: (1) levying war against the United States and (2) adhering to the nation's enemies, giving them aid and comfort. On their face, these are exceptionally serious and dangerous offenses. They necessarily involve an unforgivable betrayal of the nation and its people. A president found to have committed such acts couldn't conceivably remain in power. If he remained in office, no apologies or alternative restraints would alleviate the continuing danger he posed. Once a traitor, always a traitor.

Under Donald Trump, impeachment talk has been riddled with sometimes careless insinuations of treason. Most of those allegations relate to legally questionable dealings between Trump advisors and foreign powers—seemingly with his knowledge or tacit approval. In the estimation of many experts, though, it's highly unlikely that the law of treason as such will play a major role in the continuing Trump saga. Indeed, scholars specializing in the subject would find it quite surprising if formal accusations of treason featured prominently in *any* presidential impeachment of the twenty-first century.

With regard to levying war, it's awfully hard to imagine an American president using armed force in an attempt to overthrow the government he heads. But historically, that is what courts have required: an assemblage of people who used *actual* force or violence to execute a treasonable design against the government. And even if this requirement could be met by proof of cyberattacks, we doubt an American president and his co-conspirators would hack into government agencies to achieve distinctively warlike objectives. For purposes of the Treason Clause, there's a big difference between hacking into voting machines to change electoral outcomes (not treason) and hacking into the Pentagon to launch missiles at New York City (certainly treason).

That leaves only treason consisting of "aid and comfort" to our "enemies." Although the world is full of powers with hostile intentions, few of them qualify as "enemies" in the relevant sense. As Professor Carlton Larson explains the conventional view, "an enemy is a nation or an organization with whom the United States is in a declared or open war."[10] We haven't engaged in a "declared" war since World War II. In contrast, we've had many states of open war, including against Korea, Vietnam, Iraq, and Afghanistan. At the moment, America's unquestioned "enemies" are limited to the likes of Al Qaeda, the Taliban, and ISIS. We very much doubt that any president is likely to lend "aid and comfort" to these groups.

Some commentators have argued that Russia also ranks among our "enemies." They contend that Russia engaged in open cyberwarfare against the United States when it hacked into American computers and weaponized the resulting information to interfere with the 2016 election. This argument raises interesting and important questions about the circumstances under which cyberattacks create a state of war for purposes of the Treason Clause. For the time being, however, continued legal uncertainty about whether it is treasonous to lend "aid and comfort" to Russia militates against basing an impeachment on this theory.

In most cases, it likely would be easy enough to avoid these thorny issues, since formal acts of treason aren't the only form of betrayal that can properly subject a president to impeachment. It is beyond doubt that a president *can* be removed from office for knowingly colluding, conspiring, or otherwise working with foreign powers against the national security interests of the United States. For example, if the president improperly conspired with a hostile nation to interfere with a US election or weaken US policy on matters of strategic importance, that conduct would be impeachable in its own right. While the Constitution defines treason narrowly for purposes of criminal prosecution, this rule does not impliedly prohibit Congress from concluding that other betrayals of the nation qualify as "high Crimes and Misdemeanors."

Turning to "Bribery," the Constitution nowhere defines this term. Nor did federal law do so until 1853, when Congress passed the first bribery statute of general application. (Before then, federal prohibitions focused mainly on people who bribed judges.) A well-developed body of federal bribery law now exists, but this jurisprudence is an imperfect guide for interpreting the Impeachment Clause. Because these highly technical doctrines mix politics with broadly-applicable criminal law, Congress and the Supreme Court have painstakingly micromanaged them. The result is a set of rules that may sometimes fail to capture improper exchanges that the Framers intended to make impeachable.

Indeed, the Supreme Court has recently led an effort to narrow and revise federal bribery law as applied to government officials. In its most prominent decision, *McDonnell v. United States*, the Court explained that a broader definition of bribery would permit unaccountable federal agents to chill democracy by "cast[ing] a pall of potential prosecution" over interactions between local officials and their constituents.[11] Yet that important policy concern in criminal law is almost entirely inapplicable to impeachment. When impeachment charges are filed, there's no shortage of political accountability. And Congress, unlike prosecutors and juries, is more than capable of sensing when an apparent *quid pro quo* arrangement crossed the line. *McDonnell* thus exemplifies why it makes little sense to blindly transplant federal bribery law—or other criminal law doctrines—into the Impeachment Clause.

In defining "Bribery," it's more helpful to ask why the Constitution singled out this offense (alongside treason). As we explained in Chapter 1, the Framers feared insidious foreign influence most of all. Gouverneur Morris thus warned that the president "may be bribed by a greater interest to betray his trust."[12] "No one," Morris added, "would say that we ought to expose ourselves to the danger of seeing the first Magistrate in foreign pay." But the Framers' concern about betrayal wasn't limited to foreign powers and foreign money. Categorical rules against bribery spoke to the conditions of possibility for a liberal society in which the people were truly sovereign. As Professor Akhil Amar notes, "bribery—secretly bending laws to favor the rich and powerful—involves official corruption of a highly malignant sort, threatening the very soul of a democracy committed to equality under the law."[13] What kind of republic could America be if leaders answered only to the selfish interests of those who paid them off?

The Framers were so anxious about bribes that they built a multilayer defense system. First, in Article 1, Section 9, Clause 8, they banned federal officials from accepting any presents, emoluments, offices, or titles from foreign governments unless Congress affirmatively consented. This rule was designed to guard against unconscious division of loyalty. Further, by banning foreign emoluments, the Framers sought to prevent circumstances in which bribery might occur but be impossible to detect. Next, in Article II, Section 1, Clause 7, the Framers banned the president from accepting any emoluments from states and the federal government itself. That strict rule ensured the president wouldn't be improperly swayed by private inducements from domestic officials. Finally, the Framers struck directly at the core evil: *quid pro quo* bargains. By writing bribery into the Impeachment Clause, they ensured that the nation could expel a leader who would sell out its interests to advance his own.

This background must frame our interpretation of "Bribery." The ultimate question is whether a president exchanged money or other favors with the intent of influencing some official action or inaction. The corrupt exercise of power in exchange for a personal benefit defines impeachable bribery. That's self-evidently true whenever the president *receives* bribes to act a certain way. But it's also true when the president *offers* bribes to other officials—for example, to a federal judge, a legislator, or a member of the Electoral College (a possibility that terrified the Framers). In either case, the president is fully complicit in a grave degradation of power, and he can never again be trusted to act as a faithful public servant. While instances of outright bribery now seem rare—or hard to prove—this rule remains vital in an age of presidential kleptocracy. At the very least, it anchors our understanding of how corruption may threaten the Constitution.

The Framers had good reason to single out "Treason" and "Bribery," and to declare them impeachable. Fortunately, these offenses have historically played a negligible role in cases of presidential impeachment. Their main function in such proceedings has been to inform the meaning of their textual neighbor, "high Crimes and Misdemeanors." It's to that topic we now turn.

* * *

Few terms in constitutional law have been so fiercely contested as "high Crimes and Misdemeanors." Whenever impeachment talk emerges, the great minds of the nation race to explain why the president has (or has not) committed such offenses. Often, though, these "analyses" are merely political attacks drenched in Madison quotes. It's hard to write about impeachment without a crushing awareness of unfolding events. Even general discussions of impeachable conduct are inevitably shaped by views on the sitting president.

That's long been a feature (and a bug) of the US system. In selecting an imprecise standard, the Framers delegated to future generations a duty to decide what conduct is beyond the pale. Those decisions, in turn, aren't made in a void. They're always situated in unfolding political drama and shaped by reactions to the most recent experience of tyranny. Because many of the rules, norms, and habits that discipline our chief executive are fluid and contested, so are the outer limits on tolerable uses of power. Deciding when a president has gone too far calls for a present-day judgment based on political principle, legal theory, and moral vision.

It's therefore unsurprising that Americans have long disagreed over what it means to commit "high Crimes and Misdemeanors." In the pre–Civil War period alone, federal legislators called for impeachment over a dizzying array of offenses. A nonexhaustive list from that period includes (1) John Adams's extradition of a mutinous British Navy sailor to England, amid rumors that the sailor was a captured American; (2) Thomas Jefferson's supposed "deliberate neglect" in failing to appoint a Collector of the Port of Boston; (3) Andrew Jackson's contested decision to withdraw federal deposits from the Bank of the United States; (4) John Tyler's alleged misuse of the veto power; (5) Franklin Pierce's refusal to intervene militarily against pro-slavery forces in "Bleeding Kansas"; and (6) James Buchanan's suspected involvement in corrupt deals with members of Congress.

In each of these cases, opinions varied wildly on what kinds of presidential misconduct qualified as impeachable. Some politicians hinted that nothing short of declaring a monarchy would suffice. Others insisted that *any* unconstitutional act by the president required immediate impeachment. Even in the early years of the Republic, when Framers filled the ranks of government, disagreements on this basic question were common.

Those interpretive battles persist to the present—partly because there's never been a successful presidential impeachment. We have no clear precedent accepted by both the House and the Senate about what presidential conduct qualifies as "high Crimes and Misdemeanors." To be sure, we can consider the articles of impeachment approved by the House against Andrew Johnson and Bill Clinton, as well as articles approved by the House committee investigating Richard Nixon. But the Nixon articles were never adopted by the House, and the Johnson and Clinton impeachments failed in the Senate. Although some senators publicly justified their votes in the Johnson and Clinton cases, most senators didn't speak their minds—and the publicly available explanations don't cohere into a single majority view of the Impeachment Clause. Even if they did, we're skeptical that so-called "impeachment precedent" commands deference apart from its power to persuade future generations. Congress isn't bound by its own prior decisions.

This doesn't mean we're entirely at sea. A fair-minded study of the Constitution and our history *does* reveal some principled insights about the meaning of "high Crimes and Misdemeanors." To appreciate them, we must try to interpret that phrase as though we stand behind a veil of ignorance—unsure about when the Impeachment Clause will be applied. If you can, put the current president out of mind. Imagine that your best friend and then your worst enemy might hold our highest office. What rules, in general, should decide when either of them could be impeached?

In answering that question, it's helpful—though less so than you might expect—to return to Convention Hall. As we've seen, the Framers originally adopted "mal-practice or neglect of duty"[14] as the standard for impeachment. In late July, though, the Committee of Detail changed the standard to "Treason, Bribery or Corruption." By narrowing the grounds for removal, the committee sought to address lingering concerns that the president would be too dependent on whoever had the power to impeach. Five weeks later and without explanation, another committee shortened the list to "Treason or Bribery."

For George Mason, this was a bridge too far: "Why is the provision restrained to Treason & bribery only? Treason as defined in the Constitution will not reach many great and dangerous offences." To solve this problem, Mason proposed adding the nonspecific term "maladministration" as a more general ground for removal. Elbridge Gerry seconded Mason, but James Madison objected: "So vague a term will be equivalent to a tenure during pleasure of the Senate." Morris chimed in to suggest that a new presidential election every four years would suffice to "prevent maladministration." Without any further debate or discussion, Mason then substituted "other high Crimes and Misdemeanors." The Convention accepted this compromise and moved on.[15]

And that was the whole discussion. Unlike many other facets of impeachment, the Framers devoted essentially zero time to selecting "high Crimes and Misdemeanors" as the applicable standard.

Before we proceed, then, it's worth emphasizing that this is a case where we should be modest about reliance on originalism.

Few delegates at the Convention addressed impeachable conduct at all, and we don't know whether the views of those who did are representative of all thirty-nine men who signed the Constitution. Further, if we look beyond Convention Hall to gauge original meaning, the definition of impeachable conduct was barely discussed at most state ratifying conventions. That absence is telling. Given the diversity of state impeachment practice, it's likely that Americans around the country had divergent understandings of the Impeachment Clause that they ratified.

Even individual Framers were at times inconsistent. Just two years after objecting to "maladministration," Madison apparently reversed course. Speaking in the First Congress about presidential power, he opined that "the wanton removal of meritorious officers would subject [the president] to impeachment and removal" for "an act of maladministration."[16] It seems that Madison—a key player in the switch to "high Crimes and Misdemeanors"—didn't assign enduring significance to his earlier concerns, if he remembered having raised them in the first place.

Accordingly, if you're told that the Framers *definitely* meant a particular offense to be impeachable (or not), your first reaction ought to be skepticism. More often than not, that sort of originalist hokum is just a rhetorical gambit meant to make a disputed judgment sound neutral and objective.

*　*　*

Still, we have to start somewhere. And in interpreting the phrase "high Crimes and Misdemeanors," the Convention records do shed some helpful light. The insights they offer can then be fleshed out by considering the text itself and the structure of the Constitution.

There are three important points. The first is that nobody at the Convention objected to capturing "great and dangerous offences" beyond treason and bribery. This suggests a recognition that the scope of the Impeachment Clause had to match its broad purpose. At the very least, it's apparent that in adding this phrase after "Treason" and "Bribery," Mason didn't have a particular set of offenses in mind. Nor was he using recognized shorthand for a well-defined list that he assumed everyone would immediately recognize. Rather, he chose an open-ended term that would allow Congress to impeach for many imaginable—and not yet imaginable—"great and dangerous offences."

In thinking about what types of offenses those might be, it's useful to invoke *ejusdem generis*. While this may sound like a spell from *Harry Potter*, the reality is no less exciting: it's a canon of legal interpretation. (Okay, maybe that's less exciting.) *Ejusdem generis* says that if we list a series of items and then include a catchall phrase at the end, that phrase includes only things similar to the items that precede it. Courtesy of Justice Antonin Scalia and his coauthor Bryan A. Garner, here's a helpful example of *ejusdem generis*: "If one speaks of 'Mickey Mantle, Rocky Marciano, Michael Jordan, and other great competitors,' the last noun does not reasonably refer to Sam Walton (a great competitor in the marketplace) or Napoleon Bonaparte (a great competitor on the battlefield). It refers to other great *athletes*."[17]

In our case, the relevant list is "Treason, Bribery, or other high Crimes and Misdemeanors." Invoking *ejusdem generis*, we can presume that "high Crimes and Misdemeanors" are offenses of the same general type as treason and bribery. Treason causes the gravest possible injury to the nation and reflects a betrayal of the first order. Bribery is the ultimate corruption of office—an exercise of power for private benefit, not public good. Both offenses drastically subvert the Constitution and involve an unforgivable abuse of the presidency. It's inconceivable that someone who committed these misdeeds could ever again be trusted with "the Executive Power." Both offenses are also momentous: they have the capacity to inflict extraordinary harm on the nation, and the discovery that they occurred could disqualify any president as a viable national leader. To qualify as impeachable, offenses must share these traits.

Treason and Bribery have one more thing in common: they require proof of *intent*. To impeach on these grounds, we must assess a president's state of mind. In practice, that needn't always involve a separate factual inquiry. Some abuses of power would be facially impeachable, because there's no conceivable motive that would justify them. An order that the army kill all protesters at a peaceful rally in New York City would constitute such an abuse. But more often than not, we'd need to know *why* the president did what he did. Many otherwise lawful uses of executive power might be impeachable if—but only if—the president acted for impermissible reasons. For example, while the president can generally pardon criminals, fire the FBI director, and make false public statements, doing so as part of a conspiracy to obstruct justice is plainly impeachable. Motive matters in assessing whether the president acted corruptly or abusively.

Given the many difficulties of proving intent, this requirement is often fatal to calls for impeachment. In Nixon's case, it was only tape recordings of Oval Office conversations that incontrovertibly showed malice. Yet to borrow a phrase from commentator George Will, rarely is there a "smoking howitzer" like the Nixon tapes.[18] Instead, we ordinarily must infer the president's state of mind from all relevant circumstances.

A second source of insight into the definition of impeachable offenses comes from the Constitution's drafting history. When the Framers replaced "maladministration" with "high Crimes and Misdemeanors," they sought to narrow—not expand—the class of impeachable offenses. At the time, "maladministration" broadly encompassed gross incompetence, bad policies, and unwise personnel decisions. In contrast, "high Crimes and Misdemeanors" was understood as limited to serious misconduct that inflicted injury on the state itself. Mason and Madison thus rejected a term that allowed impeachment for strong differences over policy and personnel and replaced it with a rule of wrongdoing.

On that score, use of the word *high* is revealing. In Britain, high treason involved a crime against the Crown—as distinguished from *petit* treason, the betrayal of a superior by a subordinate. The Framers knew this and deliberately chose to incorporate the word *high* as a limitation on impeachable offenses. We can safely treat that fact as important, because the Framers knew how to denote ordinary crimes when they wanted to do so. For example:

- The Fifth Amendment requires grand jury indictment in cases of a "capital, or otherwise infamous crime."
- The Currency Clause empowers Congress to "provide for the Punishment of counterfeiting the Securities and current Coin of the United States."
- The Law of Nations Clause authorizes Congress to "define and punish Piracies and Felonies committed on the high Seas, and Offenses against the Law of Nations."
- The Interstate Extradition Clause provides that "a Person charged in any State with Treason, Felony, or other Crime" who flees from one state to another shall be returned upon request.

The Impeachment Clause thus stands out in the Constitution. By adding *high* before *Crimes* in this one provision, while excluding it everywhere else, the Framers plainly sought to capture a distinct category of offenses against the state.

Unlike some scholars, however, we don't assign any further meaning to this choice of language. While "high Crimes and Misdemeanors" was a term of art dating to 1386, and had thus accumulated centuries of intellectual baggage, there's no reason to think the Framers had all that in mind. As Alexis de Tocqueville observed, the colonists—and then the Framers—transformed impeachment when they ripped it from its English roots. In America, this power was about political accountability and popular sovereignty, not criminal punishment and parliamentary supremacy. Those differences weaken the relevance of English practice. Moreover, it's unlikely that

Americans in the 1780s knew the details of four hundred years of technical English learning on "high Crimes and Misdemeanors."

This leaves our final lesson about conduct that justifies ending a presidency: impeachment is *not* meant to function like a bill of attainder. As we explained in Chapter 1, Parliament used these bills to declare that someone's prior acts were crimes—and to impose punishment for those "crimes" without a trial or hearing. The Framers were so appalled by this practice that they forbade it at every level of government. In the same breath, they also barred *ex post facto* laws, which made illegal an act that was legal when committed—or which increased the punishment for a crime above the level authorized when the deed was done.

At the Constitutional Convention, while explaining why impeachment must reach "great and dangerous offenses," Mason observed that "bills of attainder which have saved the British Constitution are forbidden."[19] Unlike Parliament, Congress could not retroactively declare that particular presidential conduct was abusive or corrupt. Instead, it could impeach the president only for evil deeds identified as such ahead of time. Accordingly, Mason emphasized that the Constitution must use a broad definition of impeachable offenses to preserve Congress's discretion.

At even a glance, this reasoning appears inconsistent. How can a flexible standard for impeachable offenses be squared with the principle of fair notice that underlies the bill of attainder and *ex post facto* clauses? Professor Charles L. Black Jr. has offered a convincing solution. Reading the Constitution harmoniously, he concludes that the phrase "'high Crimes and Misdemeanors' . . . must not be so interpreted as to make its operation in a given impeachment case equivalent to the operation of a bill of attainder, or of an *ex post facto law*, or of both."[20] What does this mean in practice? Black explains: "[We should] treat as impeachable those offenses, and only those, that a reasonable man might anticipate would be thought abusive and wrong, without references to partisan politics or differences of opinion on policy."[21]

Put simply, the Constitution doesn't contemplate impeachment by ambush. In thinking about "high Crimes and Misdemeanors," we must recall elementary norms of fair notice and just punishment. Judgments about which conduct justifies removal must be made in the present rather than by reference to the founding era (or any other period). This rule protects the president against impeachment for reasonable, good-faith errors. At the same time, it means that presidents may not plead ignorance of the norms and customs that now define constitutional governance.

Pulling all this together, we can identify key elements of "high Crimes and Misdemeanors": like treason and bribery, they involve corruption, betrayal, or an abuse of power that subverts core tenets of the US governmental system. They require proof of intentional, evil deeds that risk grave injury to the nation. Finally, they are so plainly wrong by current standards that no reasonable official could honestly profess surprise at being impeached.

In short, when a president commits an impeachable offense, he has done something so awful that we must seriously consider removing him without waiting for the next election. We face that decision because the president has lost legitimacy and viability as our leader, and because we fear he'll inflict further damage to our polity if he remains in power.

Making these judgments requires a nuanced view of current circumstances, a realistic assessment of whether the president poses a continuing risk, and a substantive conception of how the chief executive may exercise power. The Constitution guides this inquiry but can't answer it except at a very general level. When a leader is called to answer for his sins, case-specific variables swiftly overtake broad claims about the meaning of "high Crimes and Misdemeanors." As we've seen before and will surely see again, every presidential implosion burns a different color.

Based in constitutional text, structure, and history, these principles afford us a working definition of impeachable offenses. To refine that understanding, it's helpful to consider a frequently asked question about "high Crimes and Misdemeanors": Can presidents be impeached for misdeeds that *aren't* crimes?

Our analysis of that issue begins with one of US history's greatest, weirdest villains.

* * *

He did not throw away his shot. On July 11, 1804, Vice President Aaron Burr mortally wounded former Treasury Secretary Alexander Hamilton at a duel in Weehawken, New Jersey. The tale is now widely told, thanks to Lin-Manuel Miranda's musical *Hamilton*. Less well known is what followed.

As biographer Ron Chernow reports, "when a handwritten notice of Hamilton's death went up at the Tontine Coffee House [in New York], the city was transfixed with horror."[22] The New York Supreme Court and Bank of New York were draped in black, and for a full month New Yorkers sported black armbands to mourn their fallen hero. On July 14, 1804, Hamilton's two-hour funeral procession brought the city to a halt for a slow-motion spectacle of silent despair.

And fury. As outrage persisted, New York and New Jersey indicted Burr for murder. Local papers damned the vice president as a heartless traitor and sadistic coward. His surreal confidence finally broken, Burr fled south to Georgia.

You might think that this murder would at least raise a question of impeachment. But you'd be wrong: Congress never considered impeaching Burr. To the contrary, eleven US senators formally asked the governor of New Jersey to drop all charges. This was necessary, they explained, "to facilitate the public business by relieving [Burr] from the peculiar embarrassments of his present situation, and the Senate from the distressing imputation thrown on it, by holding up its President to the world as a common murderer."[23] (As vice president, Burr also served as president of the Senate.)

Incredibly, the story only got stranger from there. Months later, Burr was forced back to the capital to preside over a highly partisan (and unsuccessful) impeachment trial for Justice Samuel Chase. As Chief Justice William Rehnquist has recounted, "this led one contemporary wag to remark that whereas in most courts the murderer was arraigned before the judge, in this court the judge was arraigned before the murderer!"[24] In the end, Burr was never punished by Congress for killing Hamilton. New Jersey dropped its murder charge, and Burr was convicted by New York only for the misdemeanor offense of dueling.

To modern sensibilities, this story is appalling. If Vice President Michael Pence were to kill Treasury Secretary Steven Mnuchin—and if Pence did not then resign—he would surely be impeached, removed from office, and charged with murder. Even given the culture of dueling that persisted in the early 1800s, Congress's response to the Burr–Hamilton incident is profoundly disturbing. We have nothing good to say about it.

Nonetheless, this tale gestures to an important difference between criminality and impeachability. Across history, not all crimes by federal officials have been seen as impeachable. This was as true for Burr in 1804 as it was for Richard Nixon in 1974, when the House Judiciary Committee rejected an article of impeachment for tax fraud. The inverse of this principle is also true: impeachment doesn't require proof of a crime. Consider the case of Judge Alcee Hastings. In 1989, the Senate convicted and removed Hastings for conspiring to accept bribes—even though he had already been *acquitted* in a criminal trial of that same offense. (In an ironic turn of events, Hastings later ran for Congress—and won. On January 10, 2007, after years of service, he formally presided over the same institution that had impeached him two decades earlier.)

These and other examples make clear that impeachment and criminal punishment are distinct. Some lawyers, however, continue to insist that an official can be impeached *only* if the official has committed a crime. Although this restrictive position enjoyed a measure of support in the early 1800s, it has long since been widely and convincingly rejected. Indeed, the first successful judicial impeachments of the twentieth century—Judge Robert Archbald (1913) and Judge Halsted Ritter (1936)—both involved misconduct that didn't break any criminal laws.

The argument that only criminal offenses are impeachable is deeply and profoundly wrong. It misunderstands the Constitution, US history, and the nature of criminal law in important ways. Nonetheless, even having died a thousand deaths, this theory staggers on like a vengeful zombie. Democrats and Republicans alike have invoked it when doing so suited their partisan needs—and then have flip-flopped when that seemed more expedient.

The wrongness of this claim offends us as scholars and troubles us as citizens. A relentless focus on criminality distorts public dialogue about impeachment. It also sabotages productive discussion about improper (though noncriminal) uses of presidential power. Because some analysts continue to conflate impeachability and criminality, we will offer a detailed explanation of why their position is wrong. This analysis, in turn, illuminates the nature of impeachment and impeachable conduct.

Starting with history, there's virtually no evidence that the phrase "high Crimes and Misdemeanors" was widely understood in the 1780s to mean indictable crimes. As our review of the Constitutional Convention revealed, the Framers were concerned with abuse of power, corruption, and injury to the nation. At no point did any delegate link the ultimate safeguard against presidential betrayal to intricacies of a criminal code (or to judge-made common law crimes). In fact, delegates did the opposite, invoking an array of broad and adaptable terms as grounds for removal. When those grounds were narrowed to Bribery and Treason, the phrase "high Crimes and Misdemeanors" was added to guarantee that impeachment could address any "great and serious offence."

This goal aligned with American approval of Edmund Burke's ongoing campaign in Parliament to impeach Warren Hastings, the former governor-general of India. Burke had charged Hastings with rampant subversion of England's unwritten constitution. He had not alleged any particular crimes. And it seems that some Framers agreed with Burke. While explaining why treason and bribery alone were too narrow as grounds for impeachment, Mason warned that "Hastings is not guilty of Treason."[25] He thus made clear that Hastings *should have been* impeachable—tacitly rejecting a constitutional standard that would prevent Congress from punishing noncriminal abuses of power.

A more capacious view of impeachment is also supported by other sources. For example, that conclusion accords with colonial practice—which, for all its variation, occasionally roamed beyond the boundaries of criminal law. It's also supported by evidence from numerous state ratification conventions. There, delegates sweepingly opined that impeachment would be appropriate if an official "deviates from his duty" or "dare[s] to abuse the power vested in him by the people."[26]

This position was echoed by leading minds of the era. In *Federalist* No. 65, Hamilton argued that impeachable offenses are defined by "the abuse or violation of some public trust." In that sense, he reasoned, "they are of a nature which may with peculiar propriety be denominated POLITICAL, as they relate chiefly to injuries done immediately to the society itself."[27] A few years later, Constitutional Convention delegate James Wilson echoed Hamilton's point: "Impeachments, and offences and offenders impeachable, come not . . . within the sphere of ordinary jurisprudence. They are founded on different principles, are governed by different maxims, and are directed to different objects."[28]

These teachings are confirmed several times over by the Constitution's structure. Consider again the Bill of Attainder Clause, which bans legislative punishment of particular individuals. If impeachments were exclusively about proving that the president committed a specific crime, then the Impeachment Clause would be at war with the basis for that rule, since it authorizes a form of trial and punishment by legislature. This tension dissipates, however, if impeachment is seen as a legislative remedy for *any* great and dangerous offense against the nation. Viewed in that light, impeachment is a fundamentally political process with a forward-looking and preventive focus. It is not a process through which Congress decides whether a particular statutory crime occurred and whether removal is warranted as a punishment.

So, too, with the Double Jeopardy Clause, which protects against being tried twice for the same crime. The Impeachment Clause expressly contemplates that an official, once removed, can still face "Indictment, Trial, Judgment and Punishment, according to Law." In other words, after a president is kicked out, he can be indicted and punished for any crimes he committed while in office. It would be inconsistent with the spirit of the Double Jeopardy Clause to envision criminal trial and punishment for the president after removal, but to insist that he can be removed only if Congress first finds that he *did* commit a crime. The better view is that impeachment does not necessarily say anything at all about criminal liability.

The Pardon Clause further supports this interpretation. Under that clause, presidents have the "Power to grant Reprieves and Pardons for Offences against the United States, *except in Cases of Impeachment*" (italics added). The categorical exception for impeachment is crucial to preserving checks and balances. If the president's top advisors commit evil deeds at his behest, he can save them from criminal punishment—but not from impeachment and removal. On that question, Congress *always* has the final word. This ensures that dangerous officials can at least be removed from positions of public trust. Further, in the improbable event that the president attempts to pardon himself for committing federal crimes (which likely would be unlawful), he can't thereby preclude his own impeachment. This limitation, like the others we have discussed, rests on the unique nature of the impeachment power.

*   *   *

The problems with treating only indictable offenses as "high Crimes and Misdemeanors" aren't limited to constitutional law.

They multiply when we consider the history and structure of criminal law, which are often overlooked in accounts of impeachment.

One possible view is that presidential misdeeds are impeachable only if they constitute *federal* crimes. But that view is hard to take seriously when measured against original public understanding. As early as 1812, the Supreme Court made clear that federal crimes are limited to those specifically defined by Congress. And the Framers, who took a narrow view of federal power in this field, didn't think that Congress was authorized to create a broad criminal code. As Professor William J. Stuntz has emphasized, the Constitution contained few explicit grants of power to create federal criminal law. These provisions were limited to "counterfeiting, piracy, 'offenses against the law of nations,' and crimes that occur within the military."[29] While further criminal prohibitions might have been seen as "necessary and proper" to carrying out Congress's other powers, Stuntz notes that "Madison and his friends did not expect that category to be large."[30]

Their prediction was a good one. Through the early years of the Republic—really, until the mid-twentieth century—federal criminal law was thin and patchy. It covered relatively few categories of offenses, and it was infrequently and irregularly enforced by tiny federal agencies. Where federal criminal codes did apply, they often had arbitrary, jagged limitations meant to respect now-obsolete boundaries on Congress's constitutional power. As Justice Story noted in 1833, many federal offenses were punishable only when committed "in special places, and within peculiar jurisdictions, as, for instance, on the high seas, or in forts, navy-yards, and arsenals ceded to the United States."[31]

This haphazard character would have made federal criminal law an improbable tool for defining "high Crimes and Misdemeanors." Why would the Framers limit the impeachment power to federal crimes, while simultaneously giving Congress hardly any power to create criminal law? Indeed, the early Congresses—filled with Framers—didn't even *try* to create a body of criminal law addressing many of the specific abuses that motivated adoption of the Impeachment Clause in the first place. Nor has any subsequent Congress purported to pass a criminal statute generally stating which acts are impeachable when committed by the president.

More recent developments don't change that bottom line. Although the scope of federal criminal law is now much broader, it still leaves many important issues to the states. Further, as we explained earlier with respect to bribery, the evolution of federal law has been shaped by many factors irrelevant to impeachment. For instance, in developing criminal law for the entire nation, legislators and courts have worried about chilling speech, destabilizing politics, inviting arbitrary enforcement, disrupting federalism, and appearing tough on crime. To the extent these concerns even bear on the definition of impeachable offenses, they apply very differently. Rules that properly bind a sitting president may not always be generalizable into federal crimes.

In the alternative, one might say that "high Crimes and Misdemeanors" occur when the president violates *state* criminal law. Here, however, we risk flipping federalism on its head: invoking state law to supply the content of the federal Impeachment Clause would grant states a bizarre primacy in our constitutional system. Especially given that impeachment is crucial to the separation of powers *within* the federal government, it would be strange for states (not Congress) to control when this power may be used. Further, if state criminal law governs, then the same act by the president might be impeachable if committed in New York and not if committed in Alabama. But why should quirks and loopholes of state doctrine block Congress from removing an out-of-control president? An examination of state criminal codes hardly inspires confidence that they're well-suited to the task: many state law books are riddled with arbitrary and outmoded rules, some of which criminalize ordinary, innocuous acts like swearing in public or spitting on sidewalks.

A more fundamental problem with reliance on criminal codes is that neither state nor federal criminal law is built for impeachment. Legislators have little incentive to craft criminal codes with attention to acts that might imperil the nation if committed by the president. Instead, legislators have responded to a very different set of concerns while deciding what conduct to criminalize. Indeed, even if a legislator *wanted* to draft a statute defining all impeachable crimes, she'd likely find the task impossible. As Justice Story cautioned in 1833, "political offences are of so various and complex a character, so utterly incapable of being defined, or classified, that the task of positive legislation would be impracticable, if it were not almost absurd to attempt it."[32]

Insisting on the equation of criminality and impeachability produces many other absurd results, too. The practical mismatch between these categories is often demonstrated with two hypotheticals sketched by Professor Black. First, "suppose a president were to move to Saudi Arabia, so he could have four wives, and were to propose to conduct the office of the presidency by mail and wireless from there."[33] If the president commits no crime *en route,* is he truly unimpeachable? Surely not. As Professor Akhil Amar has noted, "gross dereliction of duty imperiling the national security and betraying the national trust might well rise to the level of disqualifying misconduct."[34]

We can look beyond Black's absentee leader to confirm his underlying intuition. Imagine a president who announces that Catholicism shall be the official religion of the United States and orders all agencies to act accordingly; or one who promises to pardon any person who violates the legal rights of undocumented migrants; or one who promises to endorse any company that fires employees who voted against him; or one who announces that no woman or person of color is welcome in the White House as long as he occupies the presidency. Hypotheticals like these illustrate the point that some noncriminal acts must be impeachable.

Now consider Black's second hypothetical, which shows the inverse. This one hasn't aged well since 1974, when gays and lesbians lived in fear of the law: "Suppose a president did not immediately report to the nearest policeman that he had discovered that one of his aides was a practicing homosexual."[35] That would be "misprision of a felony"—a serious crime in its own right. Yet only a madman would deem it an impeachable offense.

In short, while it's sensible to seek out neutral principles that can discipline our political debates, criminal codes aren't up to the task. Even if we erroneously limited ourselves to their requirements, we'd still have to make tough, value-laden judgments about which crimes qualify as impeachable. And no principle internal to criminal law can sensibly make those judgments for us.

There's an important lesson here. In 1974, it would have been criminal—but not impeachable—for the president to conceal same-sex intimacy by White House aides. A century earlier, given prevailing laws and norms, it would have been criminal *and* at least conceivably impeachable for the president to abet such conduct. Yet in 2018, there's nothing criminal *or* impeachable. To the contrary, the only potentially impeachable offense on these facts would be to enforce an anti-sodomy law in the first place, thus defying clear Supreme Court precedent.[36]

This is just one of many examples showing that beliefs about criminality and impeachability aren't set in stone. They can diverge (or converge) in new and surprising ways, responding to fluid legal doctrine and views on appropriate uses of executive power.

* * *

Of course, the distinction between criminality and impeachment doesn't mean that criminal law is *irrelevant*. Our criminal codes identify many terrible acts that would surely warrant removal if committed by the chief executive.

Evidence of criminal conduct is relevant to impeachment determinations in other ways, too. When a president stands accused of murder, perjury, or other familiar crimes, the American people may be less likely to view this conduct as debatable or forgivable. It's hard for a president to say that he acted reasonably, or in good faith, if he broke a criminal law. Further, proof that a crime occurred can feel comfortingly objective. It relieves us of the need to exercise judgment and casts a technical gloss over bitterly divisive political questions. Within the blast furnace of political combat, we know that criminal codes identify forms of wrongdoing that society has forbidden in general—not just when faced with a specific presidential scandal. In that respect, as scholar Jane Chong observes, criminal law can serve as "a helpful reference point that we must always track to ensure we do not get so turned around that we stray into reactionary partisanship."[37]

These are all appropriate ways to reference criminal law. But it must not be forgotten that criminal codes are only a guide to wrongful acts; they aren't a comprehensive listing. The Constitution doesn't compel us to let a corrupt or tyrannical leader off the hook just because his offenses are not directly addressed by the US Code. Impeachment is mightier and savvier than that.

This point is important because there are major societal downsides to obsessing over criminality in impeachment debates. That tendency has encouraged partisans to warp the criminal law to fit their latest debates over presidential conduct. Even more troubling, it has stifled the public's ability to speak constructively about desirable, debatable, and detestable uses of presidential power. Jamming these debates into a criminal law framework often obscures what's really at stake. In most cases, a focus on criminality makes these issues seem legalistic and dry—the province of fancy lawyers, not ordinary Americans. Perhaps as a result, when faced with dueling claims that the president is a crook, people often retreat to their political predispositions. That reflexive race to partisan defaults can thwart efforts to sustain dialogue about whether the president's acts accord with our country's traditions and values. It can also accelerate a disturbing trend toward the criminalization of political differences. Eventually, the blurring of impeachment and criminality may atrophy the public's ability to evaluate whether a president's acts, criminal or not, truly pose a threat to our democratic system.

Unnerving as it may be, we can't fall back on criminal law in hopes of escaping the judgment that impeachment requires of us. Attempting to do so can be actively harmful to our politics. The Constitution *compels* us to grapple with threats that transcend crimes. It creates a powerful presidency that can directly affect every man, woman, and child touched by the United States government. If the president betrays our trust—whether or not through acts that qualify as crimes—he can destroy everything we hold dear. Impeachment is about perceiving when that occurs and responding to the disaster. When we think about "high Crimes and Misdemeanors," we must ask: Will we survive this presidency, and, if we do, what kind of nation will we have become?

* * *

That question loomed over Congress on February 24, 1868. After years of conflict with Andrew Johnson, the House of Representatives finally—and decisively—approved eleven articles of impeachment against him. Nine of them charged Johnson with violating the Tenure of Office Act, which restricted the president's power to remove cabinet members during the term of the president who had appointed them. Johnson allegedly violated this law by attempting to fire Secretary of War Edwin M. Stanton. The other two articles of impeachment charged Johnson with denying Congress's authority and bringing it into disgrace.

As many at the time recognized, the House had put forth a weak case. The Tenure of Office Act was unpopular and likely unconstitutional; moreover, Stanton had been appointed by Abraham Lincoln, so it wasn't even clear that Johnson had violated the act by removing him. The vague allegations about disrespecting and disgracing Congress, in turn, struck many as mere political rhetoric. Ultimately, after some high-velocity wheeling and dealing that we'll revisit in later chapters, the Senate fell a single vote short of convicting. Johnson got to serve out the rest of his term.

Johnson's near removal offers some enduring and underappreciated lessons about "high Crimes and Misdemeanors." Most important: it really does matter which acts are identified in articles of impeachment voted on by the House. Although impeachment proceedings are intensely political, they are also technical and legalistic. When the House decides to impeach a president on the basis of specific misdeeds, it will inevitably be held to establishing those particular claims in the Senate and in the court of public opinion.

In Johnson's case, there was a stark mismatch between the articles of impeachment and the actual reasons he was impeached. Following a bloody Civil War, slavery had finally been abolished—at least on paper. But brutal racial suppression still stalked the land. More than six hundred thousand Americans lay dead, with collateral damage to every aspect of national life. Profound questions about the future and very nature of the Union stood unanswered. As many legislators recognized, the Constitution had failed in its essential purpose and required radical transformation. Led by a fractious Republican coalition, Congress therefore embarked on a controversial reconstruction program meant to heal a broken country.

These would have been trying times for a truly great leader. But Johnson wasn't great. He wasn't even okay. Utterly devoid of presidential manner, Johnson mixed malice and incompetence with virulent racism. Universally disliked, Johnson would have been an awful president at any point. In 1868, though, his awfulness reached transcendent heights. As Professor Annette Gordon-Reed has observed, "it would be impossible to exaggerate how devastating it was to have a man who affirmatively hated black people in charge of the program that was designed to settle the terms of their existence in post-Civil War America."[38] Johnson opposed and then vetoed landmark civil rights statutes. When Congress overrode those vetoes, he refused to enforce the laws and interpreted them in bad faith. Along the way, he mangled the basic duties of his office and trashed every ounce of goodwill he was offered. "[W]ithin a year of [his] elevation to the presidency," writes historian Michael Les Benedict, the "preliminary Reconstruction program enacted by Congress lay in utter ruin."[39]

After repeated, unsuccessful efforts to compromise, Republicans in Congress finally concluded that Johnson had to go. At this point, they searched long and hard for an ironclad offense that would justify his removal. But rather than rely on the true reasons for their campaign, Republicans resorted to the Tenure of Office Act. Having selected a dubious impeachable offense, they were stuck with it. In the case they made to the Senate, Johnson's removal of Stanton—rather than his reactionary and neo-Confederate vision of the post–Civil War presidency—took center stage.

This was unfortunate. The shaky claims prosecuted by Republicans obscured a far more compelling basis for removal: that Johnson's virulent use of executive power to sabotage Reconstruction posed a mortal threat to the nation—and to civil and political rights—as reconstituted after the Civil War. In 1868, these were not ordinary policy disagreements. In many ways, the country was in the throes of a second founding. Yet Johnson abused the powers of his office and violated the Constitution to preserve institutions and practices that had nearly killed the Union. He could not be allowed to salt the earth as the Republic made itself anew.

Historians have long debated whether different arguments would have ended Johnson's presidency. For example, perhaps it would have been wise to impeach him for failing to "take Care that the Laws be faithfully executed"—in particular, the series of laws comprising Reconstruction. Historians have also debated whether removing Johnson would have mattered in practice (given the politics of the era) and whether the act of impeaching him was sufficient in its own right (since Johnson thereafter deferred to Congress on Reconstruction). We'll revisit some of those questions in subsequent chapters. But in hindsight, there can be little doubt that House Republicans failed to plead and prosecute their best case on the merits.

The Johnson proceedings thus teach a crucial lesson. The Impeachment Clause directs attention to *particular* misdeeds, not the ambient badness of a presidency. It's therefore essential that the House formulate articles of impeachment that effectively capture the full gamut of alleged "high Crimes and Misdemeanors." It's through these articles that the House defines the terrain on which it will join battle with the president. When the House contemplates formal accusations that the president committed impeachable offenses, those charges must stand on their own.

A difficulty may therefore arise in cases—like Johnson's—where the offense consists not of a single atrocity, but rather an accumulation of bad acts into a terrifying pattern. On the one hand, accuracy and specificity are key attributes of "high Crimes and Misdemeanors." They separate that standard from "maladministration," and help ensure that impeachment trials don't become free-ranging meditations on shifting, scattershot allegations. On the other hand, an unyielding fixation on discrete deeds can blind us to patterns that turn individually troubling acts into a dangerous abuse of office. To adapt a term from debates over privacy law, consider this a "mosaic theory" of impeachable offenses: individual tiles might say little, but viewed together they can compose a shocking picture.[40]

In some cases, a mosaic approach is therefore necessary. Indeed, as attorney John Labovitz recognized in 1978, "the concept of [a discrete] impeachable offense guts an impeachment case of the very factors—repetition, pattern, coherence—that tend to establish the requisite degree of seriousness warranting the removal of a president from office." The question, he added, "is not whether a string of zeroes will sum to one, but whether a number of fractions will."[41] At times, a single evil act might say everything necessary to justify impeachment. In other cases, though, that determination requires reference to a broader course of conduct that slowly reveals a monster lurking in the Oval Office. In Johnson's case, for example, none of his particular vetoes, speeches, nonenforcement policies, misinterpretations of the law, or neo-Confederate acts were "high Crimes and Misdemeanors" in their own right. But they almost certainly qualified as impeachable in the aggregate.

On this score, the Nixon impeachment hearings are instructive. After thorough fact-finding and debate, the House Judiciary Committee reported three articles of impeachment to the full House. The committee's first article, "Obstruction of Justice," leveled the following accusation:

> On June 17, 1972, and prior thereto, agents of the Committee for the Re-election of the President committed unlawful entry of the headquarters of the Democratic National Committee in Washington, District of Columbia, for the purpose of securing political intelligence. Subsequent thereto, Richard M. Nixon, using the powers of his high office, engaged personally and through his close subordinates and agents, in a course of conduct or plan designed to delay, impede, and obstruct the investigation of such illegal entry; to cover up, conceal and protect those responsible; and to conceal the existence and scope of other unlawful covert activities.[42]

This allegation was followed by nine paragraphs identifying "the means used to implement this course of conduct." Those means nonexhaustively included many lesser offenses: perjury; withholding evidence; interfering with ongoing FBI investigations; endeavoring to misuse the CIA; disseminating secret information to people under investigation; making and supporting false public statements about investigations into his illegal conduct; and encouraging prospective criminal defendants to expect favored treatment in return for their silence or false testimony.

This article of impeachment wisely mixed the particular and the pattern. While it charged Nixon with a single overarching offense, the supporting evidence canvassed years of conduct and dozens of discrete acts—few of which would have been grounds for removal viewed in strict isolation. Only through painstaking effort, and sensitivity to the bigger picture, did the House Judiciary Committee assemble a clear and damning account of Nixon's abuses. Sometimes "high Crimes and Misdemeanors" occur in slow motion and require panoramic vision.

* * *

Lawyers specialize in thinking about things while pretending not to. As Professor Thomas Reed Powell caustically remarked in 1935, "if you think that you can think about a thing inextricably attached to something else without thinking of the thing which it is attached to, then you have a legal mind."[43] In this chapter, we have identified general principles of constitutional law that must frame any account of impeachable offenses. This analysis should stand for many years to come, under presidents of different backgrounds and ideologies. Yet it would be strange to pretend we can discuss "high Crimes and Misdemeanors" today without *any* reference to Donald Trump.

So we won't pretend. Instead, we'll offer a few thoughts on specific questions that have arisen in the early Trump presidency.

But first, a disclaimer: impeachments are dynamic processes that must respond to new information and evolving political realities. Whether presidential conduct justifies removal from office can't properly be decided in a void. That's especially true when the public doesn't yet have a full understanding of the facts or their legal implications. As we write in mid-March 2018, Special Counsel Robert Mueller and several congressional committees are investigating relationships between Russia and the Trump campaign. Those investigations are exceptionally important. Their conclusions will shape public views of whether Trump engaged in, knew about, or recklessly tolerated collusion with a hostile foreign power. It would be imprudent to make strong claims about Trump's conduct without a full record of the relevant facts. Accordingly, at this juncture we must confine ourselves to some general observations about the nature of Trump's alleged "high Crimes and Misdemeanors."

Among the gravest allegations shadowing this presidency is that it may have come into being illicitly. There is now a plausible basis for speculation that senior figures in Trump's campaign—and possibly the president himself—conspired with the Kremlin in manipulating the 2016 election. For example, it has already been established that the president's son and campaign manager knowingly met with Russian agents to obtain information that they hoped would harm Hillary Clinton's candidacy. Further, it is now apparent that an astonishing number of senior Trump advisors have lied about meeting with Russians, lied about who was present, and lied about what they discussed. Perhaps most alarming, since taking office, Trump has ostentatiously refused to fulfill one of his most basic duties as president: protecting the nation and its political system from damaging cyberattacks by a hostile foreign power.

In creating the impeachment power, the Framers worried most of all about election fraud, bribery, traitorous acts, and foreign intrusion. Willful conspiracy with a hostile foreign power to influence the outcome of a presidential election directly evokes all of these concerns. Although the meaning of "high Crimes and Misdemeanors" is often open to dispute, here there's little room for serious disagreement. Needless to say, any such duplicity would be especially severe if it could be shown that the foreign power had assisted the winning candidate in exchange for promises to bend US policy in its favor. The evil posed by that sordid arrangement would be compounded further still if the foreign government had also offered the continuing benefit of withholding embarrassing or incriminating information about the president (or his associates). These misdeeds involve an extreme and corrupt betrayal of the United States, and it would therefore be appropriate to impeach a president who owed any part of his election to them. Simply put, a president found to be engaged in such extraordinary treachery could never again be trusted to lead the US government or conduct its foreign affairs.

Some observers, however, have voiced doubt that conduct before a president is elected or sworn into office can ever justify impeachment. They note that it is logically impossible to abuse power before one actually possesses it.

With respect to pre-inauguration conduct meant to distort an election, we think that argument is both incorrect and irrelevant. The Framers were practical men. While creating the Constitution, they repeatedly described corrupt acquisition of the presidency as a paradigm case for impeachment. It would be passing strange to think that this concern covers illegal acts by an incumbent (who already holds power), but is utterly inapplicable to an insurgent (who improperly obtains power). Reading the Constitution that way transforms a workable blueprint for self-governance into an exercise in abstract formalism. The Constitution's commitment to popular sovereignty—and its defenses against foreign influence over federal officials—strongly imply that someone who gains power by working with a hostile nation cannot retain the fruits of his wrong. Although our system affords no process for nullifying or rerunning a corrupted election, it does provide a rough approximation: stripping the treacherous candidate of his ill-gotten gains.

In any event, we doubt that a president who has already betrayed the nation this way would cease all impeachable conduct the instant he is sworn into office. If his collusion with a foreign power involved expectations of continuing influence over US policy, any official actions he took consistent with that expectation would constitute "high Crimes and Misdemeanors." If the foreign nation threatened to expose the president's electoral malfeasance, or sought to blackmail him with other compromising information, any official actions he took to conceal that fact or improperly favor the foreign power also would be impeachable. Further, if suspicion of wrongdoing emerged and the president obstructed justice, that conduct would independently justify his removal. For instance, it would be an impeachable offense in that scenario to pardon co-conspirators, fire investigators, order prosecutors to drop the case, intimidate witnesses, and orchestrate a cover-up. It's therefore unlikely to be decisive whether pre-inauguration conduct is impeachable in its own right. A president who wins by corrupt means will almost inevitably abuse power after swearing the oath of office.

For that reason, among others, it is significant that Trump has already taken steps that raise credible questions about obstruction of justice. To note just a few examples, he secretly demanded "loyalty" from then-FBI Director James Comey; requested that Comey cease investigating his campaign for improper contact with Russia; fired Comey over his handling of the Russia investigation; bragged about firing Comey in a meeting with the Russian ambassador; and then made multiple inconsistent statements about why he had fired Comey in the first place. While many facts critical to an assessment of Trump's conduct remain unknown, this highly irregular pattern of behavior cries out for congressional scrutiny. Regardless of whether Trump's conduct satisfies the elements of an obstruction charge under applicable provisions of the US Code, it might well justify impeachment hearings in the House.

Some of Trump's most extreme defenders have argued that the Constitution categorically prohibits impeachment on the basis of Trump's decision to fire Comey. In their view, because Trump has broad constitutional authority to hire, fire, and supervise executive branch employees, it isn't possible for him to "obstruct justice" in exercising that power. This argument bears a striking resemblance to Nixon's infamous assertion, "When the president does it, that means it's not illegal." And it is equally mistaken.

The basic flaw in this claim is that it purports to describe a zone of absolute, unchecked, and uncheckable power. Such a limitless view of the president's authority is jarringly out of key with the rest of the Constitution, which stands for the principle that *nobody* is above the law. In conferring powers upon the president, the Constitution does not also immunize him from continuing oversight and accountability. As Jane Chong accurately observes in the *Lawfare* blog, "There are no realms of impunity and no exercises of power that can be meaningfully described as categorically exempt from serious congressional scrutiny."[44]

That scrutiny properly encompasses hearings on whether to end a presidency. Concluding otherwise would blast a massive hole in the Impeachment Clause. After all, the formal powers vested in the chief executive are vast. Put to nefarious ends, they could wreak havoc on our democracy. It is inconceivable that the architects of checks and balances forbade us from removing presidents who use lawful powers to achieve tyrannical ends. If anything, the opposite is true. When the president corruptly exercises his power in destructive ways, impeachment serves as the ultimate safeguard for our political order. Indeed, the paradigmatic case for impeachment involves abuses of "the executive Power" that portend future harm and that can't be addressed through less extreme measures.

Thus, the president's broad power over foreign affairs wouldn't save him from impeachment if he gave our most vital national security secrets to China during a negotiation in exchange for a private benefit to him or his businesses. The president's power as commander in chief of the armed forces wouldn't prohibit impeachment if he deliberately ordered US soldiers to massacre innocent civilians. And the president's power to nominate judges wouldn't shield him if he announced that he hates courts and will refuse to nominate any judges throughout his term in office. As these hypothetical examples show, it would be irresponsible and dangerous to conclude that Congress may not impeach the president based on how he wields the powers of his office.

For a more concrete example, consider Nixon. As head of the executive branch, he ordinarily would have been free to determine the priorities of the White House, the IRS, the CIA, and the FBI. In fact, he would have been *expected* to do so. Further, many of the specific orders that he issued to federal employees between June 1972 and August 1974 surely fell within the lawful scope of his constitutional power as president. But for good reason, these facts did not deter the House Judiciary Committee from probing how Nixon had wielded his authority throughout this period. Nor did it stop the committee from exploring the motives for Nixon's actions. And in the end, the committee had little trouble finding that Nixon had acted with the corrupt and criminal purpose of obstructing justice. On this basis, among others, it decisively approved articles of impeachment against him.

Similar logic applies to pardons. While the president has an absolute power to pardon, Congress has an absolute power to impeach the president for abusive or corrupt exercises of the pardon power. In our view, Trump might have crossed that line on August 25, 2017, when he pardoned Joe Arpaio (the former sheriff of Maricopa County, Arizona). In July 2017, Judge Susan Bolton of the U.S. District Court for the District of Arizona had found Arpaio guilty of criminal contempt of court. She concluded that Arpaio had willfully and repeatedly violated a federal judicial order requiring him to respect the rights of undocumented migrants. Although Judge Bolton didn't mention this fact in her order, it was widely understood that Arpaio had perpetrated a campaign of terror and atrocities against vulnerable Hispanics within his jurisdiction. Against that background, Trump's decision to pardon Arpaio was widely seen as a presidential endorsement of violent racism.

There are two reasons this pardon may qualify as an impeachable offense. First, it amounted to a frontal assault on the judiciary's ability to enforce the Constitution. Here we agree with Professor Noah Feldman: "When a sheriff ignores the courts, he becomes a law unto himself. The courts' only available recourse is to sanction the sheriff. If the president blocks the courts from making the sheriff follow the law, then the president is breaking the basic structure of the legal order."[45] By pardoning Arpaio, Trump signaled that thugs who brutalize minorities and break the law may be shielded from justice. He also undermined the judiciary as a guardian of the rule of law. Using the pardon power this way thus involved a gross abuse of presidential authority. If Trump were to issue a series of similar pardons, that course of conduct would surely constitute a removable offense.

But the Arpaio pardon may also have qualified as impeachable for a very different reason. Trump made this decision amid widespread concern that he would try to stymie Special Counsel Robert Mueller. As lawyer Bill Yeomans has remarked, the Arpaio proclamation might have been meant as a "warning pardon that announced the weaponization of the pardon power."[46] It would be extremely troubling if Trump's motive in pardoning Arpaio was to dangle a get-out-of-jail-free card in front of Michael Flynn, Paul Manafort, Jared Kushner, or anyone else who might testify against him. Using the pardon power as part of a plan to prevent witnesses from testifying, or to discourage them from telling the truth, might well be impeachable. While we do not yet know enough about Trump's motives to make any such assessment, it is a question that Congress—and Mueller—should investigate.

Of course, Russia-related misconduct does not exhaust the long list of Trump's alleged "high Crimes and Misdemeanors." The very first resolution calling for his impeachment instead targeted Trump's support for "white supremacy, bigotry, racism, anti-Semitism, white nationalism, [and] neo-Nazism." It also sought Trump's removal for "inciting hate and hostility" and "sowing discord among the people of the United States, on the basis of race, national origin, religion, gender, [and] sexual orientation." The resolution supported these claims with detailed references to Trump's hateful and offensive remarks since taking office. On December 6, 2017, however, the House of Representatives rejected this resolution by a vote of 364–58.[47]

We anticipate that future impeachment resolutions will include similar allegations. They may also note that Trump frequently uses his bully pulpit to issue reckless threats against well-armed adversaries, and to make disturbing and undemocratic statements. For example, he has described the news media as "the enemy of the American people"; called upon employers to fire employees for their political speech; threatened to punish businesses that don't support him; denounced his own Justice Department and Federal Bureau of Investigation as "the deep state"; and retweeted inflammatory anti-Muslim videos. Wholly apart from what a court would say, Congress is free to decide in an impeachment hearing that some of Trump's public comments have violated the Free Speech Clause, the Free Exercise Clause, and the Equal Protection Clause. In addition, future impeachment resolutions may emphasize that Trump has brandished half-truths and lies in ways that exceed anything in living political memory. It is no exaggeration to say that his style of political communication hinges on an instinctual disregard for the constraints of objective truth. That manner of rhetoric has no rightful place in a democracy. It is dangerous in its own right and evokes a dark history of demagogues who sought only to consolidate power.

There comes a point at which a president can properly be impeached for his statements. Nixon reached that point: the House Judiciary Committee included his public falsehoods in its article of impeachment for obstructing justice. By the same token, Congress may choose to consider Trump's public remarks bearing on the Russia investigation if it opens an impeachment hearing. More generally, a president may be impeached for his public statements when they are intimately connected to—or essential to the execution of—a broader course of corrupt and abusive conduct.

But rarely, if ever, will words alone suffice for impeachment. That's true even of offensive statements that target vulnerable minorities and undermine democratic institutions. Impeaching solely on the basis of a president's public remarks would verge dangerously close to accepting "maladministration" as a removable offense. Politicians frequently make imprecise, hyperbolic, insulting, flattering, and misleading comments. A politician who didn't could never make his way to the White House. Allowing Congress to remove a president on the ground that he has made divisive and incendiary public statements would only invite structural instability.

A remarkable number of Trump's public comments have involved neither politics nor policy, but rather his global business empire. This leads us to a final alleged impeachable offense: receipt of unlawful emoluments. The Foreign Emoluments Clause prohibits the president, among others, from "accept[ing] any present, Emolument, Office, or Title, of any kind whatever, from any King, Prince, or foreign State," unless Congress consents. The Domestic Emoluments Clause, in turn, forbids the president from receiving "any other Emolument from the United States, or any of them."

Until Trump took office, most people didn't know (or care) what an *emolument* was. By January 2017, however, this term was in common use. It even topped the charts on Merriam-Webster. com. As far as words go, that's a very big deal.

This surge of popular fascination with the Emoluments Clauses reflects a widespread consensus that Trump is violating them. The nature of Trump's violation is straightforward. Because of his ownership stake in the Trump Organization, Trump's private financial interests are intertwined with a global business empire subject to many possible burdens and benefits at home and abroad. As a result, in his dealings with governmental officials, Trump might be guided not only by the national interests of the United States but also by those of the business that bears his name.

The purpose of the Emoluments Clauses is to eliminate precisely this kind of blurred loyalty. As the Framers recognized, leaders with divided interests cannot faithfully serve those who elected them. Private financial entanglements with foreign powers—or with elements of their own government—risk influencing even the most virtuous leaders. The Emoluments Clauses thus impose clear and categorical limitations. Their prophylactic rule is designed to avoid situations in which the American people must try to read the president's mind, searching for hints that he may have been seduced to compromise our national interest for his private profit. When the president makes trade deals, deploys soldiers, negotiates treaties, and allocates tax burdens, we shouldn't have to worry that his own bank account is on the line.

Trump's flagrant and continuing violation of the Emoluments Clauses is deeply troubling in its own right. But that pattern of illegal conduct also connects to broader concerns that he has infected our political system with elements of kleptocracy. By undermining the wall of separation between his family business and the US government—and by undeservedly elevating his own children to prominent public positions—Trump has acted more like a third-world dictator than the leader of a democratic nation. Further, since taking office he has used Twitter to attack journalists who criticize his properties; he has repeatedly visited and promoted Trump-branded restaurants, hotels, and golf clubs; and he has directly threatened the business interests of his prominent political critics. As corruption expert Seva Gunitsky notes: "This is the kind of thing you see in broken states."[48]

As we write, there are several lawsuits pending in federal court that challenge Trump's receipt of illegal emoluments. We are involved in two of those cases, and it is our considered view that the courts can (and must) enjoin Trump's constitutional violations. But the existence of this litigation does not prevent Congress from taking immediate action. For example, Congress can require Trump to publicly disclose the full extent of his emoluments. It can also pass a law to limit and regulate his financial entanglements with foreign states. It would become especially important for Congress to act if the judiciary (wrongly) concluded that it lacked the power to address these issues—or if Trump refused to comply with a court order to stop accepting emoluments.

Although less extreme measures might well suffice, Congress also could address Trump's ongoing violations of the Emoluments Clauses in the context of an impeachment proceeding. There is historical support for that view. At the Virginia Ratifying Convention, Edmund Jennings Randolph stated that a president "may be impeached" for "receiving emoluments from foreign powers."[49] If the House of Representatives were to seriously consider articles of impeachment on this basis, it would surely want to investigate a number of factual issues beforehand. These would include the nature and scope of Trump's unlawful emoluments; whether there is any evidence suggesting that Trump has been improperly influenced; and how else Trump's illegal acts have harmed US interests. In drafting its articles of impeachment, the House might also choose to describe Trump's misconduct as "Implementing Kleptocracy." This formulation would encompass receipt of emoluments—but it would also capture an array of corrupt, nepotistic, and financially self-interested actions that have undermined the integrity of US public policy and self-governance.

*　*　*

In *Through the Looking Glass*, Humpty Dumpty instructs Alice that, "When *I* use a word, . . . it means just what I choose it to mean—neither more nor less." In response, Alice poses her memorable challenge: "The question is . . . whether you *can* make words mean so many different things." To which Humpty briskly responds: "The question is . . . which is to be master."

With their cynical views of interpretation, Humpty Dumpty and Gerald Ford would've gotten on famously—especially if they happened to discuss impeachment. But even words as pliable as "high Crimes and Misdemeanors" *are* subject to meaningful limitations. The text, structure, and history of the Constitution—coupled with centuries of popular understanding and political practice—limit the universe of impeachable acts. The Constitution relies on Congress to respect those constraints. As we'll see in the next chapter, that is only the beginning of Congress's constitutional duty to exercise good judgment in defending the Republic from tyranny.

3
TO IMPEACH OR *NOT* TO IMPEACH

On February 12, 1998, Senator Robert Byrd of West Virginia cast his vote on whether to remove President Bill Clinton from office. A respected elder statesman, Byrd had served in the Senate for thirty-nine years and was recognized as an authority on its traditions. Friends and foes alike described him as an "institution within an institution." To many, he embodied aspirations that the Senate might serve as a responsible chamber for national deliberation. His remarks on whether to convict Clinton thus carried special weight.

Byrd was unsparing in his criticism of the president: "Mr. Clinton's offenses do, in my judgment, constitute an 'abuse or violation of some public trust.'" Clinton had willfully lied under oath, breaking his promise to "see to it that the laws be faithfully executed." He had also "undermine[d] the system of justice and law on which this Republic . . . has its foundation." Byrd elaborated: "Does not such injury to the institutions of Government constitute an impeachable offense, a political high crime or high misdemeanor against the state?"

"But the matter does not end there," Byrd cautioned. Impeachment involves a "uniquely and especially grave" judgment that affects the entire constitutional system. Senators could therefore vote to acquit even if they thought the president's conduct was indeed impeachable. As Byrd explained, "simple logic can point one way while wisdom may be in quite a different direction." In the Senate chamber, he added, "the voice of the people in things of their knowledge is as the voice of God." And when it came to Clinton, "the people's perception of this entire matter as being driven by political agendas . . . tip[s] the scales for allowing this President to serve out the remaining 22 months of his term." Even if the president were guilty as charged, removing him would "only serve to further undermine a public trust that is too much damaged already." Byrd then concluded, "I will reluctantly vote to acquit."[1]

With unusual candor, Byrd embraced and exercised the power *not* to impeach. As we've discussed, the Constitution explicitly states that Congress may not end a presidency unless the president has committed an impeachable offense. But nowhere does the Constitution state or otherwise imply that Congress *must* remove a president whenever that standard is met. Even when members of the House and Senate believe that the president has committed "high Crimes and Misdemeanors," they possess a legally unlimited prerogative not to end his term in office.

This negative power can operate at any stage of the impeachment process. Byrd invoked it at the last possible moment. Far more often, however, it is deployed silently and strategically at the very beginning of a scandal. Motivated legislators may oppose, ignore, or sabotage efforts to investigate presidential misdeeds, thus preventing definitive proof from coming to light. In the face of any such evidence, they might seek to discredit investigators, confuse the public, distract the press, or promote a milder punishment. They may also refuse to call for impeachment, urge their colleagues to avoid the "i-word," and criticize anyone who puts that option on the table. At all times, legislators can privately help a president defend against impeachment talk and publicly campaign against it. Once the House has opened impeachment hearings, it can decline to move forward for a host of reasons that have nothing to do with a failure of proof. And senators, in turn, are free to vote against conviction even if they think the president is guilty as charged.

Like all grants of discretion in the Constitution, this one is open to abuse. No document can guarantee the wise or responsible exercise of the powers that it establishes. Legislators might reflexively oppose removal out of personal or partisan loyalty to the president—or for other unworthy reasons. But in the hands of a conscientious legislator, the power *not* to impeach allows full consideration of all factors relevant to ending a presidency. In other words, it allows Congress to exercise judgment.

* * *

Whereas Byrd recognized the need for judgment in impeachments, many legislators prefer to deny their own agency. It can be intimidating to accept responsibility for such politically sensitive decisions. One version of false denial occurs when legislators insist that they are bound by original intent or the criminal code. Another version, relevant here, is the claim that evidence of "high Crimes and Misdemeanors" *requires* that they advocate for impeachment or conviction. During the Clinton hearings, this was a common refrain from Republicans; if Donald Trump is someday impeached, we can expect to hear it from many Democrats.

If that claim were true—if the impeachment *power* were actually an impeachment *duty*—then legislators have broken their oaths countless times. Don't take our word for it; take theirs. For the past 229 years, hardly a day has passed without an outraged legislator accusing the president of tyranny, corruption, or criminality. Yet rarely are such claims followed by impeachment resolutions in the House. It would be strange if this fact proved abdication of duty rather than commendable restraint. The better view is that legislators have long recognized their own discretion, except perhaps in the most extreme cases.

Indeed, Congress has repeatedly declined to act despite credible suspicion of impeachable offenses. James Polk invaded Mexico in 1848 without seeking a declaration of war. Warren Harding flouted Prohibition by downing whisky at smoke-filled poker nights in the White House. Franklin D. Roosevelt defied the Lend-Lease Act during World War II by sending military shipments to

England. And Gerald Ford's pardon of Nixon led many to question whether he had struck a deal with the devil. Yet in none of these cases did the House seriously contemplate impeachment.

The Iran-Contra Affair offers an especially striking example. In the early 1980s, Ronald Reagan supported a Nicaraguan rebel group known as the Contras. When Congress got word, it passed a series of laws limiting all aid to the group—direct and indirect, military and nonmilitary. Ignoring those statutes, the Reagan administration secretly used the National Security Council (NSC) to solicit covert foreign aid for the Contras. NSC Director Robert McFarlane and Marine Lt. Col. Oliver North oversaw the cabal—and were encouraged in their efforts by Reagan's claim that the Contras were the "moral equivalent of the Founding Fathers."[2] Meanwhile, Reagan urged McFarlane and Admiral John Poindexter to organize a complex arms deal with Iran in hopes of addressing an ongoing hostage crisis. These orders broke numerous trade embargoes and Reagan's own pledge not to negotiate. The resulting transactions, which slowly evolved into an arms-for-hostages exchange, at times involved an exiled Iranian businessman, the Israeli government, and other exotic third parties. Iran ultimately paid out $48 million— much of which was then secretly diverted to the Contras by Oliver North. His unlawful plan was approved by Poindexter, who had succeeded McFarlane as director of the NSC. These transactions failed miserably at addressing the hostage crisis. But they succeeded in flouting almost every applicable statute, executive branch policy, and rule of constitutional law.

As details of the scandal came to light, an outraged public demanded answers. Poindexter resigned and North was relieved of his duties, though not before they both destroyed reams of evidence. Multiple investigations were launched in Congress and the executive branch, focused largely on a single issue: Did Reagan know about funds flowing from Iran to Nicaragua?

Insisting that he didn't recall most of the key facts, Reagan built a defense on negligence and ignorance. In this telling, subordinates took advantage of his loose management style to engage in illegal activities that they believed would further his goals, but of which he was unaware. Investigators and the public generally accepted this story, though it raised a significant question of its own: Where was the president in all this? As commentator Anthony Lewis remarked, "Mr. Reagan did not act in this affair with the minimum attention required of his office. He was not a president."[3] Congressional investigators reached an even more damning conclusion: Reagan had "created or at least tolerated an environment where those who did know of the diversion [of funds] believed with certainty they were carrying out the President's policies."[4]

These findings would undoubtedly have justified further hearings and a vote on articles of impeachment—especially given hints of a cover-up and doubts about Reagan's complete honesty. As Senator Daniel Inouye noted at the time, Iran-Contra involved unconstitutional "secret policy making." Congress had uncovered "a tale of working outside the system and of utilizing irregular channels and private parties accountable to no one on matters of national security."[5] These extraordinary violations of the separation of powers posed a direct threat to the constitutional system.

Yet the House stayed its hand. According to Representative Lee Hamilton, this was partly because nobody found a smoking gun: "If you are going to impeach a president you've got to have very direct proof and we just didn't have it."[6] Reagan had lied to Congress, violated statutes, and failed to supervise key subordinates, but there was never clear evidence that he had known specifically about diversion of Iranian funds to the Contras. Whether he had committed "high Crimes and Misdemeanors" could plausibly be argued both ways.

Perhaps more important, Reagan remained popular. Polls showed that Americans liked and trusted him—and didn't feel the same way about Vice President George H. W. Bush, who would be elevated if Reagan were removed. Further, key players in Congress feared disaster if another presidency went down in flames just thirteen years after Watergate. As Representative Hamilton later admitted, "we really felt that the Reagan presidency was on the brink, and the whole process of government could collapse, literally . . . it really was a constitutional crisis for us at that point."[7] Naturally, the Cold War also loomed over this analysis. Legislators feared that an impeachment would disrupt Reagan's ongoing nuclear disarmament talks with Soviet leader Mikhail Gorbachev. Finally, Reagan was halfway through his second term. Removing him did not seem worth the trouble, especially after he cooperated with investigators, installed a well-respected chief of staff, and signaled openness to enhanced oversight of covert actions.

All these factors affected the House's final decision not to accuse Reagan of impeachable offenses. They also help explain why House members only briefly discussed impeaching Vice President Bush—despite evidence that he had known about some illegal aspects of Iran-Contra. Later, while serving as president, Bush brought the story to an end by pardoning six Reagan administration officials involved in the scandal. This self-interested pardon effectively doomed an independent prosecutor's lingering campaign to reveal the full scope of executive branch misconduct.

As the Iran-Contra saga demonstrates, invoking impeachment is always a matter of congressional judgment. Suspicion of "high Crimes and Misdemeanors" may begin the story but can never end it. At every step along the way—from the earliest whispers of impropriety to a final vote in the Senate—legislators must choose whether and how to proceed. Those decisions reach beyond the president's alleged misdeeds. They often encompass big questions about what's best for the Republic, and small questions about what's best for each legislator and political party.

Every impeachment is unique. That's why analyses of this power often struggle to descend from lofty generalizations. Still, it's possible to map out the major questions that Congress usually must resolve in cases of presidential wrongdoing. We do so here in three steps. First, we explain why the Constitution is properly interpreted as vesting broad impeachment discretion in the House and Senate. Second, we describe other powers that Congress can deploy in response to presidential malfeasance—including its authority to censure the president. Finally, we propose a general framework for assessing the biggest risks that Congress must consider in deciding whether to impeach. These include the risks of impeaching too early and too late, as well as the inherent risks that accompany even a well-timed, well-justified impeachment.

*　*　*

If you spend enough time drinking at bars in Washington, DC, you'll hear a lot of jokes about Congress. Almost without fail, they end with the same punchline: "and then Congress did nothing." Sometimes these jokes are funny. Most of the time they're sad. But their bottom line is right. As a matter of constitutional law—if not political reality—Congress enjoys nearly unbounded discretion in deciding whether and when to exercise its authority. *Inaction* thus ranks among Congress's mightiest (and most well-exercised) powers. For an especially high-profile example of this point, consider the Senate's handling of a recent Supreme Court nomination.

Justice Antonin Scalia passed away on February 13, 2016. Within weeks, Senate Majority Leader Mitch McConnell publicly declared that the Republican-controlled Senate would not hold a confirmation hearing on *any* nominee put forth by Barack Obama. McConnell justified this move by arguing that it was Obama's last year and the issue should be settled in the November 2016 election. This was an embarrassingly weak and indefensible position, squarely at odds with centuries of legislative practice. Yet McConnell refused to budge even after Obama nominated Chief Judge Merrick Garland of the District of Columbia Court of Appeals—a widely respected centrist. When Trump won the presidential election, McConnell's cynical gambit guaranteed that an unyieldingly conservative judge could be nominated and confirmed. And that's exactly what happened. On April 8, 2017, Neil Gorsuch was sworn into the seat once occupied by Scalia. He has already proven himself a reliable warrior for conservative causes.

In the period between Scalia's death and Trump's electoral victory, some argued that the Senate was violating Article II, Section 2 of the Constitution by refusing to consider Garland's nomination. That section provides: "[The president] shall nominate, and by and with the Advice and Consent of the Senate, shall appoint . . . Judges of the supreme Court." Constitutional critics of the Senate asserted that the word *shall* in this sentence applies both to the president and to the Senate. They added that Article II, Section 2 thus required the Senate to perform its "advice and consent" function by meeting with and voting on judicial nominees. As attorney David Gans wrote, "the Constitution does not require the Senate to confirm a particular nominee, but it does require the Senate to consider the nominee."[8]

The Senate's treatment of Chief Judge Garland was exceptionally dishonorable. It violated longstanding practice and shattered many of the norms still applicable to judicial nominations. But we're skeptical that the Senate violated the Constitution. While Article II, Section 2 requires Senate consent in order for a judicial nominee to be confirmed, it doesn't impose an affirmative duty on the Senate to take specific actions when presented with a nominee—much less to do so within a particular time frame. In practice, it would be impossible to draw a principled, enforceable line between ordinary foot-dragging (valid) and failure to give a nominee "true" consideration (supposedly invalid).

Especially given that the Senate's role in the nomination process is to serve as a check on the executive, we should be wary of insisting that it can do so only one way. As Professor Michael Ramsey has observed, the Constitution "often provide[s] for one part of government to propose an action subject to the approval of another part." That's an ordinary feature of Senate treaty approval, proposal and passage of bills, and ratification of proposed constitutional amendments. Ramsey adds: "The Constitution is not read in any of these situations to impose a duty on the second entity to act formally on the proposal. If the second entity fails to approve, for whatever reason and in whatever manner, the measure does not take effect."[9] (The noteworthy exception to this rule is Article I, Section 7, which provides that a bill passed by Congress becomes law within ten days unless the president vetoes it.)

This background explains why it is possible for Congress to remain a celebrated bastion of do-nothingness. In our separation of powers, rarely is it affirmatively commanded by the Constitution to do something. As any savvy lobbyist knows, congressional inaction is frequently and strategically deployed as a deliberate course of conduct by the majority. Where Congress is vested with constitutional powers, it is almost always vested with corresponding discretion about whether and when to use them.

That lesson applies with full force to impeachment. Too often, this power is described as though it operates mechanically, springing to life whenever triggered by "high Crimes and Misdemeanors." That perspective is not only wrong but misleading. The Framers didn't establish the House as a roving commission to smite every wrongdoer. Instead, they entrusted the impeachment power to an institution with the capacity and legitimacy to make sensible political judgments for the whole nation.

This discretion is confirmed by constitutional text. Article I, Section 2 provides that the House "shall have the sole Power of Impeachment." Article I, Section 3 states that the Senate "shall have the sole Power to try all Impeachments." This simply isn't the kind of language that the Constitution uses to mandate official action. While it is true that the president "shall be removed from office" if impeached and convicted, the word *shall* in this sentence addresses the consequences of conviction, not the decision whether to bring charges in the first place.

In contrast, consider how the Constitution describes the Senate when it convenes as a court of impeachment: "When sitting for that Purpose, they shall be on Oath or Affirmation. When the

President of the United States is tried, the Chief Justice shall preside: And no Person shall be convicted without the Concurrence of two thirds of the Members present." This is what mandatory constitutional language looks like. To adjudicate articles of impeachment, the Senate *must* be on "Oath or Affirmation" and the chief justice *must* preside if the president is in the dock. Further, to convict the defendant, two-thirds of the Senate *must* support that outcome. Nothing about this text admits of discretion.

In short, the Framers knew how to issue commands—and nowhere did they instruct the House and Senate to take aim at every potentially impeachable offender. Instead, they endowed legislators with the *option* of acting, but not with the *duty* to act in every instance where removal would be justifiable. Congress thus bears the heavy burden of exercising judgment.

*   *   *

Denying the existence of congressional discretion, partisans supporting an impeachment often suggest that the House should function only as a "grand jury." On that account, which is borrowed from the criminal justice system, the bar for impeaching is both low and mandatory. The House need only determine whether there is probable cause to believe that the president committed "high Crimes and Misdemeanors." If there is, the House must immediately force the Senate to hold a trial.

Grand jury analogies, however, are badly misplaced when it comes to impeachment. Lacking an affirmative duty to impeach, the House is never obliged to take that drastic step unless it concludes that doing so is in the greater interest of the nation. This requires a far more sensitive judgment than any grand jury is expected to make. And for good reason: accusing the president of "high Crimes and Misdemeanors" is an extraordinary act in its own right. As Senator Byrd warned, impeachment is "the greatest censure, the greatest condemnation, that the House can inflict upon any President."[10] Further, a Senate trial of any chief executive is both costly and divisive. The House cannot responsibly impose that burden on the nation based merely on suspicion of wrong-doing. On the contrary, House members should vote to impeach only if they genuinely believe that the accusations are well supported and warrant the president's immediate removal from office. We must therefore reject grand jury analogies, which are often deployed to relieve the House of responsibility for its most consequential decision.

If the criminal justice system is to be our reference point, then prosecutors offer a far superior analogy for the House. Discretion is essential to the prosecutorial role. Considerations of fair play and justice properly guide decisions about whom to prosecute, what charges to bring, and what punishments to seek. Those decisions must also account for sound public policy, the allocation of limited resources, and sustaining governmental legitimacy. Just as prosecutors need not hound every potential lawbreaker, the House need not impeach all "high Crimes and Misdemeanors." For politicians and prosecutors alike, the rule of law is most nobly served when tempered by values of mercy and wisdom. As Professor Akhil Amar writes, that is particularly true when the House votes on articles of impeachment, since "the ordinary locus of pre-trial mercy in our constitutional system—the President's pardon power—is inapplicable."[11]

Of course, discretion takes on a very different cast in the realm of impeachment than in standard criminal cases. Rarely will a single prosecutorial decision risk catastrophic harm. In contrast, a single decision to impeach the president—or not to impeach him—could have extraordinary consequences. That's why fact-finding in the House must always be followed by careful analysis of a tough political judgment: given what we've learned, what's the best course forward for the American people?

In answering that question, the Constitution offers little direct guidance. Apart from requiring proof of "Treason, Bribery, or other high Crimes and Misdemeanors," it allows the House to impeach—or not—for any reason. Thus, House members may decline to impeach because the nation faces more urgent issues; they definitely lack two-thirds support in the Senate; they don't believe a decisive majority of the public would support their decision; or they have good reason to believe other political remedies can better address the president's misconduct going forward.

Most of what we've just said applies to the Senate, too, with a crucial difference. Whereas the House decides whether to set in motion the vast and unsettling machinery of impeachment, that's a foregone conclusion for the Senate. The harm is done; those costs are sunk. For senators, the only question is whether the president should be removed from office (and, if so, whether he should be disqualified from future office holding). That's no small matter, obviously. Yet compared to the House, the Senate's range of options is narrower and the scope of its discretion more clearly defined. If we need a criminal justice analogy for the Senate, the best candidate is "judge"—though senators may consider practical, moral, and political factors that have no place in a well-constituted court of law.

There's actually useful precedent on this point, for a change.[12] While prosecuting Clinton's trial in the Senate, Representative Bob Barr repeatedly referred to senators as "jurors." Agitated, Senator Tom Harkin took to the Senate floor: "I object to the use and the continued use of the word 'jurors.'"[13] Chief Justice William Rehnquist agreed: "The chair is of the view that the Senator from Iowa's objection is well taken, that the Senate is not simply a jury; it is a court in this case. And therefore counsel should refrain from referring to the Senators as jurors." Later, Harkin explained his motives for raising this objection: "As Alexander Hamilton said, we are judges, and judges can take into account a lot of things other than the facts and the law."[14] That's a questionable statement about real judges, though it's certainly true of the Senate sitting as a court of impeachment.

In sum, there can be no doubt that the House and Senate wield considerable discretion on the matter of impeachment. Arguments to the contrary are usually partisan ploys rather than good-faith interpretations of the Constitution. The important questions concern *how* discretion should be exercised, not whether it exists at all.

* * *

In Chapter 4, we'll examine why the Framers gave the impeachment power to Congress. At this point, though, it's helpful to consider an implication of that choice. Unlike the Supreme Court or state officials (who were also considered), Congress is well equipped to corral a rogue president through less extreme measures. As the saying goes, when all you have is a hammer, the world is full of nails. But not every presidential misdeed—not even every "high Crime[] and Misdemeanor[]"—should be met with a hammer. In deciding whether to pull impeachment from its toolbox, Congress must consider the possibility that its other powers may suffice.

We recognize that it might sound unrealistic these days to urge that Congress act effectively and creatively during a national crisis. Frozen by dysfunction, trapped in cycles of recrimination, awash in dark money, and captured by powerful interests, our national legislature is in abysmal shape. Fans of alliteration now call it the "broken branch."[15] Experienced observers caution that "it's even worse than it looks."[16] And serious scholars write books with titles such as *The Decline and Fall of the American Republic*. According to Professors Eric Posner and Adrian Vermeule, ours is an era "after the separation of powers," dominated by an ever-more-imperial presidency and an embarrassingly outmatched legislature.[17]

There's no denying the force of those concerns. Still, as Barack Obama learned repeatedly, and as Trump has already discovered, tales of Congress's death (and the president's imperium) have been somewhat exaggerated.

In any event, to ask about alternatives to ending a presidency is to presume that we're already in impeachment territory. As a matter of political and institutional reality, that would occur only if there were substantial legislative support behind calls to rebuke or restrain the president. Keep in mind that congressional paralysis isn't inevitable. It's a consequence not only of institutional failures but also of broken, gerrymandered, and polarized politics. Changed facts on the ground could alter those dynamics and generate a temporary consensus about addressing presidential misconduct. Thus, when the stars are aligned such that impeachment is on the table, other responses to the president may also be available.

Congress's arsenal should not be underestimated. The basic genius of the Constitution is to divide powers among branches that possess the self-interest and sheer capacity to counteract one another. When roused to action, Congress has many methods of constraining a president and thwarting his abuses. Before concluding that impeachment is necessary, it's important to review these powers and to decide whether an alternative strategy would be more appropriate.

Let's start with some of Congress's most straightforward options. Naturally, Congress might invoke its power to legislate (and to override presidential vetoes). By passing new laws, Congress can impose sweeping, durable limits on the president and the rest of the executive branch. The power of the purse, in turn, allows Congress to exercise far-reaching control over the conduct, policies, priorities, and very structure of the executive branch. Finally, Congress's powers over personnel give legislators a major say in who occupies judgeships, cabinet positions, and agency roles. That indirectly enables Congress to shape policy and to influence cultures of independence and integrity within the president's domain.

When exercised directly against the president, these powers allow Congress to coerce obedience to its will. But they also have a subtler dimension. Used properly, they can shrink the scope of the president's authority to act unilaterally. As Justice Robert Jackson famously wrote, the president's powers "are not fixed but fluctuate depending upon their disjunction or conjunction with those of Congress."[18] If Congress legislates on issues of great concern to the president, it can reduce his power to what Jackson called "its lowest ebb." This would undermine the president's *formal* prerogative to pursue significant initiatives without congressional support.

In the same breath, Congress can undermine the president's *informal* authority. On many issues, the Constitution offers little more than a rough sketch for how the political branches should interact. As a result, the governing authority actually available to the president and Congress at any given point isn't determined only by law. Instead, it's largely determined by shifting dynamics of public support. As Professor Josh Chafetz writes, "within the confines laid out by the [Constitution], it is public engagement in the public sphere that determines where . . . the power to decide really lies."[19] If the president's abusive conduct undermines his standing with the public, Congress can seize the high ground. Having done so, it can then attempt to realign national politics behind its initiatives—including efforts to keep the rogue president under control.

Relatedly, Congress can hold the president and his staff accountable through aggressive oversight. Both houses of Congress enjoy a power of investigation that the Supreme Court has deemed "penetrating and far-reaching."[20] This includes the authority to compel testimony and hold uncooperative witnesses in contempt. Through its vast investigatory power, Congress can keep a close eye on the president, interrogate and publicly shame administration officials, and review many top-secret materials.

If its investigations reveal troubling information about the president, Congress's right to share that news with the American people is protected by the Constitution's Speech and Debate Clause. Under that provision, an array of official acts by legislators and their staffs are shielded from criminal prosecution, civil discovery, and other burdens that might chill their deliberations. As relevant here, the Speech and Debate Clause safeguards the prerogative of individual legislators to publicly release confidential information about the executive branch.

Savvy use of these oversight powers allows Congress to trigger an even broader network of checks on the presidency. In traditional accounts, the federal system is balanced between three branches of government and a fourth estate, the press. But as

Professor Jack Goldsmith has observed, the "modern accountability system" involves a host of decentralized, nontraditional actors. Civic groups at home, human rights groups abroad, lawyers and watchdogs within the executive branch, and new species of journalist hold the government responsible for its misdeeds. Goldsmith notes that these players "help ensure that the other institutions of government know about the president's actions, can require him to account for them, and can punish him if they think he is engaged in the wrong policy or acting unlawfully."[21] Congress's power to check the president can thus activate—and be activated by—a broader alarm system around the White House.

In extreme cases, Congress may seek to restrain the chief executive by carefully raising the question of impeachment. Even when the odds of removal from office are very low, serious legislative consideration of impeachment can strike fear into a president. In 1813, for instance, John Adams confided in Thomas Jefferson that calls for his removal over a decade earlier had offered "a hint or two . . . on the Subject of Terrorism."[22] Here he referred to the explosive *Hermione* controversy in 1799. That year, American officials seized and detained Jonathan Robbins, a mutineer on Her Majesty's armed frigate *Hermione*. Adams ultimately surrendered Robbins to the British military, despite a last-minute claim by Robbins that he was American. Although Adams remained secure in the presidency, opposition leaders demanded impeachment for this decision and apparently made a lasting impression in doing so.

As we'll see in Chapter 5, threats of impeachment talk can raise many difficult strategic questions. So can reliance on any of the other constitutional powers that Congress might invoke to address a rogue president. And there's no denying that those alternatives may, in some cases, be inadequate to the task of thwarting tyranny. Even when Congress sustains consensus and aggressively asserts itself, a president can always do a lot on his own—especially in the realms of foreign affairs and national security.

That said, Ezra Klein hit on an important truth when he observed that "Congress is a tiger that we pretend is made of paper."[23] The legislature wields exceptional and wide-ranging powers. With sufficient commitment to country over party, Congress *could* effectively assert itself against the president and avert the need for impeachment. Identifying when that's the best option is always a context-sensitive judgment. It may not be an easy call to make; however, it's a choice we can't avoid.

* * *

When evidence of presidential abuse comes to light, a resolution of censure may emerge as an attractive middle ground between impeachment and more quotidian legislative checks. Congress unquestionably has the authority to censure a president. The trick is ascertaining what effect, if any, a censure will have.

Congress's power of presidential censure isn't made explicit in the Constitution. Whereas censure of legislators is authorized by the Rules and Expulsion Clause, which empowers each house to "punish its Members for disorderly Behaviour," no comparable language addresses censure of the president. Still, resolutions of censure are consistent with all relevant constitutional rules. First, because a resolution of censure is merely an expression of opinion rather than an individualized punishment by the legislature, the Bill of Attainder Clause poses no obstacle. Second, while impeachment can result only in removal and disqualification, the Constitution doesn't forbid other sanctions *outside* of an impeachment proceeding. Finally, Congress's duty to "keep a Journal of its Proceedings"—considered alongside the Speech and Debate Clause—supports the authority of either house (or both concurrently) to pass a resolution expressing views on public issues.

A censure may sound like very weak medicine. In many cases, a legislative slap on the wrist is unlikely to convince a tyrant to confess error and mend his ways. Intense skepticism is usually the right attitude toward censure. But history suggests that there are occasions when a resolution condemning the president can send a powerful message.

Andrew Jackson offers a telling example. In 1832, Jackson vetoed an act to recharter the Bank of the United States and then moved to withdraw all federal deposits. These decisions were enormously controversial and incited a backlash by Jackson's enemies, who held a majority in the Senate. Led by Henry Clay, Daniel Webster, and John C. Calhoun, they put forth this proposal: "*Resolved*, That the President . . . has assumed upon himself authority and power not conferred by the Constitution and laws, but in derogation of both."[24] After ten weeks of debate, the resolution passed 26 to 20. Jackson's fury knew no limits. As a biographer explains, "Jackson could not get it out of his head that a verdict had been rendered against him, and against his vision of the Presidency."[25] Jackson responded to the Senate with a "Protest" defending himself and denying the legality of the Senate's action. In a stunning breach of protocol, the Senate refused to print or acknowledge the president's response in its own journal. The House, in turn, passed a resolution criticizing the Senate for its handling of the situation.

This episode stuck with Jackson. In his Protest, he wrote that the censure was a "judgment of *guilty* by the highest tribunal in the Union." It would inflict a stigma "on the offender, his family, and fame . . . handing down to future generations the story of his disgrace." To Jackson, these were the "bitterest portions, if not the very essence" of the Senate's punishment.[26] Three years later, when Jackson's allies retook the Senate, they ordered that the censure text be stricken from the 1834 journal. That night, historians report, "the Senate galleries were so raucous and the atmosphere so tense that [Jackson's allies] sent for guns."[27] Once the deed was done, a courier rushed to Jackson bearing a poignant tribute: the pen that erased his infamous censure. Needless to say, these were not the actions of people who thought that censure was a mere slap on the wrist. Jackson took it *very* seriously indeed.

Less dramatic but no less revealing are two cases where impeachment and censure were debated simultaneously. The first occurred in January 1848, after James Polk sent General Zachary Taylor beyond the Nueces River in Mexico, triggering hostilities without a declaration of war. Whigs in Congress passed a resolution denouncing Polk's gambit as "unconstitutional." But they stopped short of calling for impeachment, leading Polk's defenders to level charges of cowardice: "They have said by their votes that the President has violated the Constitution in the most flagrant manner . . . and I here demand of them to impeach the President."[28] Incredulous, a Tennessee Whig named Washington Barrow responded: "Impeach the President! Do they take us to be fools? . . . [Instead we] have placed a rebuke of him upon [the House Journal], which will continue to blister his name so long as he lives, and will be affixed to his memory while the history of the country endures."[29] In Polk's case, censure didn't convince the president that he should withdraw American forces from Mexico. Nor did it destroy his reputation in the history books. Instead, it was the only official action against Polk available to a party that lacked the votes to impeach.

The near opposite dynamic unfolded in Bill Clinton's case. There, House Republicans *did* have the votes to impeach the president for his misconduct but feared that a successful censure resolution would lose them their pro-impeachment majority. The issue came to a head in December 1998, when several representatives floated the idea of censuring Clinton rather than impeaching him. House leaders refused to allow a floor vote on any of these proposals. Although dressed in legalese, their objections were based on fear that fence-sitters would switch their votes for impeachment if censure were an option. As it turns out, they were right. Several House members who voted for impeachment later stated that they would have preferred only to censure the president. The Clinton case thus produced an unusual alignment: House leaders opposed censure, while the president, many Democrats, and some Republicans supported it. In fact, Clinton later criticized Republican leaders for refusing to put censure to a vote, emphasizing in his autobiography that censure "was the preferred option of 75 percent of the American people."[30]

As this history shows, censure has an indeterminate character. In some cases, formal legislative condemnation may tarnish a president's legacy and warn him off from further abuses. Moreover, a censure resolution signals to future generations that the president did something terribly wrong—thus ensuring that his misconduct isn't cited as precedent. But censures are only worthwhile under highly specific circumstances. Where a president isn't troubled by his standing in the court of history, and isn't amenable to course corrections, censure is a largely pointless undertaking that may divert energy and attention from more necessary measures.

That's to be expected. The appropriate response to presidential wrongdoing is always context-dependent. Given what the president did, how the president is likely to react, and what the nation will think, Congress must decide between impeachment and alternative remedies. In making this choice, Congress is well-served to thoroughly consider the substantial risks associated with any impeachment. We now turn to that analysis, beginning our discussion with an oft-overlooked point: impeachment isn't a single decision. This judgment is entrusted to an institution with 535 members, who must continuously reassess their position in real time as the process unfolds.

* * *

Chief Justice William Rehnquist cut a dramatic figure as he presided over the Clinton impeachment. Ever since Thomas Jefferson's stinging rebuke of "needless official apparel," Supreme Court justices had all worn plain black robes.[31] (Jefferson particularly despised "the monstrous wig which makes the English judges look like rats peeping through bunches of oakum.") But Rehnquist had personally redesigned his robes in 1995, adding four gold stripes on each sleeve. A lover of operettas, he was inspired by a production of *Iolanthe* in which the Lord Chancellor's robe also sported gold stripes. The chief's colleagues were unimpressed; they had already rejected his plea to upgrade their wardrobes. When the cameras started rolling in January 1999, though, he certainly looked the part of Chief Justice of the United States.

Rehnquist brought more than a fancy title and flashy robes to the Senate. He was also a bona fide expert on impeachment. Years earlier, in *Grand Inquests*, he had chronicled the failed efforts to remove Andrew Johnson and Justice Samuel Chase. This study led Rehnquist to view the impeachment power as a "wild card."[32] Improper calls for removal, he worried, risked destabilizing the separation of powers between Congress and the other branches. Overall, the thrust of his book was a stern warning against partisan impeachments. It's no small irony that he later oversaw the divisive impeachment trial of Bill Clinton.

In describing impeachment as a "wild card," Rehnquist offered the right metaphor but an incomplete lesson. It's true that an impeachment can scramble the separation of powers. But this is hardly the full extent of its power to disrupt. In theory, a bitterly contested impeachment could unravel the very bonds that hold the nation together. Of course, the inverse is no less true. A failure to impeach when faced with tyranny could spell the end of US constitutionalism. In these respects, impeachment can serve as both savior and destroyer of American democracy.

This duality frames the issue of when Congress should impeach and when it should stay its hand. By their nature, impeachments have the potential to cause and prevent many kinds of harm. It thus makes little sense for anyone to be pro- or anti-impeachment in the abstract. Assessing what might happen in any given case requires a deeply fact-intensive analysis—and an appreciation that impeachments can unleash forces impossible to predict or control.

That's not the only complication. In analyzing how Congress should exercise its discretion, we must always keep in mind what part of the impeachment process we're discussing. The American public is not shy about debating whether a president should be removed from office. But that framing of the question begins at the end, putting ourselves in the role of senators voting on self-written articles of impeachment. This habit leads us to gloss over the many choices that legislators must make during a full impeachment process. In roughly sequential order, those include (1) holding public hearings on alleged presidential misconduct; (2) investigating the president; (3) publicly or privately using the "i-word"; (4) designating a committee to consider removal; (5) debating and voting on articles of impeachment; (6) voting in the House on those articles; (7) establishing process and procedure for the Senate impeachment trial; (8) conducting the Senate trial; and then (9) voting in the Senate on whether to convict the president.

By the time the process arrives at the final step, millions of less-noticed decisions have shaped how we got there and what's likely to happen next. The factors relevant to each of those choices could occupy books of their own. We'll simply note that in deciding whether to impeach, we're considering a series of events, not a single yea or nay vote. This perspective highlights the fact that impeachments are more than direct reactions to bad things the president may have done. They're dynamic processes in which both Congress and the public play a major role. Every step along the road changes the landscape in ways our analysis must take into account. Legislators' actions and choices at early stages of the process shape the circumstances under which they act later on.

Of course, Congress is hardly a monolith. When we say that "Congress" must make decisions, we're really saying that hundreds of legislators must separately and collectively pick a course of action. To be sure, those legislators are organized by political party and membership in various committees, caucuses, and leadership structures. But this organization often looks more impressive on paper than it feels on a day-to-day basis. Accordingly, individual legislators may not know how their colleagues will vote—and may thus struggle to ascertain the likely consequences of their own decisions. Amid fast-moving developments, power in Congress is everywhere and nowhere.

In short, impeachment analysis is fact intensive, constantly evolving, and partly recursive. Nonetheless, it's possible to identify some general guideposts. We'll do so here by asking three questions: What are the risks of impeaching *too quickly*? What are the risks of impeaching *too late* (or not at all)? And what risks are unavoidable even in a justified, well-timed impeachment? Although somewhat artificial, this framework can help us identify some of the most important considerations in any debate over impeachment.

* * *

Let's start with the risks of moving too quickly.

How might that come to pass? In general, we suspect most people agree that impeachments should be careful, deliberative, and thorough. But when we're faced with crisis, or when partisans sense blood in the water, caution can fall by the wayside. Ours is not a patient culture. If support for impeachment grows, a public addicted to speed may chafe at the tedium of congressional process or Justice Department investigators. It's in the heat of such passion that Congress might buckle, forgetting that we can't afford to screw up an impeachment.

A significant risk of moving too quickly is sacrificing a complete investigation. In most cases, only fools or hacks approach impeachment with their minds inalterably made up. Before removing a president, it is necessary to see the full picture that compels such rough treatment. Except in the most extraordinary circumstances, impeaching with a partial or plausibly contested understanding of key facts is a bad idea. We may subsequently learn new information that casts the whole course of events in a very different light. Moreover, the House might rush to judgment but then fail to prove its case in the Senate—or in the court of public opinion.

That's why a neutral entity, trusted by a broad cross-section of the public, must be given time, resources, and investigatory powers to build a reliable factual record. Historically, the House and Senate have investigated through their committees. They've also relied on evidence from special prosecutors, independent counsels, and ad hoc commissions. Effective investigations, however, usually take months or years. To achieve their purpose, they look beyond whether crimes were committed and instead assess the full scope and circumstances of potentially impeachable conduct. Critically, although they may involve occasional public hearings, most investigatory activities must be kept secret until they have nearly reached an end. Impeaching before these investigations have concluded may prevent the creation of a complete and respected account of what the president allegedly did wrong.

If Congress moves quickly to impeach, it may also lose a different source of useful information: the president's response to allegations of wrongdoing. Does the president admit error, apologize, and clean house? Does he prove his innocence, or at least his reasonable good faith? Or does he lie and obstruct until the bitter end? Maybe he fires investigators and stonewalls prosecutors? If ordered by a court to take an action or to abate illegal conduct, does he comply in good faith or does he defy the judiciary, either overtly or by a mere semblance of compliance?

These data points are invaluable when Congress asks whether leaving the president in office would pose a continuing threat to the nation. They can also clarify why the president did what he did and shape public views on whether he remains a viable leader. In some circumstances, moreover, the president might commit additional high crimes while trying to conceal his misconduct. A race to impeachment may thus deny Congress insights that can be gleaned only from the president's real-time reaction to a national inquiry.

Indeed, how the president handles scrutiny might reveal whether he'd accept alternative forms of corrective action. In the face of high crimes, it's easy to assume that half measures are inadequate. That assumption, though, may be unfounded. Many forms of presidential wrongdoing are effectively redressable through ordinary uses of legislative or judicial power. In assessing whether options short of impeachment will suffice, it's essential to know whether the president will go to war with the other branches rather than tolerate new limits on his authority. The answer to that question, moreover, might evolve as the terrain shifts during an impeachment inquiry. Presidents who initially respond with denunciation or outright defiance may suddenly crack under mounting pressure. The very first steps of an impeachment can thus reveal both that the president abused his power *and* that removing him from office isn't necessary.

Shooting from the hip on impeachment is also dangerous because it can short-circuit public deliberation. Mustering two-thirds of the Senate is no easy task. For this to occur, and to avoid a crushing backlash, there must be a relatively durable bipartisan consensus in support of removal. Even for a president with low popularity ratings, that kind of national will takes time to emerge. The *process* of impeachment, drawn out through investigations, hearings, and debates, allows the nation an opportunity to deliberate. If the process functions well, Congress may account for a more mature public sentiment than could have existed beforehand. In contrast, if the process is seen as hasty, incomplete, or illegitimate, Americans may lose faith in it. Worse, they may close their minds to new evidence, freezing attitudes before all the facts are in.

While evaluating alleged presidential misconduct, Congress must carefully avoid crying wolf. If legislators are quick on the trigger in urging impeachment—or in suggesting that possibility—each subsequent call may be taken less seriously. A nation constantly warned that the president is a despot can grow numb to those accusations, especially if prophesies of doom aren't immediately realized. That's why Congress should always tread carefully around references to removing the president. When impeachment talk is normalized as an aspect of partisan discourse, it is easily trivialized. Promiscuous invocation can thus prevent the impeachment power from achieving its purpose. (As we'll see in Chapter 5, this concern is now at a historical high point.)

Ultimately, the greatest risk of striking too early is that Congress might fail where it should succeed. Impeachment is not a bullet that can be readily fired twice during a single presidency. The resources and energy that must be marshaled for a Senate trial on articles of impeachment are too great for the nation to sustain them year after year. If Congress shoots and misses, the president will be practically untouchable. Wounded but not dead, the president could pursue his worst and most tyrannical impulses without fear of premature expulsion from office. History teaches that abuse of power rarely ceases of its own accord. The nation would thus remain in grave and continuing danger.

In short, the risks of impeaching too quickly are significant. Which raises a question: How can we tell when we're moving too quickly? Abusive presidents and their supporters will insist until the end of time that it's too early to consider such drastic measures. Their victims and political foes, in contrast, may start pounding an impeachment drum while the oath of office is sworn. Responsible legislators may struggle with when to finally declare, "Enough!"

This is where generalizations start running dry—and where it's vital to recall that different stages of the impeachment process present their own questions. Tweeting *#ImpeachPOTUS* isn't the same as voting for articles of impeachment. Over time, legislators properly assign different weights to the importance of gathering information, seeing how the president responds, gauging the political landscape, and allowing citizens to deliberate. That calculus must also be informed by the nature of the impeachable offense. If the president has a twitchy thumb near the nuclear codes, impeaching him yesterday wouldn't be too quick. But if he doesn't threaten immediate damage, and if Congress can otherwise stabilize a crisis, it may be worth taking time to build an unassailable case. Beyond that, the Constitution offers no magic formula. Knowing when it's too early is ultimately a matter of judgment.

* * *

What about the risks of moving too slowly, or not at all, when the president is believed to have committed impeachable offenses?

Specificity is elusive here. The risks of not impeaching are as diverse as the forms of potentially impeachable conduct. Failing to remove a chief executive who is secretly a Russian agent could be catastrophic. Declining to remove a president who has obstructed investigations into his son's tax fraud would be harmful, but not earth-shattering. In theory, the risks of a decision against impeaching the president for high crimes range from very bad consequences to the destruction of the nation and the death of millions.

If abiding the president's abuses *doesn't* pose risks within that spectrum, then those abuses aren't really "high Crimes and Misdemeanors." Impeachable offenses are necessarily defined by substantial risk of future danger. While backward-looking in its assessment of specific acts already committed by the president, the orientation of an impeachment is primarily prospective and probabilistic. The all-important question is whether we must remove a leader whose continuation in office poses a grave risk.

Consider Andrew Johnson's case. The House spent years locked in a scorched-earth battle with the president before deciding that it had to impeach him. Failing to take that step would have left the federal government at war with itself. These escalating interbranch hostilities risked permanently destabilizing the separation of powers. More important, leaving Johnson in office would have allowed him to continue destroying rights and programs crucial to a fragile nation. Left to his own devices, Johnson could have undone still more of the Union victory and might well have pointed the nation toward further bloodshed. Under these circumstances, Congress properly concluded that the risks of not impeaching were overwhelming. While the effort to oust Johnson didn't succeed, it achieved its primary goal. In exchange for a few key votes in the Senate, he acceded to most of Reconstruction and appointed moderates to his cabinet.

If the House hadn't impeached Johnson in 1868, it risked leaving the country stuck with a leader who pretended to hold exceptional power but couldn't actually lead. This concern may arise in other cases, too. A president seen as a villain will hemorrhage legitimacy—the lifeblood of effective presidential leadership. He may also discover that Congress, the judiciary, and his own bureaucracy are willing to take extraordinary measures to control his authority. Disabled, but still vested with "the executive Power," that wrongdoer in chief would be forced to resign or to stumble along, presiding over a resistant and ungrateful nation. Although alarming under any circumstances, a collective loss of trust in the chief executive could be disastrous were a crisis to occur. There are times when the nation urgently needs a leader who can capably perform all the duties of the office. In some cases, declining to impeach may leave the ship of state without a functioning captain.

A related concern is that presidents weakened by proof of "high Crimes and Misdemeanors"—and laboring under the shadow of potential impeachment—may take desperate steps to regain authority. Even when compromised by public knowledge of their misdeeds, presidents command a bully pulpit, the military, and endless ways to reshape the narrative. It's hard to imagine a crooked president, or one with an outsize ego, simply resigning himself to irrelevance. More likely, he'd try to assert control, even if that required new and creative abuses of power. As a result, we could never know whether to trust him again. His every action, no matter how legitimate, would be undermined by suspicion of ulterior and unsavory motives.

The United States faced a version of this problem in the late 1990s. First came *Wag the Dog*, a dark comedy in which a spin doctor distracts voters from a presidential sex scandal by inventing a fake war with Albania. Then, only a few weeks later, came news of Clinton's relationship with Monica Lewinsky. And then, six months after that announcement, came Clinton's missile attacks on targets in the Sudan and Afghanistan. At the time, Clinton's critics raged about a devious effort to shore up his popularity and distract the public. Looking back, that criticism isn't compelling. Clinton's targets were all associated with Al Qaeda and Osama bin Laden. But following news of Clinton's trysts, his opponents openly wondered whether his military judgments, sexual escapades, and public relations tactics had cross-fertilized.

Of course, a weakened and unreliable president isn't the only potential downside of inaction. Failing to impeach a president for "high Crimes and Misdemeanors" may result in irreparable damage to the constitutional system. That is particularly clear when the impeachable offenses at issue undermine democracy or threaten the separation of powers. In such cases, only by removing the president from office can Congress undo the immediate damage and prevent continuing constitutional harm.

Furthermore, declining to impeach for "high Crimes and Misdemeanors" may forever change how the American people understand their own democracy. People aren't good at living with tension. If they decide to support the continuation of a presidency despite evidence of misconduct, they will be motivated to believe in the wisdom of their own decision. This feeling can distort and mitigate whatever disgust they originally felt toward the president. Eventually, to avoid cognitive dissonance, many Americans might come to view the president's wrongdoing as tolerable, or even admirable. When the sun keeps on rising, their original moral revulsion may fade into a sense that the president's abuse wasn't really so bad. Legislators and journalists may be especially susceptible to this pressure: while resisting impeachment calls, they may come to view their fates as enmeshed with the president's and thereby lose perspective on the gravity of his misdeeds. As solid red lines dissipate in a haze of convenience and rationalization, abuses that once seemed unthinkable can be normalized. The president might even be *praised* for his next impeachable act, and the one after that.

Declining to impeach for severe misconduct can also establish many kinds of bad precedent within the federal government. Presidents tend to move forward rather than backward in their claims to power. Decisions not to impeach signal to future chief executives that they, too, can cross whatever bridge proved safe for a predecessor. Worse, such decisions may later be cited as proof that the president didn't *really* commit "high Crimes and Misdemeanors," thus permanently raising the bar on what counts as an impeachable offense.

But the harm doesn't stop there. Tolerating corruption and abuse of power in the White House sends a terrible message. It may lead other officials and bureaucrats to ask, *If the president can do this, why can't I?* That's how destructive cultures take root in the halls of power. And it can stoke cynicism about governmental ethics and integrity that lasts for decades.

House Republicans repeatedly cited this concern in their case against Clinton. Indeed, Representative Henry Hyde highlighted it in his closing argument: "The issues we're concerned with have consequences far into the future, because the real damage is not to the individuals involved, but to the American system of justice, and especially the principle that no one is above the law."[33]

To Hyde's credit, this wasn't a trivial or unreasonable point. Clinton's conduct had sent *exactly* the wrong message about the rule of law, respect for women, and basic decency. Ultimately, though, many Americans concluded that removal wasn't justified on those grounds alone. In their view, the impeachment process itself had offered a more than sufficiently harsh rebuke for Clinton's wrongdoing. The president's offenses, moreover, didn't portend national peril if he were allowed to serve out the remaining twenty-two months of his term. As Professor Keith Whittington has noted, Clinton was "a generally competent president who could be trusted to exercise the duties of his office in a manner that was within normal bounds of political tolerance."[34]

Needless to say, all of the risks discussed so far pale in comparison to the worst-case scenario: that by sitting on our hands and not impeaching, we destroy civilization itself. That isn't intended as hyperbole. Impeachment is the final limit on a person who commands the most powerful military, largest nuclear arsenal, and most deadly cyberwarfare capabilities on the planet. In the twenty-first century, all that's truly required for global disaster is the kind of president who would needlessly launch or trigger cataclysmic warfare.

Shy of global Armageddon, not impeaching for the highest of "high Crimes" also risks the end of our constitutional order. This nightmare could take many forms. Most of them would involve the president corrupting the electoral system to his own advantage. Along the way, the president would presumably violate many other rights and degrade democratic institutions. Maybe there would even be a steady beat of impeachment calls, defeated or dismissed until the president's abuses are substantially normalized. Eventually, the president and his allies in Congress would openly wonder whether we *really* need to hold elections at all.

Here we encounter a tragic aspect of the impeachment power: as democracy itself strains under presidential assault, impeachment may grow both more imperative *and* more dangerous. If a tyrannical president sabotages free speech, voting rights, and fair elections, the nation may reach a point where only impeachment can save it—but where our political system can't withstand the strain of an impeachment (or muster the will to undertake one). By the same token, populist demagogues who sow discord and division can nurture tyranny even as they destroy the political consensus necessary to thwart it. Impeachment is a mighty weapon, but also an imperfect one.

Pulling this all together: when the nation is confronted by evidence of "high Crimes and Misdemeanors," there is a point at which *not* impeaching becomes the more dangerous choice. When that is a possibility, Congress must steel itself for combat. Most important, it should immediately open an investigation so that it can exercise its judgment with an understanding of all relevant facts. It's incumbent on Congress to assess whether the president can be brought into line or whether he will remain a threat. If only impeachment and removal can safeguard the system and set it aright, then Congress has a duty to act.

* * *

Finally, what risks do we face even if Congress impeaches and removes the president *precisely* when that's the right move to make?

Power can never be exercised without consequence. That is doubly true for the great powers of the Constitution, including impeachment. When Congress ends a presidency before its natural life span, there's no avoiding profound and enduring national trauma. If the president's "high Crimes and Misdemeanors" aren't widely felt, the removal process itself will be. During an impeachment, important aspects of federal governance are necessarily affected. So are America's influence and authority in the world, and Americans' national self-conception. As scholar Jane Chong writes, even when impeachments herald a necessary course correction, they "involve[] a measure of violence from which our constitutional democracy can only slowly and by no means inevitably recover."[35] While the pain may be worth the price, it's virtually impossible to know in advance. Impeachments take place in a sea of variables that continually shift and reshape themselves. Congress can exercise some control over that process, but not very much.

An unavoidable risk of any impeachment is that the Congress, the president, and the chief justice are diverted from the ordinary business of governing for a prolonged period. To be sure, many aspects of federal administration don't involve the heads of each branch and would continue uninterrupted. Yet there are always matters that require the nation's most senior decision makers. For months (or even years), they would devote significant time to an internal crisis of governance rather than to shaping and administering policy. Beset by an impeachment, they may struggle to give other issues, including emergencies, the attention that they deserve. Friends and foes abroad would swiftly notice that America's leadership is distracted, and our country's standing in the global community could suffer as a result.

Impeachments are especially hard on presidents. No matter how brave a face they put on, laboring under a grand inquest by the House of Representatives is a brutal, taxing experience. John Adams, as we've seen, viewed even hopeless impeachment calls as a lesson on "Terrorism." And James Buchanan, while protesting demands for his removal, warned that trying the president on articles of impeachment "would be an imposing spectacle for the world."[36] At stake, he pleaded, was not only expulsion from political office, "but also what is of infinitely greater importance to [the president], his character, both in the eyes of the present and of future generations."

Fear of that judgment can crush a person. In the final days of his presidency, Richard Nixon bitterly observed to General Alexander Haig, "You fellows, in your line of business, you have a way of handling problems like this. Somebody leaves a pistol in the drawer."[37] As historian John A. Farrell recounts in his excellent Nixon biography, senior officials were so concerned by the president's mental state in August 1974 that they took drastic steps: "To ensure against a military coup, a nuclear Gotterdammerung, or some other frantic act, the secretary of defense instructed the Joint Chiefs that any eleventh-hour orders from the White House must be vetted by the chain of command."[38]

Impeachment was also a strenuous ordeal for Clinton— despite the fact that he retained strong public support and allies in the Senate. In his autobiography, *My Life*, Clinton weaves together the story of his impeachment and the flow of executive business. His thoughts on major policy decisions, missile strikes, and Middle East negotiations are interspersed with detailed renderings of maneuvers to save his presidency. As you might expect, he denies that his judgment was compromised: "The best way to win the final showdown with the Far Right was for me to keep doing my job and let others handle the defense . . . that's what I tried to do."[39] But even to a casual reader, Clinton's pride in his other accomplishments can't eclipse the overwhelming sense that everything he did was shadowed by impeachment. Every decision could affect the proceedings; every choice could be attacked as an effort to wag the dog. Because Clinton saw congressional attacks as a partisan ploy, he viewed high popularity and the appearance of leadership as crucial to his defense strategy. Impeachment was always in sight.

Obviously, presidents who commit evil deeds and bring impeachments on themselves deserve little pity. Our point here isn't that impeachments should be avoided because they might upset presidents. Rather, it's that when the House impeaches a president, it distracts and weakens the commander in chief of the military, our main global emissary, and the head of a vast bureaucracy. Given the president's singular role in American life and public administration, undercutting our head of state always presents substantial risks—no matter how well justified.

* * *

In theory, impeachments can also have long-term consequences for checks and balances. There's no turning back from such a raw display of legislative power. By effectively decapitating the executive branch, Congress sends a resounding message about limits on the presidency. The precedent it establishes is bound to shape the national mood and constitutional architecture. At the extreme, if Congress were to take an excessively broad view of impeachable offenses, it might tilt our system toward parliamentary rather than presidential democracy.

Without dismissing this point, we should note that it is typically overstated and undertheorized. Reflecting on Johnson's case, for instance, lawyers often assert that his trial caused a lasting diminution of the executive. Yet as historians remind us, Johnson's failed effort to consolidate power in the presidency (often through racist, populist appeals) was itself a departure from nineteenth-century norms. And if Congress hadn't impeached, it would have kept invoking other powers to combat Johnson. The result may have been new and more permanent restraints on the presidency. Moreover, from 1868 until the early 1950s, many politicians saw the Impeachment Clause as a dead letter. To the extent impeaching Johnson made use of this power seem unappealing, it may actually have increased executive authority by tainting the notion of ending a presidency.

Nixon's case offers slightly more support for the idea that impeachments can redefine the separation of powers. After his resignation, Congress ringed the presidency with innovative limits to thwart abuse of power. Many of the nation's campaign finance, transparency, and ethics rules date to this period. And nobody would describe Gerald Ford and Jimmy Carter as strong leaders who effectively stood up to Congress. Here, though, it wasn't the threat of an overreaching, aggressive legislature that kneecapped the executive. Rather, the wound was self-inflicted, and a transformative response was overdetermined after Nixon's crimes came to light. Within a decade, moreover, Ronald Reagan took office and catapulted the presidency to new heights of dynamism. Partly in reaction to a perceived debasement of the executive branch after Watergate, Reagan and his advisors built new legal theories to justify their sweeping vision of presidential command.

In contrast to the Watergate proceedings, the Clinton impeachment produced no durable effect on the separation of powers. Republicans built their case for impeachment on a decidedly uncontroversial premise: presidents shouldn't perjure themselves or obstruct justice. Condemning such conduct didn't budge the status quo or repudiate a novel claim to power by Clinton. In the end, moreover, the Republicans' impeachment campaign came to be viewed largely as an act of partisan animus. Its ultimate failure thus served only to confirm prevailing and preexisting views of when removing a president is justified under the Constitution.

Based on this history, we believe that impeachment would be most likely to reshape the separation of powers under two circumstances. First, if Congress were to successfully impeach and remove a president primarily on the basis of policy or partisan disagreement. And second, if Congress used an impeachment to draw a line in the sand, marking a prohibition against conduct that otherwise might have recurred in future presidencies.

In the thick of an impeachment campaign, however, it may be unclear whether these descriptions apply. Presidents invariably argue that attacks on them are partisan and based on specious principles. Their allies warn that the presidency itself will go down in flames if Congress proceeds. Advocates of impeachment, in response, insist that they're vindicating neutral, well-understood, and settled requirements. They present themselves as defenders of a balanced system that the president upended through his wrongdoing. The success or failure of an impeachment—and its long-term consequences for checks and balances—hinges largely on which framing of the dispute is ultimately accepted by the American people. But that outcome can be very difficult, if not impossible, to anticipate when an impeachment first begins.

In any event, when gauging the risks of an impeachment, it shouldn't be presumed that weakening the presidency is automatically a bad thing. There's nothing magical or necessary about the current distribution of power among the branches of government. If anything, modern presidents probably have too much authority in the US constitutional system, not too little.

This speaks to an important tension that may emerge in impeachment debates. As a president grows more powerful, it simultaneously becomes more important to keep him in check and more difficult to do so. Presidents who have unduly aggrandized their authority will always insist that distracting or weakening them through an impeachment will endanger the nation. That claim, however seductive, cannot carry the day. Whatever other challenges we face, a president who has abused power and corrupted his office cannot be trusted to lead us through them.

* * *

The inherent risks of impeachments multiply when we shift our gaze beyond checks and balances in the federal system. As Alexander Hamilton recognized in *Federalist* No. 65, the prosecution of impeachments "will seldom fail to agitate the passions of the whole community, and to divide it into parties more or less friendly or inimical to the accused." Frequently, he added, impeachments will connect with "pre-existing factions, and will enlist all their animosities, partialities, influence, and interest on one side or on the other."

This prediction led Hamilton to fear that impeachments would be "regulated more by the comparative strength of parties, than by the real demonstrations of innocence or guilt." But his observation also points to a distinct risk: that impeachments will unleash and concentrate the ugliest forces in US politics. Virtually every source of dysfunction in our democracy—hyperpartisanship, dark money, fake news, manufactured outrage, cultural warfare—could be magnified tenfold by an impeachment. Even more than presidential elections, the drawn-out, high-stakes drama of an impeachment proceeding might embitter Americans against one another, further fraying our sense of devotion to a shared national project.

An impeachment might also foment widespread feelings of alienation and disenchantment. Sustained inquiry into scandal, corruption, and abuse in the White House can destroy any remaining faith in politics and politicians. That risk is increased when the president is literally placed on trial. The resulting cynicism may persist a generation or longer, seeping like a poison into American life. Even when that feeling is justified by the failure of political elites, it can have unnerving collateral consequences. Reactionary and extremist politics flourish when Americans abandon established political institutions. More than any other congressional act, impeachments can birth a cycle of angry, existential politics, breaking settled political structures and surfacing latent divisions.

Don't get us wrong: sometimes that's necessary. We offer no brief for a "see no evil, hear no evil" mentality. Nor are we so petrified of change that we'd prefer a known tyrant to unknown tumult. As Lord Acton warned, power corrupts—and absolute power corrupts absolutely. In our system of government, only the president can edge close to absolute power. If that happens and results in "high Crimes and Misdemeanors," removing the president from office would be worth a period of disruptive political reconstruction. Indeed, sometimes the end result may be beneficial. Rallying a majority against an abusive president could trigger productive dialogue about reform and reformation. The dilemma is that we can't know in advance whether an impeachment will raze or reinvigorate the cultures, norms, and institutions that define our democracy.

The Nixon case exemplifies both possibilities at once. Scholars have shown that Watergate permanently scarred a generation of Americans. Public attitudes toward politics have never recovered. Yet Watergate also unified much of the nation in fury and horror. Familiar political divisions collapsed in a widely shared recognition that the president was a menace. From the ashes of Nixon's resignation rose new laws to shield integrity in politics.

Perhaps the single greatest risk of any impeachment, no matter how justified, is that a minority will view it as a gussied-up coup d'état. In most cases, the Constitution's supermajority voting rule for the Senate will help to avoid that outcome. But a president could still be removed with millions of Americans in bitter dissent. Those citizens might simply walk away from our shared democratic project, concluding that their votes and voices don't matter. Or they might drift ever more deeply into revolutionary politics, concluding that our democracy is rotten to the core. In the worst of all worst cases, they might even take up arms—especially if the ousted president refuses to depart gracefully and instead terrorizes the polity that rejected him.

If this sounds extreme, recall that we've already seen such threats from allies of President Trump. Roger Stone, for instance, has predicted that impeaching Trump would cause "a spasm of violence in this country, and insurrection, like you've never seen." "Both sides are heavily armed," he added, so politicians voting to impeach Trump "would be endangering their own life."[40] While we doubt Stone knows of what he speaks, his threats remind us that we've never seen a president removed from office under protest. Nixon resigned and then retreated to California, where he paced the beach of San Clemente in solitude. Not every president would go quietly into the darkness. That, too, is an unavoidable risk of impeachment.

* * *

Like many foreign scholars before him, Viscount James Bryce was fascinated by the constitutional power to end a presidency. After careful study, he concluded: "Impeachment . . . is the heaviest piece of artillery in the congressional arsenal, but because it is so heavy it is unfit for ordinary use. It is like a hundred-ton gun which needs complex machinery to bring it into position, an enormous charge of powder to fire it, and a large mark to aim at."[41]

The Constitution never *requires* Congress to deploy this weapon. Instead, it puts the option on the table and vests Congress with virtually unlimited discretion in deciding whether (and how) to use it. By virtue of that design, Congress cannot escape final responsibility for the prudent exercise of power. Legislators should therefore acknowledge the judgments they must make and address them forthrightly in dialogue with the public.

Indeed, some especially thoughtful members of Congress have described their role in exactly these terms. Consider this statement by Representative Jerrold Nadler, currently the top Democrat on the House Judiciary Committee:

[I]f we decide that the evidence isn't there for impeachment—or even if the evidence is there we decide it would tear the country apart too much, there's no buy-in, there's no bipartisanship and we shouldn't do it for whatever reason—if we decide that, then it's our duty to educate the country why we decided it.[42]

Although these remarks referred specifically to a possible Trump impeachment, the general decision-making process that Nadler described reflects the major lessons of this chapter. It also displays a commendable understanding that Congress must respond to voters while also affirmatively educating the public about when impeachment is appropriate.

In that respect, and many others, Congress must take the lead in ending an abusive presidency. When confronted by evidence of "high Crimes and Misdemeanors," Congress should immediately open a comprehensive investigation to ensure that its judgment can be applied to a correct view of the facts. If the House finds that the president has committed arguably impeachable offenses, it should deliberate alongside the nation and consider whether any steps short of impeachment may suffice. At that time, the House must consider all the risks of impeachment—those discussed here and many more—and set a course that it deems in the best interest of the Republic. If the House decides that impeachment is necessary, both houses of Congress should act at every step to keep the process fair and legitimate, which may help hold the nation together.

By their nature, attempts to end a presidency are traumatic. As Senator Byrd acknowledged in the Clinton proceedings, there may be "no happy ending, no final act that leads to a curtain call in which all the actors link hands and bow together amid great applause from the audience."[43] We can hope only that the nation survives with its spirit intact and the strength to rebuild all that's been broken.

4

CONGRESS, THE DECIDER

Whether our nation's leader is being elected or removed, it goes without saying that *who decides* the identity of the American president makes an enormous difference. Never has this been clearer than on December 12, 2000, when five Republican-appointed Supreme Court justices decided that George W. Bush, a Republican, would be the forty-third president.[1] The constitutional reasoning offered to justify this outcome was hard to credit. The justices in the majority had spent decades advocating judicial restraint, deference to states, and a very narrow view of the Equal Protection Clause. Yet suddenly, they turned that jurisprudence on its head, reversing a decision by the Florida Supreme Court to continue counting certain disputed ballots. Even many conservatives blushed at the Court's results-oriented analysis. When later challenged, Justice Antonin Scalia rarely bothered invoking the Constitution. Instead, he barked at critics to "get over it," asserting that the Court had risked its neck to save a nation in crisis. "We were the laughing stock of the world," he said. "It was becoming a very serious problem."[2]

Scalia got one thing right: the 2000 presidential election was a disaster. Something had to be done about it—and quickly. Scalia's framing, though, concealed a sleight of hand. The question wasn't *whether* to act but rather *who* should do so. As briefed to the Supreme Court by one of us, *Bush v. Gore* was a case about the allocation of power. In responding to calls for a recount in certain Florida counties, whose word would be final?

To many observers, there was a clear answer: the Florida Supreme Court. As the highest authority on applicable state law, it had decisively addressed the "hanging chad" issue by ordering a recount. The US Supreme Court had never second-guessed a state court under remotely similar circumstances, and the Constitution afforded no recognized basis for doing so. If confusion persisted after a recount in Florida, the House of Representatives was empowered by the Twelfth Amendment to resolve any controversies in the Electoral College.

But the *Bush v. Gore* majority disdained these alternatives. In its view, leaving control to Florida and the House risked further chaos. Convinced that only they could restore order, five justices decided to seize control of the situation. They made their power play by stretching the Equal Protection Clause far past the limits of any prior interpretation. Once they reconfigured the dispute as a violation of the Constitution, they placed themselves in the driver's seat. Their word would now be final on the issue that mattered most: ending the Florida recount. Removing any doubt about its goals, the majority ignored a natural implication of its own reasoning and opted to halt the recount outright rather than ordering it redone correctly. As those five justices knew well, this particular remedial order effectively declared Bush the victor.

The majority achieved its goal, but it paid a high price. As Justice John Paul Stevens prophesied in dissent, *Bush v. Gore* forever damaged "the Nation's confidence in the judge as an impartial guardian of the rule of law."[3]

There are many lessons of *Bush v. Gore*. One of the most important is that the Court treads on brittle ice when deciding who will lead the nation. The 2000 election proved this about *selecting* presidents. And as we'll see, the Framers believed this would be true in *removing* them for misconduct. It's exceptionally important for judges to protect the ground rules of free and fair elections. But nothing good comes of a perception that unelected judges decide who occupies the Oval Office.

More fundamentally, *Bush v. Gore* also cast in stark relief a question that is often overlooked in public debates over constitutional law: *Who decides?* On most issues that matter, Americans have different views about what the Constitution forbids, allows, and requires. That's partly because the Constitution itself rarely speaks with perfect clarity. Most of the time, it uses vague standards such as "cruel and unusual punishment," "due process of law," or "unreasonable searches and seizures." Sometimes it says nothing at all about how government should operate, forcing us to infer rules from its underlying structure. And in many cases, its principles come into unavoidable conflict. As Justice David Souter wrote in 2010, "We want order and security, and we want liberty. And we want not only liberty but equality as well."[4] History teaches that the Constitution leaves broad room for good faith disagreements on matters of interpretation.

When faced with such uncertainty, it's crucial to determine who has the power to make a final decision. Different institutions have their own vision of what the Constitution means. They also have unique incentives, political sensibilities, personality quirks, and decision-making processes. Asking nine unelected federal judges to interpret "the free exercise" of religion isn't the same as asking the Treasury Secretary, the Senate Judiciary Committee, the governor of Alabama, or the New York City Council. These differences in outlook often loom largest when a question involves the separation of powers or federalism. Each branch and level of government has its own conception of how the Constitution allocates authority.

Indeed, deciding who will decide a constitutional question is sometimes the most significant choice. Far too often, abstract discussions of power and restraint fail to grapple with this point. Constitutional law unfolds and takes shape *within* institutions of government, not in a philosophical ether. As a result, the answer to many legal questions may depend on when they're asked and who can answer them, especially in the heat of political combat.

Yet as *Bush v. Gore* proves, it's not always clear at the outset who will get the final say. In constitutional law, many disputes over the plan of government expand to encompass the very battleground on which they're fought. That's possible because the Constitution's lack of specificity affects not only the division of power but also the refereeing of those divisions.

When they addressed impeachment, though, the Framers took a *very* different approach. Here is a rare case where the Constitution leaves no doubt about who's in charge. Not even a court as ambitious as the *Bush v. Gore* majority could say otherwise. The House "shall have the sole Power of Impeachment." The Senate "shall have the sole Power to try all Impeachments." The president has no role except as suspect and defendant. The vice president, in turn, is barred from his usual role presiding over the Senate when the president has been accused. The chief justice takes the vice president's place as presiding officer at a presidential impeachment trial—though by virtue of the Senate's "sole power," any of the chief justice's rulings can be overturned by majority vote.

Simply put, Congress has the first and final word on matters of impeachment. The Constitution couldn't be clearer about who decides.

It's impossible to overstate the significance of Congress's exclusive role. Nearly every aspect of impeachment involves difficult judgments on which the Constitution offers little guidance. What are "high Crimes and Misdemeanors"? How much proof is required? What if 10 percent of the nation would violently resist removal, despite shocking misdeeds? By virtue of its sole jurisdiction, Congress alone must chart our nation's course through the fog.

In that effort, the House and Senate can never escape themselves. Unlike the courts, which strive for detachment and neutrality, Congress is political to the core. Its members stand for election on a regular basis, and famously obsess over public opinion. Their habit of mind is pragmatic, not formalistic. Their view of impeachment's risks, consequences, and alternatives is steeped in political reality as they comprehend it. So is their assessment of the president as a friend or foe. They understand the use of power because they live and breathe it. Their habits are defined by partisan combat, legislative process, campaign finance, and serving constituents. To many legislators, impeachments are a disruptive and unwelcome break from ordinary governance.

By entrusting the impeachment power to Congress, the Constitution shapes when and how it will be exercised. By dividing it between the House and Senate, and by imposing a two-thirds voting rule for conviction, the Framers set a high bar for removal. These limits, based in constitutional structure, define the political circumstances in which Congress can succeed in ending a presidency. This imaginative constitutional design was intended to roughly calibrate the impeachment power to the broader system of checks and balances.

Too often, Congress's role in impeachment is taken for granted or dismissed as mere politics. Scholars instead focus their energy on generating endless lists of what conduct does (and doesn't) qualify as impeachable. That's unfortunate. The Framers agonized over who should decide matters of impeachment and saw their selection of Congress as a crucial limit on this dangerous power. Appreciating why they made that choice allows a far more sophisticated understanding of impeachment's role in our democracy. So, too, does a deep dive into how Congress has historically approached its awesome responsibility.

*　*　*

As one of us knows from personal experience in South Africa, the Marshall Islands, and the Czech Republic, writing a democratic constitution is mind-blowingly hard. The decision points are endless. That's true even if a choice is made at the outset to build a presidential system with a separation of legislative, judicial, and executive powers. It's especially challenging to ensure that the branches of government constructively balance one another rather than spiraling out of control. In this search for equilibrium, shields against a rogue president are among the most bedeviling variables.

The Framers thought so, too. In 1788, while criticizing a draft of the Virginia Constitution, James Madison bluntly conceded that "a Court of Impeachments is among the most puzzling articles of a republican Constitution."[5] Alexander Hamilton took a similar view in *Federalist* No. 65: "A well-constituted court for the trial of impeachments is an object not more to be desired than difficult to be obtained in [an elected] government."

As described in Chapter 1, the complexities of this question led some Framers to give up on the very idea of presidential impeachment. To them, allowing anyone to hold such an extreme threat over the president would undermine the executive branch. Viewing the system on paper, they didn't see how impeachment could fit the grand design of checks and balances.

After centuries of national experience, it may now seem natural that this power should reside in Congress. The Framers, however, had few useful models. England divided impeachment between the houses of Parliament, but the Framers consciously rejected many aspects of English practice. Given their republican objectives, most of them were wary of replicating parliamentary systems wholesale. Meanwhile, the Framers' experiences in colonial and state government only confirmed how difficult it was to design an impeachment process. With palpable frustration, Madison wrote that "the diversified expedients adopted in the Constitutions of the several States prove how much the compilers were embarrassed by the subject."[6]

Over the summer of 1787, as the Constitutional Convention debated whether to allow presidential impeachment, it considered a dizzying array of options for who would do the deed. That discussion began on May 29, when Edmund Randolph introduced the "Virginia Plan." Under this far-reaching scheme for the federal government, the judiciary would handle "impeachments of any National officers."[7] That same day, Charles Pinckney of South

Carolina proposed that the "House of Delegates" would bring impeachment charges, which would be tried before the Senate and the judiciary.[8] These proposals remained the sole contenders until June 2, when John Dickinson of Delaware threw a curveball: "the Executive [should] be made removable by the National Legislature on the request of a majority of the Legislatures of individual States."[9] In his view, "the happiness of this Country . . . required considerable powers to be left in the hands of the States," and these powers included impeachment.[10]

On June 13, Randolph and Madison struck back, proposing that "the jurisdiction of the national Judiciary shall extend to . . . impeachments of any national officers."[11] But two days later, William Paterson scattered the state of play by offering his own scheme of government, the "New Jersey Plan." In this proposal, the president could be removed by Congress "on application by a majority of the Executives of the several States."[12] The following Monday, June 18, Hamilton shared a very different vision for the Constitution. Like Dickinson and Paterson, he saw an important role for the states in matters of impeachment: all such proceedings would be tried before a court consisting of each state's most senior judge, though only if such judges were insulated from politics by a permanent salary and protections for their tenure in office. Randolph, who had initially agreed with Madison that the judiciary should handle impeachment, ultimately came around and endorsed Hamilton's view.

In late July, the Committee of Detail—which was charged with turning a mess of ideas into a working draft—proposed that impeachments would be tried "before the Senate and the judges of the federal judicial Court."[13] But when the committee issued its final report on August 6, it had shifted away from that position. Instead, it supported impeachment by the House and trial by the Supreme Court.[14] That remained the operative rule until September 4, when a different committee proposed replacing the Supreme Court with the Senate.[15] As we'll see, this decision was linked to the invention of the Electoral College. After impassioned debate, with Madison speaking eloquently in opposition, the Convention decided that the Senate alone would render verdicts on articles of impeachment.[16]

In many historical accounts, the Framers are portrayed as confident world builders, forging a nation from their collective genius. Here we see them playing with fire, scared of their own creation. The Framers didn't reach an agreement on who would wield the removal power until the final two weeks of the Convention. By then, their deliberations over who could end a presidency had stretched on for months. At various points, they considered the Senate, the Supreme Court, the Senate and the Supreme Court, a forum of state judges, a vote of state legislatures, and a vote of state governors. It's safe to say they left almost no stone unturned. Why, then, did they settle on the House and Senate?

* * *

To answer that question, it's helpful to ask a different one: Why did the Framers split this power in half? The notion that there should be an "impeacher" and a "court of impeachments" was familiar from Parliament, but that didn't make it self-recommending. Indeed, some of the proposals offered in Philadelphia involved only a single actor: the federal judiciary, or a gathering of state officials. To this day, many foreign nations with unicameral legislatures give representatives sole control over presidential impeachments.

Yet the Framers rejected that model. Although there is no clear record of why they did so, Hamilton later offered a convincing two-part account in *Federalist* No. 66. First, he reasoned that splitting impeachment "avoids the inconvenience of making the same persons both accusers and judges." To a lawyer like Hamilton, it was obvious that nobody who spends years building a case can possibly judge his or her own position impartially. The human mind doesn't work that way. Nor do the political forces and factions that drive an impeachment campaign. Especially in a nation committed to an adversarial system of justice, removal proceedings couldn't be seen as fair unless they were adjudicated by a neutral decision maker.

Second, Hamilton also explained that splitting impeachment "guards against the danger of persecution, from the prevalency of a factious spirit in either of those branches." This argument identified a safeguard against abuse of the impeachment power. The Framers knew that partisan rivalries and popular outrage could prevail over responsible governance. We suspect they also recognized that "high Crimes and Misdemeanors" was an unstable standard. Although they couldn't eliminate the risk that impeachment would be misused, they could mitigate it through constitutional structure. By requiring that two institutions separately agree—and that the accuser be put to its proof—they shielded the president from a "factious spirit" in any single branch. This helped to preserve executive authority and independence.

Once they split impeachment, the Framers quickly agreed that only the House was fit to serve as prosecutor.[17] When the president has betrayed or imperiled the nation, who should accuse him other than elected representatives of the people at large? As James Iredell explained at the North Carolina Ratifying Convention, "this power is lodged in those who represent the great body of the people, because the occasion for its exercise will arise from acts of great injury to the community."[18] Given the fraught political judgments that surround impeachment, the House alone could wield this power with a mantle of democratic legitimacy.

In one important respect, that was even truer in 1789 than it is today. Initially, the House was the *only* branch of government directly elected by the people. Judges have always been appointed by the president, with the advice and consent of the Senate. And senators, in turn, were originally chosen by state legislatures. Direct election of senators didn't begin until the Seventeenth Amendment was ratified in 1913—largely because the Senate blocked many earlier proposals that would have changed its selection process. As a result, the House alone faced popular elections for the first 124 years of US history. By virtue of this electoral mandate, it could credibly claim unique authority to speak for the American people.

That democratic aura eclipsed even the president's. Whereas members of the House of Representatives are directly elected every two years, presidents have always been chosen by the Electoral College. At heart, the Electoral College is an undemocratic and unrepresentative institution. The Framers designed it to ensure that only elite, distinguished characters would select the chief executive. Consistent with that vision, many states didn't allow direct elections for Electoral College delegates until the 1820s. But even after that development, which gave the process a more populist tint, the Electoral College remained an arbitrary filter between the people and the presidency. To this day, while failing to achieve any worthwhile purpose, the Electoral College continues to skew the course and outcome of elections. In practice, it serves mainly to promote minority rule and to provide small states with an undemocratic advantage over larger states. In consequence, when the House rises to accuse a president of "high Crimes and Misdemeanors," it is fortified by the distinctive legitimacy conferred through frequent, direct elections.[19] Not all presidents can claim a comparable mandate, especially if they took office after losing the national popular vote.

This discussion points to a distinct explanation for why the Framers may have assigned impeachment to the House. As they knew, the Electoral College was an odd duck. It had no continuing life and no stable membership. Each elector cast two ballots, one of which had to be for someone who lived in another state. Electors, moreover, were required to convene separately, each in their own state. Together, these rules made coordination virtually impossible. The Framers therefore anticipated that the Electoral College would usually fail to select a president. As Professor Michael Klarman notes, "the vast geographic scope of the country, combined with the relatively primitive state of transportation and communication, would prevent presidential candidates from becoming widely known or coordinating their campaigns across states—especially in the absence of national political parties."[20] Indeed, George Mason predicted that the Electoral College would come up short "nineteen times in twenty."[21] To address that situation, the Framers decided that if no candidate had a simple majority in the Electoral College, the House would choose the president from the top five vote getters. In light of these complex expectations, entrusting impeachment to the House created a certain symmetry. The House would often end up selecting the president, and the House would then have the sole power to initiate his removal.

At least, that may have been the theory. In practice, the early emergence of national political parties narrowed most Electoral College votes to just two candidates. To the extent the Framers anticipated symmetry in the House's powers of presidential selection and removal, their reasoning didn't hold up.

Of course, that wasn't the only flaw in framing-era justifications for vesting the impeachment power in the House. Although the Framers often referred to the House as speaking for the people at large, this simply wasn't true in 1789. Back then, an overwhelming majority of people living in the United States couldn't vote, including most women, blacks, Native Americans, and white men who didn't own property. It took decades of struggle, and a bloody Civil War, to expand the franchise. The House didn't speak for all Americans until well into the twentieth century.

Even today, this characterization of the House is open to doubt. The right to vote remains besieged on many fronts. Political parties have mastered gerrymanders that effectively waste millions of votes and massively skew representation along partisan lines. Blacks and Hispanics have been targeted by a swarm of discriminatory voter ID laws and other barriers that repress their political voice. Many states have failed to protect their voting machines from cyberattack, all but inviting electoral chaos that could sow doubt about the House's legitimacy. And to this day, the House lacks direct representation for millions of Americans living in Puerto Rico, Guam, and other territories—all of whom can be gravely affected by presidential decisions.

In these and many other respects, idealistic claims that the House speaks for all Americans have always fallen short of reality. But the Framers' reasoning doesn't ultimately depend on a belief that the House is a perfect avatar of the people. Rather, it depends on the recognition that the House is the best we've got in deciding whether and when to confront an out-of-control president.

*   *   *

Although the Framers celebrated the House as a bastion of democracy, they didn't give it sole control of impeachment. Writing for a public audience, Hamilton explained this decision by reference to general principles of fair adjudication. Behind closed doors in Philadelphia, however, there was a far more profound reason why the Framers constrained the House.

Simply put, many of the Framers feared too much democracy. They worried that "factious spirits" and "democratic licentiousness" could doom the young nation.[22] As Professor Klarman explains, this "deep distrust" affected "nearly every substantive choice made in the Constitution that bore on the new federal government's susceptibility to popular influence."[23] The Framers sought to ensure that elite Americans—educated, wealthy, virtuous, and dignified—would play a significant role in administering the country. That was particularly important for the great powers of the Constitution, such as impeachment. An ugly or ignorant mood could easily sweep the populace, agitating representatives into an unjustified assault on the executive branch. Convinced that the House would uncontrollably boil over with irrational fury, the Framers generally agreed that it couldn't have the final say on ending presidencies.

In practice, this meant establishing a court of impeachment in which the House would prove its case. By vesting control in a more deliberative and insulated body—one less prone to splashes of democratic excess—the Framers aimed to temper popular passions.

Describing the second stage of impeachment as a *trial* furthered this goal by evoking Americans' historic obsession with the forms and fixtures of legal process. The president would not be expelled from office after a few hasty votes. No, the president would literally be placed on trial for his "high Crimes and Misdemeanors."

And who better to preside over a trial than judges? To quite a few Framers, it was self-evident that the Supreme Court should decide cases of impeachment. The justices would be elite, independent, and divorced from the daily drama of politics. Further, assigning this role to the Court would address lingering concerns that the Senate was already too powerful.

Although the Framers didn't take that path, plenty of other countries have done so. Impeachments are tried before the judiciary in about forty nations worldwide, including Burkina Faso, Cape Verde, Djibouti, France, Mali, South Korea, and Venezuela. In fact, three US states also involve their courts. New York tries impeachments before a body composed of its senate and high court, or "the major part of them."[24] Missouri uses a special commission of seven "eminent jurists" selected for that purpose by its senate.[25] And Nebraska uses seven district court judges chosen by the chief justice of the Nebraska Supreme Court.[26]

A majority of the Framers, however, voted against relying on the judiciary. There were four major reasons for that decision. Together, those rationales illuminate how some Framers hoped the impeachment power would operate in practice.

One of the most significant objections to trying impeachments before the Supreme Court was that the president might have appointed one or more of the justices. George Mason and Roger Sherman both raised this concern.[27] At bottom, they worried about independence: the entity charged with trying the president should not be populated by his appointees and thereby subject to his influence. In that circumstance, an appearance (and reality) of bias could undermine the whole process—especially if the president had nominated allies who shared his corrupt or abusive views.

A version of this issue arose in 1974. With Watergate hearings in full swing and the nation paying close attention, the Court had to decide whether Richard Nixon should be ordered to surrender his tapes. At the time, Nixon had appointed four members of the Court: Warren Burger, Harry Blackmun, Lewis Powell, and William Rehnquist. Of that group, only Rehnquist recused himself, because he had worked closely with key players in Watergate. The final vote in *United States v. Nixon* was eight to zero—and rightly so. But surely the public outcry would have been furious if the Court had ruled in the president's favor, with Nixon's appointees casting the decisive votes. And if that sounds bad, imagine the public reaction if Nixon's appointees had been in a position to control his actual impeachment rather than a case about access to evidence. Many of us would view that situation as intolerable and potentially illegitimate.

Next consider a variation on the same Watergate theme: What if Nixon had been removed from office, Gerald Ford had refused to pardon him, and Nixon was then convicted of federal crimes? This hypothetical exemplifies a second reason for the Framers' skepticism of the Court: it might later sit in judgment of the president in an appeal arising from the conduct that got him impeached. Given the possibility of an impeachment followed by criminal charges, it would be incongruous and unfair for the same tribunal to have the final word in both proceedings.[28]

A third objection to the Court involved its size. The Constitution does not say how many justices must sit on the Court, but the Framers expected a small number. Their expectations proved well founded. The Court's membership started at six and has topped nine only once, from 1863 to 1866. The Court's size raised concerns at the Constitutional Convention that it would be too easy to manipulate so few people. As Gouverneur Morris warned, "the Supreme Court were too few in number and might be warped or corrupted."[29] Hamilton later made a similar point in *Federalist* No. 65: "The awful discretion which a court of impeachments must necessarily have, to doom to honor or to infamy the most confidential and the most distinguished characters of the community, forbids the commitment of the trust to a small number of persons." In contrast, Hamilton reasoned, it would be far more difficult for anyone to corrupt a larger body of decision makers.

Finally, some Framers doubted that the fledging federal courts were up for the task. As Hamilton famously remarked in *Federalist* No. 78, the judiciary was the "least dangerous" branch. Lacking the sword or the purse, it possessed "merely judgment." He couldn't but wonder: Did the Court have sufficient fortitude to decide impeachments under crushing political pressure? And if unelected judges did manage to reach a verdict, could they reconcile the public to their final decision—especially if they had rejected charges brought by the House on behalf of all Americans?

Morris gave similar concerns a different spin. If vested with a role in impeachments, he warned, the Court would inevitably be "drawn into intrigues with the Legislature and an impartial trial would be frustrated."[30] In his view, the judiciary couldn't resist creeping politicization and secret conspiracies if thrust into a high-stakes political process.

Pulling these objections together, we can develop a sharper sense of what the Framers sought in an impeachment tribunal: (1) independence from the president in its selection process; (2) no other role in judging the president's misdeeds; (3) enough members to resist corruption; and (4) the legitimacy, competence, and courage to adjudicate disputes between the House of Representatives and the president of the United States. With the Supreme Court disqualified, this left only one viable option in the federal government: the Senate.

*   *   *

James Madison led a valiant charge against trying impeachments in the Senate. Drawing on all his powers of persuasion, he warned that this would make the president dangerously dependent on Congress.[31] Coming from one of history's foremost constitutional architects, that objection had to be taken seriously. Charles Pinckney echoed Madison's anxiety and painted a troubling picture: "If [the president] opposes a favorite law, the two Houses will combine [against] him, and under the influence of heat and faction throw him out office."[32]

This concern resonated with a preexisting fear among some delegates that the Senate was too powerful.[33] It already boasted authority over appointments and treaties. Adding impeachment to the mix risked exalting Congress's upper chamber above all other branches. Moreover, presidential abuse of the appointment and treaty powers might in some cases require impeachment. Could the Senate serve as a fair judge if it had been complicit in the president's decisions?

Yes, it could. Or so concluded most of Madison's peers.

The Framers trusted the Senate. They imagined a legislative chamber not unlike the Constitutional Convention itself: virtuous, well-educated, and wealthy elites, steeped in republican values and committed to the national interest. With only twenty-six members, the Senate would be large enough to avoid corruption but small enough to engage in productive deliberations. Critically, unlike members of the House, senators would also serve six-year terms in office. Insulated from the pressure of regular elections, they could resist flashes of factional tumult and display comparatively greater independence of vision. In deciding affairs of state, the Senate would rely on its own wisdom and even temper.

The Senate also shone where the Supreme Court was lackluster. None of its members would owe their selection to the president. It would have no role in adjudicating the president's criminal liability after the impeachment process. And unlike the Court, its power and legitimacy couldn't be doubted. As Hamilton observed in *Federalist* No. 65, "Where else than in the Senate could have been found a tribunal sufficiently dignified, or sufficiently independent?"[34] Assembled as an extraordinary court, the nation's leading statesmen would render the final verdict on presidents accused of great offenses against the people.

Even then, the Senate would be held to a high standard. Only by a two-thirds vote could it convict the president on articles of impeachment. Although there is no shortage of speculation about why the Framers included this supermajority voting rule, the historical record is empty of direct evidence. Setting the decision in broader context, however, suggests a likely genealogy.

In the eighteenth century, majority rule was the default for any legislative assembly. Leading authority supported that understanding, including John Locke's *Second Treatise of Government*. Benjamin Franklin thus spoke conventional wisdom in Philadelphia when he described majority rule as "the common practice of assemblies in all countries and ages."[35] This rule applied even when the British House of Lords sat as a court of impeachment.

In Western constitutional thought, the innovative idea that certain legislative decisions should be subject to a two-thirds vote dates to the 1770s. During the American Revolution, John Dickinson was assigned the daunting task of proposing a governmental plan for the independent colonies. Following substantial revisions, his draft was adopted in 1781 as the Articles of Confederation. In a break from British practice, the Articles selectively imposed a two-thirds voting requirement: nine out of thirteen states had to agree before Congress could make certain kinds of decisions— for example, entering treaties, coining money, and raising an army. The contemporary debate over this rule revealed that it was implemented not only to ensure a strong national consensus but also to force public deliberation on matters of state.

At the Constitutional Convention six years later, there was little recorded discussion of the two-thirds rule. This suggests that in the interim, it had been accepted in American political theory. At one point, Hugh Williamson of North Carolina even suggested that *all* congressional acts should require two-thirds approval. The Convention, though, applied a supermajority standard to only a handful of issues. Inconveniently for historians, it did so behind closed doors. But that doesn't leave us entirely in the dark.

On the face of the Constitution, it's clear that the Framers reserved two-thirds votes for issues of towering importance. In addition to treaties and impeachment trials, this requirement applies in five cases: (1) overriding a presidential veto; (2) expelling a member of Congress; (3) proposing a constitutional amendment; (4) permitting someone who participated in a rebellion to hold office; and (5) deciding whether a president may return to office after having been declared unable to discharge his powers and duties pursuant to the Twenty-Fifth Amendment. In these scenarios, the Constitution deploys a special voting rule to compel unusually searching reflection and widespread public agreement.

Applying that rule to impeachment makes sense. Here more than anywhere else, the Senate must strive for impartiality, wisdom, and rigor. By requiring decisive majority support for conviction, the Constitution holds the House to a demanding standard of proof. To secure sixty-seven votes, the House typically will have to surmount partisan divisions and convince some of the president's political allies to jump ship. Where that occurs, it's likely that most Americans favor conviction. In contrast, where the House fails to secure sixty-seven votes in the Senate, removal likely isn't the best course for the nation—at least, assuming that the Senate has considered the case in good faith. As Justice Story observed, "if the guilt of a public officer cannot be established to the satisfaction of two thirds of a body of high talents and acquirements, which sympathizes with the people, and represents the states, after a full investigation of the facts . . . the evidence [must be] too infirm, and too loose to justify a conviction."[36]

A two-thirds rule also shores up the standard for impeachable offenses. "High Crimes and Misdemeanors" is a malleable phrase. One way to prevent it from being bent out of shape is to require bipartisan agreement on any particular application. That's exactly what the Framers achieved. Studying the supermajority voting rule, Woodrow Wilson remarked that the president would be convicted only for offenses causing "indignation so great as to overgrow party interest."[37]

* * *

Reviewing all of these structural safeguards, you can feel the Framers' anxiety. Impeachment was the power they most grudgingly included in the Constitution. Unsure who should hold it, they settled on Congress as the least bad option. Then they piled on limits to prevent impeachment from getting out of hand. In total, they devoted six separate clauses to the subject. Those provisions establish important ground rules for ending a presidency.

Yet in exercising the impeachment power, the House and Senate are left largely to their own devices. We've already explored their discretion in defining impeachable offenses and deciding whether to impeach. Now we arrive at an equally formidable prerogative: control over procedure. With only a few exceptions, including the Senate's two-thirds voting requirement, the House and Senate can establish their own rules for impeachment. They enjoy broad latitude in structuring investigations, hearings, deliberations, and votes. They can also decide the burden of proof, the rules of evidence, whether to hear testimony, the role of lawyers, and when proceedings should be public. In answering these and other important questions, Congress must rely on its own best judgment.

To most well-adjusted adults, the phrase "legal procedure" inspires a pang of boredom. But it shouldn't, at least not here. Procedure is where romantic ideas about legislators as the voice of the people collide with institutional reality. Good process is crucial to making thoughtful, accurate, and legitimate decisions. It's through these rules that Congress evaluates the evidence and structures its deliberations. Mastering them can make all the difference in supporting and opposing an impeachment. Moreover, if many Americans conclude that a president hasn't been given a fair shake, they may refuse to accept Congress's decision. Impeachments must therefore *be* fair and *appear* fair. This requires a strange and volatile brew of law, politics, and judicialized ritual unlike anything else in the US system of government.

It all begins in the House. The most important thing to understand about the House is that it runs by majority rule. As a result, whichever party controls the House also controls impeachment, so long as its members are willing to vote with their leadership. The House can alter almost any of the rules that we're about to describe, which are based on past practice.

There are many ways to initiate an impeachment. For example, the House may choose to act on a citizen petition, a grand jury charge, or the request of a state legislature. In the late twentieth century, federal law also permitted the appointment of an "independent counsel" whose authority included impeachment referrals to the House. Independent Counsel Kenneth Starr acted pursuant to these provisions when he submitted his report on Monica Lewinsky and Whitewater. But Starr's handling of Clinton's case, among other debacles, inspired devastating criticism of the independent counsel law. When those provisions lapsed in 1999, Congress did not renew them. Ever since, sensitive cases involving abuse of power have been instead handled by "special counsel" pursuant to Department of Justice regulations. Although these regulations are silent on impeachment referrals, there are many ways for a special counsel to raise alarms in Congress.

In any event, impeachments are usually triggered through a more mundane process: the filing of a resolution by a member of the House. In Andrew Johnson's case, Representative Thaddeus Stevens prevailed on the House to create a Joint Committee on Reconstruction, which swiftly called for Johnson's removal. The House passed that resolution 126 to 47, and then established a committee to draft articles of impeachment. In Richard Nixon's case, the House was a tad more direct: it passed a resolution authorizing the Judiciary Committee "to investigate fully and completely whether sufficient grounds exist for the House of Representatives to impeach President Richard M. Nixon."[38] After performing a comprehensive investigation, the committee approved three articles of impeachment, though Nixon resigned before they reached the full House. Finally, in Bill Clinton's case, the House followed its Nixon precedent and passed a resolution authorizing the Judiciary Committee to investigate impeachment. Relying on a report from Independent Counsel Starr, the committee drafted four articles. Representative Henry Hyde then proposed those articles as a resolution in the full House; by majority vote, the House ultimately approved two of them (perjury and obstruction of justice).

As this summary suggests, the House traditionally addresses most matters relating to presidential impeachment through its committees. The Judiciary Committee plays an especially important role. It usually takes the lead in investigating misconduct and drafting articles of impeachment. In that process, it isn't bound by technical rules of evidence or an agreed-upon definition of "high Crimes and Misdemeanors." Instead, its members have broad authority to subpoena documents, call witnesses, hold hearings, make legal determinations, and undertake any other activities necessary to fulfill their mandate. Congress's investigatory powers are at their zenith in the realm of impeachment. They should ordinarily overcome almost any claim of executive privilege asserted by the president. In addition, the committee is free to make use of evidence provided by a special counsel. Ultimately, the committee must decide what the president did, whether that conduct is impeachable, whether impeachment is warranted, and what articles of impeachment (if any) to propose to the full House.

Because they're where major decisions get made, House committees should work hard to build and maintain public credibility. Historically, however, they have taken inconsistent approaches to their role. The Joint Committee on Reconstruction didn't dwell on technicalities: given Johnson's decision to fire Secretary of War Edwin M. Stanton, it immediately concluded that he had violated the Tenure of Office Act and recommended impeachment. In contrast, the Judiciary Committee devoted extraordinary resources to investigating Nixon. It established a special staff to focus on impeachment, hired John Doar as special counsel, and spent ten months engaged in intensive fact-finding. It also deliberated over the standard for "high Crimes and Misdemeanors" and prepared scholarly reports on the history of impeachment. Many of its most important decisions were bipartisan, and the committee allowed Nixon's defense lawyer—James St. Clair—to participate in its proceedings. Unfortunately, the Judiciary Committee acquitted itself less well in Clinton's case. Relying almost completely on the allegations set forth in the Starr Report, it failed to undertake independent fact-finding. After a series of ostentatiously partisan hearings, dominated largely by questioning of Starr and testimony from legal academics (including one of us), the committee passed four articles along party lines. This process set an ugly tone that contributed to the Clinton impeachment's eventual failure.

When presented with proposed articles of impeachment, the House may hold a floor debate and then vote by simple majority on each article. If the articles fail, the president is not impeached. That has happened several times. As we've noted, the House rejected two of four proposed articles in Clinton's case. And before Johnson was finally impeached, the House rejected multiple resolutions—including one backed by the Judiciary Committee—calling for his impeachment. On many other occasions, the House has effectively killed impeachment resolutions from individual representatives by voting them down, tabling them, or burying them in committee. As we'll discuss in Chapter 5, that occurred under Thomas Jefferson, Grover Cleveland, Herbert Hoover, Harry Truman, Ronald Reagan, George H. W. Bush, and George W. Bush. It has also occurred several times since Donald Trump took office.

If the full House approves articles of impeachment, it must select "managers" from among its ranks to serve as prosecutors in the Senate. The managers typically should be supporters of impeachment and can be chosen in several ways: general ballot, a resolution naming individual members, or selection by the Speaker of the House (though only if the Speaker has been so authorized by resolution). There are few fixed requirements. The House can set its own criteria for selecting managers and assigning responsibilities. In Clinton's case, for instance, the House chose thirteen Republicans as managers—though many of them lacked the temperament or skills necessary to prosecute a case, and thus harmed their own cause. Clinton, in turn, hired five all-star professionals as his private defense attorneys. While the Constitution is silent on this point, the Senate has long allowed the president to defend himself through counsel. That's a sensible rule. When impeachments arrive at the Senate, they enter a strange and disorienting world.

* * *

Traditions define the Senate. The rules that it devised for Johnson's impeachment trial in 1866 were used, almost verbatim, for Clinton's trial in 1998. The major difference is that there are now one hundred senators rather than fifty-four (in 1866), or twenty-six (in 1789). As anyone who has served on a jury knows, it's hard enough to decide tough cases when there are only twelve decision makers. Organizing one hundred people into an effective, deliberative court is almost impossible—especially when dealing with larger-than-life personalities. Still, the Senate soldiers on, aided by a culture of decorum and a flickering sense of national responsibility.

The Senate's role begins when it is formally notified by the House that articles of impeachment have been approved. The Senate must inform the House when it is ready to first receive the managers. Subsequently, the managers appear before the bar of the Senate to orally accuse the president of "high Crimes and Misdemeanors," and to "exhibit" the articles of impeachment against him.

The Senate then summons the chief justice, who replaces the vice president as the Senate's presiding officer. This is essentially a conflict of interest rule: the vice president would ascend to the presidency upon a conviction, so he is excluded from any role in the president's trial. Today, we might expect that the vice president's ambition could be slightly counterbalanced by loyalty to his running mate—though it's hardly clear that adding another, competing conflict of interest solves the problem. But in 1789, a very different concern prevailed. Before passage of the Twelfth Amendment, the vice president was whoever received the second-most votes in the Electoral College. Because the Framers did not anticipate that political parties would organize partisan tickets, they worried that the Electoral College might sometimes pick the president's arch-rival (rather than his trusted ally) to serve as vice president. If that were to occur, the vice president would have everything to gain—and little to lose—from a verdict against the president.

Notably, this is the only impeachment-related conflict of interest rule made explicit in the Constitution. Other recusal decisions depend entirely on individual assessments of fairness and integrity. Pursuant to those principles, when House members have participated in impeachment votes and have then been elected to the Senate, they have nearly always recused themselves from the trial.[39] But some politicians have displayed less zeal for ethics. In Johnson's impeachment, for example, Senator Benjamin Wade refused to step aside even though he was next in line to the presidency under then-operative succession rules. At that same trial, the presiding chief justice, Salmon Chase, nurtured a burning presidential ambition. Yet there's no evidence that he considered recusing himself. Although we don't endorse these decisions, we've described them to show that swapping the vice president for the chief justice doesn't fix all conflicts.

Once the chief justice has arrived in the Senate, but before consideration of the articles, each senator must swear a special oath: "I solemnly swear (or affirm) that in all things appertaining to the trial of the impeachment of [the president], now pending, I will do impartial justice according to the Constitution and laws: So help me God." Although the Constitution provides that senators "shall be on Oath or Affirmation" when trying impeachments, this language was devised by the Senate itself.

Oaths may sound trite or chintzy, but they help to personalize and internalize the responsibilities of constitutional law. As Professor Richard Re explains, "for each official, the critical moment of constitutional obligation is the moment of taking the oath and thereby promising to adhere to a certain role defined by certain powers and duties."[40] Most famously, the president swears a constitutionally specified oath of office, the only one that the Constitution spells out word for word: "I do solemnly swear (or affirm) that I will faithfully execute the Office of President of the United States, and will to the best of my Ability, preserve, protect and defend the Constitution of the United States." In addition, Article VI requires that all state and federal officials "shall be bound by Oath or Affirmation, to support this Constitution."

It's therefore striking that the Framers added an extra oath here. After being sworn into office, legislators can exercise all their other powers without taking additional oaths. Indeed, House members can debate and vote on articles of impeachment in the ordinary course of business. Only in the Senate, and only for impeachments, is a further oath required. The Constitution thus impresses on each senator the unparalleled gravity of his or her decision in the case at bar. It also signifies that the Senate now sits as a court rather than as a legislative body and can exercise adjudicative powers elsewhere denied to it.

With the chief justice presiding and all members sworn, the Senate issues a writ of summons to the president. That sets in motion any pretrial pleadings that the parties may wish to file. Then the trial begins. Lawyers for both sides make opening and closing presentations, each of which can last many days. They may offer whatever evidence and argument the Senate sees fit to allow. If evidentiary questions arise, the chief justice may rule on them himself or put the issue to a vote of the Senate. If the Senate disagrees with any decision by the chief justice, it can overrule him. In Clinton's trial, Chief Justice William Rehnquist issued only a single substantive decision: that the House managers had to "refrain from referring to the Senators as jurors." Rehnquist otherwise kept a low profile. He later quipped, "I did nothing in particular, and I did it very well."[41]

Impeachment trials can be taxing for senators. In most settings, they spend the bulk of their time speaking and glad-handing; suddenly, their main role is to sit silently and pay careful attention. For some, staying awake throughout the proceedings proved too much of a challenge during the Clinton trial. Senators can't even ask questions directly. Rather, they must submit them in written form to the chief justice, who poses them orally to the lawyers and witnesses.

Of course, that assumes there *are* witnesses. The Constitution doesn't give the House, or the president, any right to present specific kinds of evidence. Nor does it prescribe rules of evidence. Here, too, the Senate must exercise judgment. In Clinton's trial, it initially appeared that no witnesses would testify. Only after a party-line vote, with Republicans in the majority, did the Senate compel Monica Lewinsky, Vernon Jordan Jr., and Sidney Blumenthal to appear. The three witnesses were then deposed privately, with tape recordings made available to senators in a secure room. Nobody offered live testimony in the Senate chamber at any point during the Clinton impeachment trial. The proceedings consisted largely of opening and closing statements, three private depositions, and over 150 questions posed orally to lawyers for both parties.

Even without courtroom drama, impeachment trials raise sensitive questions about transparency. Under Senate rules, most of the proceedings—including evidentiary submissions and oral presentations—are open to the public. The senators' deliberations, however, occur in closed session. In this respect, they are like the Supreme Court's private conferences. But unlike the Court, the Senate does not later release any reasoning to explain its decision. After deliberations conclude, the Senate votes separately on each article of impeachment. Senators may vote guilty or not guilty. (In Clinton's case, Senator Arlen Specter of Pennsylvania cited Scottish law to cast a third ballot—"not proven"—which was recorded as a vote of not guilty).[42]

If the president is convicted on any article of impeachment, he must be removed from office. The Senate may then vote separately on whether to disqualify him from future office-holding. It may not consider any other punishments or sanctions at that time.

* * *

In structuring impeachment proceedings, the Senate has virtually unbounded discretion. The Senate's "sole Power to try all Impeachments" thus includes the authority to redefine or eliminate almost every standard feature of a judicial trial.

This issue arose in Clinton's case. From day one, it was clear that the House managers could never convince sixty-seven senators to convict the president. Dreading the prospect of a full-blown trial, Senate leaders spent weeks debating an alternative associated with Senators Slade Gorton (Republican) and Joseph Lieberman (Democrat). Under this creative proposal, the Senate would hold a preliminary vote after hearing opening statements. If none of the articles received two-thirds approval—a foregone conclusion—then the Senate would end proceedings right away, without hearing testimony or further argument. At first, the Gorton-Lieberman proposal commanded strong support. And when the plan ultimately collapsed, it did so not because of any legal defect but because outraged House Republicans browbeat their Senate colleagues into allowing a broader presentation.

Here we encounter one of impeachment's most striking oddities. The Senate must "try all Impeachments." But its proceedings needn't be anything like judicial trials, which have been refined over centuries to achieve fairness, accuracy, efficiency, and many other goals. The Senate itself must decide whether and to what extent the strictures of the Due Process Clause even apply to impeachment trials. More broadly, the Senate must decide what it means to "try" an impeachment, knowing it's almost unimaginable that the Supreme Court would review any decisions it makes. Thus, as attorney Russell Spivak has remarked, "the rules . . . are governed by the whims of the 100 men and women with offices in the Dirksen, Hart or Russell buildings."[43] While senators agreed in Clinton's case to use a general procedural framework first designed for Johnson's trial, they exercised creativity and discretion where those rules didn't squarely address the question at hand.

Gorton-Lieberman was an especially extreme example of how the Senate might reimagine a trial. Now let's consider something more pedestrian. Under most circumstances, judges neither collaborate nor communicate off the record with parties appearing before them. Doing so would normally be regarded as fatal to the integrity of the proceedings. But these rules don't necessarily apply to impeachment trials. During Clinton's case, for example, Republican senators regularly huddled with the managers (and their allies in the House). Democratic senators, in turn, kept in frequent contact with the president's team to plan strategy. Some senators even turned double agent. According to Clinton, "one Republican senator who was opposed to impeachment kept us informed of what was going on among his colleagues."[44] The relentless swirl of innuendo around Washington, DC, meant that the Senate simultaneously plotted with parties and judged their case.

A related anomaly in Clinton's trial was the absence of a gag rule, which later led Judge Richard Posner to denounce the proceedings as "a travesty of legal justice."[45] In a normal case, the judge waits until the end to announce the ruling. Not here. Before and throughout the Clinton trial, many senators took strong public positions on the ultimate issue of conviction. The senators' incessant, self-congratulatory rhetoric about their own open-mindedness therefore rang hollow. Moreover, as Judge Posner observed, "the normal order of a trial—hearing, then verdict—was reversed, just as [in] *Alice in Wonderland*. Having made up their minds before hearing the evidence and arguments, the Senators were inattentive as well as biased adjudicators."[46]

Yet another peculiarity in Clinton's trial was the absence of an agreed-upon standard of proof. In most civil cases, the plaintiff must prove it's more likely than not that the defendant broke the law. Put differently, the plaintiff must establish her case by a "preponderance of the evidence." Criminal cases work differently. There, prosecutors must convince juries of guilt "beyond a reasonable doubt." Given how hard it can be to prove that a person engaged in willful wrongdoing, there's a world of difference between "preponderance of the evidence" and "beyond a reasonable doubt."

Scholars have long debated the appropriate standard of proof in an impeachment trial. Everyone agrees that the House must prove its case by more than a fifty-one/forty-nine margin. It would be crazy to end a presidency on the basis of a razor-thin probability that the president committed "high Crimes and Misdemeanors." On the other hand, requiring proof beyond a reasonable doubt would set the bar too high. We're not obliged to leave a president in power when the Senate believes that he almost certainly committed treason but can't escape a hint of doubt. That strict rule would defeat impeachment's purpose of securing the nation against threats from the Oval Office. So what's the standard? We favor Professor Charles L. Black Jr.'s charmingly noncommittal view that managers must prove the president's guilt by "an overwhelming preponderance of the evidence."[47] To this, we'd add just one important caveat. Where the president is accused of conduct that suggests imminent and existential peril if he remains in office, it would be proper to gently lower the evidentiary threshold.

One reason scholars still debate this question is that the Senate has never seen fit to answer it. Exercising its treasured power of nondecision, the Senate has affirmed that each senator can adopt his or her own standard of proof for impeachment. In fact, the Senate has taken this approach to many substantive questions that arise during the proceedings. The result is that impeachment trials involve one hundred judges with different views about making public statements, coordinating with the parties, setting a standard of proof, evaluating evidence, and defining "high Crimes and Misdemeanors." Unlike judicial trials, where most procedures and standards are knowable in advance, impeachments are tried before a court that often lacks consistent or agreed-upon rules, changes them midway, or refuses to reveal them to the parties. Greg Craig, one of Clinton's lawyers, recalls that "when the Senate decided what the rules were going to be for our trial, they really made them up as they went along."[48]

It would give the Senate too much credit to describe the absence of rules as based entirely on respect for each senator's individual prerogatives. That's only part of the story. A more important factor is that impeachments strain Congress's institutional capacity. The House is not a district attorney's office. The Senate is not a court. People aren't elected to those bodies because they possess the skills, training, or temperament we'd expect of prosecutors and judges. Focused on the ordinary business of government, Congress has few incentives to maintain the resources or expertise necessary for a smooth impeachment process. Further, true to their political instincts, legislators prefer to keep all options open. Committing in advance on major questions can tie their hands later, when it might be convenient to take a different view. This would never fly in a court of law, where the parties have a right to regular procedure. But in the House and Senate, important aspects of the impeachment process are always up for grabs.

* * *

In describing the ad hoc quality of impeachments, we don't mean to suggest that due process has no role in this story. Far from it. Congress's discretion only makes it *more* important that legislators adhere to values of justice and fair play. That's true both of the procedures they establish and the substantive decision they render on removing a president. Legislators will always scheme and skirmish. Party loyalty doesn't dissipate overnight. But ultimately, the House and Senate have a constitutional duty to reach an equitable, well-supported outcome that can be accepted as legitimate by nearly all Americans.

This vision of impeachment mixes principle with pragmatism. As we've seen in earlier chapters, it's consistent with the Constitution's original public meaning and structure. It's also grounded in constitutional text: at minimum, the textual requirement that senators "try" impeachments demands a more impartial and judicial outlook than normal legislative decision-making. The same is true of the Senate's special oath and the selection of the chief justice as presiding officer. Although the House and Senate are irreducibly political, the Constitution makes clear that impeachment calls for a profoundly different mentality.

Stated simply, impeachments are no place for small minds or low politics. Here Congress can vindicate, or obliterate, our governmental structure. Exercising this power demands seriousness of purpose and an honest engagement with constitutional values. While disagreements are inevitable, it's incumbent on Congress to act in good faith. At all stages of the process, legislators must be guided by principled impartiality.

Impartiality has a distinctive meaning in this context. Unlike in a courtroom, it's impossible to expect a truly neutral decision maker. Nobody in the House or Senate is indifferent to the president. Nearly everyone voting on his fate will identify as his ally or opponent. To demand perfect neutrality in that circumstance would be to ask the impossible. Instead, impartiality is a matter of degree and attitude. It requires discipline, empathy, and self-reflection. It also requires a principled commitment to the structure and culture of our democratic constitution, apart from mere party or personal interest. As Professor Black observed, it's helpful to ask how we would answer questions if we had opposite feelings about the president threatened with removal.

An important dimension of impartiality concerns partisanship. When an impeachment is purely partisan, or appears that way, it is presumptively illegitimate. Except in extraordinary circumstances, the president shouldn't be removed from office by a single party. In most cases, that isn't even possible. While House majorities come and go, mustering sixty-seven Senate votes usually requires some bipartisan consensus. But even where one party has the votes necessary to expel a president, it should think twice—and then think twice again—before doing so exclusively along partisan lines. When only Republicans (or only Democrats) view the president's conduct as justifying removal, there's a strong risk that policy disagreements or partisan animus have overtaken the proper measure of congressional impartiality.

The presumption against partisan impeachments is also supported by pragmatic concerns. As Professor Keith Whittington has explained: "If the impeachment power is perceived to be little more than a partisan tool for undermining elected officials and overturning election results, then the value of elections for resolving our political disagreements is significantly reduced. We do not want to be in a situation in which neither side trusts the other to [abide] by election results."[49] The risk of destabilizing our political system mustn't be underestimated. It's easy to envision how a successful partisan removal could unleash a cycle of bitter, destructive recrimination. Accordingly, impeachment should almost always be confined to cases where there is some bipartisan consensus that the president is too dangerous to be allowed to remain in office.

We can imagine only one exception to this principle. An impeachment along political party lines would be acceptable where the president has captured or corrupted his own political party and the public has elected the competing party with a mandate supporting removal. In that event, many of the president's original supporters have either abandoned him or been decisively outvoted in a subsequent election. Partisan impeachments are nightmarish but are most justified when born of a popular command to eject a tyrant (and his political allies) from power.

The ideal of impartiality runs both ways. Just as the president's opponents must act responsibly, so must his own party. The

Senate's two-thirds rule generally makes removal impossible unless some members of the president's team are willing to do him in. And as we've discussed, blocking an otherwise-justified impeachment can pose extraordinary risks to the nation. That makes the president's political party *particularly* responsible for proper use of this power. Even if voting for removal harms their policy goals or their standing in the next election, constitutional good faith may require the president's comrades to take that step. Refusing to impeach a known tyrant out of partisan self-interest would constitute a failure of governance at least as profound as urging impeachment solely for partisan reasons.

In all these respects, Congress must strive toward principled impartiality at every step of an impeachment. The outcome of the proceeding, and its public reception, may depend on how well Congress succeeds in living up to this high standard.

Of course, that's not to say Congress should *completely* tune out politics. We doubt it could do so even if it tried. By temperament, many of its members are operators and pragmatists. They're accustomed to cutting deals, weighing consequences, and negotiating competing interests. They're also immersed in political party structures that affect their daily lives in countless ways. Most important, they're sensitive to the wishes of their party, donors, and constituents. Going too far out on a limb can invite sudden unemployment.

In some respects, Congress's political character can be a virtue, not a vice. Impeachment is a political remedy wielded by politicians to address a political problem. Their mastery of politics makes legislators savvy judges—both of the specific charges and of the broader circumstances. Nobody else in the federal government better comprehends the use and abuse of power, or can more capably assess whether the president has truly crossed a line.

Moreover, during impeachments, Congress must keep a clear-eyed view of the shifting political landscape. These dynamics are crucial to assessing the risks and propriety of ending a presidency—and of failing to end it. They're also important to carrying out the process in a way that minimizes harmful consequences. At times, presidents may counterattack through partisan channels, requiring Congress to defend itself and its proceedings in the public eye. There, too, Congress can be well served by its political acumen, as long as it doesn't lose sight of the big picture and its ultimate obligations under the Constitution.

* * *

If that all sounds a bit romantic, that's because it is. The Constitution calls for greatness at moments of national crisis. In thinking about Congress as the decision maker on impeachments, we benefit from identifying principles to which legislators should aspire. Even if Congress falls short, at least we know what its members must aim for in treacherous times.

Now we'll pivot back to earth. History and political science offer useful lessons about what factors tend to drive Congress's decisions in this field. Although every impeachment has its own unique DNA—and it's impossible to state with certainty which variables matter most—it's possible to identify and evaluate a number of important considerations.

Let's start with public opinion polls on whether the president should be impeached and removed from office. For obvious reasons, everyone involved in the process keeps careful track of those figures. And appropriately so. Public opinion data may provide valuable insight into how Americans would respond to an impeachment, whether an impeachment effort is likely to succeed, and whether the president is perceived as a viable leader.

Although Americans now take for granted easy access to such information, for most of US history it had to be gauged impressionistically. During the Johnson impeachment, and through the following decades, Congress lacked access to reliable, scientific data about what the American people preferred. As Professor Sarah Igo explains, "only in the years after World War I did mass surveys telling Americans 'who we are,' 'what we want,' and 'what we believe' enter the public domain."[50] Even then, the first scientific poll on presidential impeachment wasn't conducted until 1973.

Watergate was thus the nation's first experience with impeachment polling. Support for impeachment began at 19 percent in the summer of 1973. It rose to 38 percent in October 1973 after the "Saturday Night Massacre," when Nixon ordered the dismissal of Special Prosecutor Archibald Cox, and his attorney general (and deputy attorney general) resigned in protest. Pro-impeachment sentiment trended upward until August 1974, when Nixon finally resigned. Yet notwithstanding clear evidence of criminality and abuse of power, measurable public support for Nixon's impeachment never topped 57 percent.[51]

There's an important lesson here. In the 1970s, many Americans didn't appreciate what it meant to impeach a president. Pollsters discovered that confusion persisted even when surveys described the impeachment process in greater detail. Watergate-related polls may thus have misstated public support for ending Nixon's presidency. And that deficiency in impeachment polling remains with us. Peter Hart, a professional pollster, has candidly remarked that "the electorate doesn't fully understand impeachment . . . their understanding of impeachment is *I'm sending a message of disapproval*" (italics added).[52] Consistent with that view, a July 2014 poll found that 18 percent of the public believes "Congress should attempt to impeach a President in order to express dissatisfaction with his policies or the way the president is handling his job."[53] In many other polls, large numbers of Americans have supported or opposed impeaching specific presidents for reasons flatly at odds with the design of impeachment in the constitutional system.

People are certainly entitled to their opinions, but in this nation impeachments are not decided by referendum. Legislators swear an oath to uphold the Constitution and are obliged to take its design seriously. They must therefore handle polling data with care. Although Congress properly cares about public opinion, there are also times when it must lead the nation by exercising and explaining its own considered judgment.

A related factor that has historically affected impeachments is the president's approval rating. At every step of the process, from opening an investigation to conviction, Congress is less likely to confront a popular president. That partly reflects electoral self-interest, since presidential popularity can have a big effect on the outcome of congressional races. But there's also a simpler reason: if the American people support the president, they're more likely to forgive his sins, oppose his adversaries, and resist any effort to unseat him from power. This helps explain why Ronald Reagan wasn't impeached for Iran-Contra and why the Senate didn't vote to convict Clinton. Throughout their scandals, both Reagan and Clinton maintained relatively strong overall approval and likability measures. In stark contrast, Nixon's public approval declined from 68 percent in January 1973 to 24 percent at the time he resigned in August 1974. We don't have data for Johnson, but the record suggests that he was hated by most of the voting public.

It's unnerving to consider the significance of presidential popularity in impeachments. Approval ratings can be affected by a thousand variables, ranging from economic growth to developments in foreign policy to the president's general affability. The fact that a president excels at speechifying may have little to do with whether he's a tyrant. Yet in practice, presidents who are good at maintaining a positive public image may have more leeway to get away with "high Crimes and Misdemeanors."

In assessing polls on impeachment and public approval, it's important to parse the data. We can start by identifying two groups of key players in Congress. One group consists of the House and Senate leadership, the committee chairs, and other party elders who command respect. The second group consists of legislators whose votes will likely control whether an impeachment succeeds. While legislators in both groups will care about national data, they'll usually care most about polls of their own constituents and political party. Where support for impeachment is concentrated in a few regions or in a single party, national polls may fail to predict outcomes. As journalist John F. Harris writes of Clinton's case, "Members of Congress were not driven by the logic of national majorities, but by two other imperatives: one was the imperative of individual congressional districts; the other, the politics of the party caucus."[54]

This leads to another major factor in impeachments: political party control of Congress. The impeachments of Johnson, Clinton, and Nixon all occurred while their opponents controlled both the House and Senate. That isn't a coincidence. Legislators maintain a deep reservoir of goodwill for presidents from their own party. For self-evident reasons, it's unappealing to impeach a president who would otherwise support favored policies (and whom many legislators likely endorsed). Polling expert Nate Silver thus notes that "members of a party tend to stick together, until the wheels come off—and even then the wagon sometimes gets repaired again."[55] A president's approval ratings would have to be radioactive, threatening ruin and destruction in the next election, before his own party would consider pursuing an impeachment.

When a party controls the House or Senate, it has powerful tools to set the agenda and keep its ranks in line. Disloyal members can be punished with loss of prized committee assignments, campaign funds, and legislative pork. If the president's party controls a chamber, these threats may allow its leadership to push wobbly members into resisting calls for removal. In contrast, when the president's opponents control a chamber, their leadership can exert great pressure on swing votes to support impeachment. The Republican campaign to remove Clinton offers an especially clear demonstration of these strategies. As Clinton recounts in his autobiography, "One Republican committee chairman was plainly distraught when he told a White House aide that he didn't want to vote for impeachment but would lose his chairmanship if he voted against it. Jay Dickey, an Arkansas Republican, told Mack

McLarty he might lose his seat on the Appropriations Committee if he didn't vote to impeach me."[56]

Closely related to party control, but sometimes distinct from it, is the president's relationship with party leaders in the House and Senate. Politics are about more than polls and policies. At times, personalities make all the difference.

Consider two stories with very different endings. When revelations of Clinton's wrongdoing came to light, impeachment was not a foreordained conclusion. At least some congressional Republicans would have favored a less extreme response, such as a resolution of censure. But instead, the Starr Report ballooned into our nation's second impeachment. This was partly due to legitimate outrage at Clinton's misconduct. It was also the product of a cynical (and misguided) political calculation by Republicans. Yet a major explanation for the impeachment was personal. House Republican leaders hated Clinton with every fiber of their being. A total breakdown in communication between the White House and Congress, alongside years of slow-boiled venom, had destroyed relationships that might otherwise have calmed things down.

Iran-Contra shows what can happen when those relationships are intact. Ronald Reagan was a Republican's Republican. House Speaker Tip O'Neill was a rock-ribbed Democrat. They weren't friends. At best, they were frenemies. Journalist John Farrell recalls that O'Neill "stood like an oak, skewering the president as a tool of the wealthy, a creature of the country club, as a mean old 'Ebenezer Scrooge.'"[57] Reagan, in turn, reportedly described O'Neill as Pac-Man: "a round thing that gobbles up money."[58] But even amid bruising political battles, they would occasionally socialize and meet for drinks. More important, they tried—at least most of the time—to put country above personality and party. When Iran-Contra broke, the House would have been justified in holding impeachment proceedings. But O'Neill went to the White House and met alone with Reagan. According to *Boston Globe* reporter Robert Healy, O'Neill made clear that there would be no impeachment. The nation was still traumatized by Watergate. For all their rivalry, O'Neill would not put the country through that nightmare again. Whether or not this was the right move, it shows what can happen when lines of trust and communication are open.

These stories gesture to still another variable that can influence impeachment decisions: the state of partisanship and institutionalism in Congress. What do the key players and swing voters care about? Are they unthinking, unshakable party loyalists? Or are they more independent-minded in outlook, concerned primarily with preserving democratic institutions and the separation of powers? Every session of Congress has its own gaggle of partisan zombies. Every session also has a core of elder statesmen, moderates, and mavericks—though recently those ranks have thinned to almost nothing. Whether an impeachment takes flight will often depend on which group controls the levers of power. In some extreme cases, the determining factor may be what it takes for even diehard partisans to reach their breaking point.

Nixon's case is illustrative. Even as evidence against the president piled up, many Republican voters stood by him. Indeed, on the day he resigned from office, over 50 percent of registered Republicans approved of his performance. But in Congress, the picture looked very different. At first, partisan loyalties had held firm. In February 1974, Representative William L. Hungate bitingly remarked that "there are a few Republicans who wouldn't vote to impeach Nixon if he were caught in a bank vault at midnight."[59] By August, however, Nixon's support had collapsed. His threat to the nation was clear, and his compulsive lying had alienated allies. A convening of Republican Party elders finally concluded that Nixon had to go. On Wednesday, August 7, 1974, Senator Barry Goldwater, Senate Minority Leader Hugh Scott, and House Minority Leader John Rhodes entered the Oval Office. After some awkward pleasantries, Goldwater cut to the chase: "[J]ust about all of the guys have spoken up and there aren't many who would support you if it comes to that." One day later, Nixon announced his resignation.[60]

Goldwater, like many other congressional Republicans, had snapped after a long and tortured investigation of Nixon's misdeeds. It wasn't just the underlying acts that offended him, but also the cover-up. On a call with General Alexander Haig, Goldwater had warned that Nixon "has lied to me for the last time and lied to my colleagues for the last time."[61]

Goldwater's phone call brings us to a distinct factor in impeachments: whether congressional leaders believe that the president is cooperating with them and respecting their prerogatives. As we discussed in Chapter 3, this affects perceptions of whether less extreme measures will suffice. It also affects the personal and political dynamics that can determine outcomes in Congress. Offending House and Senate leaders, and obfuscating facts, casts the worst possible light on alleged high crimes and greatly increases the odds of removal. History could not be clearer on this point. Nixon resigned after repeatedly shooting himself in the foot. Reagan survived Iran-Contra partly by collaborating with investigators, cleaning house, and promising newfound respect for the will of Congress. And Clinton suffered in the House from a perception that he had acted in bad faith during and after Starr's investigation.

*　*　*

Of course, impeachments aren't only about partisan dynamics and personal relationships; they're also about the original sin itself, the "high Crimes and Misdemeanors." We can't predict whether Congress will impeach without knowing what the president has done and what evidence has come to light. Although impeachment and proof of "high Crimes and Misdemeanors" don't always march together, evidence of presidential misconduct certainly matters. Usually there are three key questions: (1) What did the president do? (2) Why did the president do it? (3) Does this conduct justify impeachment?

Inevitably, each of these questions will be clouded by some uncertainty. In assessing whether Congress is likely to impeach, it's useful to determine how clearly we can answer each of them. It's also helpful to identify swing votes in the House and to ask whether they and their constituents may take a different view based on the news sources and information culture that they favor. Questions about what happened—and about how much we can trust the available evidence—may look very different on Fox versus MSNBC.

This brings us to a final variable: Who is next in line to the presidency? Legislators never lose sight of that question. Indeed, in Johnson's case this was among the most decisive considerations. After Abraham Lincoln's assassination, Johnson had taken office without naming a vice president. As a result, Benjamin Wade—the president pro tempore of the Senate—would ascend if Johnson was removed. Wade was among the most radical of Republicans and had burned bridges with many of his colleagues. They feared that if he took Johnson's spot, Wade would drive the party to ruin in the 1868 presidential election. Anxiety about elevating Wade thus pervaded the Senate and shaped its decision. As one newspaper explained in a burst of candor, "Andrew Johnson is innocent because Benjamin Wade is guilty of being his successor."[62]

Over a century later, Nixon tried (and failed) to create a similar dynamic. By late 1973, impeachment was in the air and Nixon was on the defensive. But the cagey president had an ace in the hole: his vice president, Spiro Agnew. By almost every relevant measure, Agnew was painfully unqualified for our highest office. In private, Nixon and John Ehrlichman jokingly called him "the assassin's dilemma."[63] Nixon was sure that Congress wouldn't impeach if doing so meant elevating Agnew. Unfortunately for Nixon, Agnew was caught in a corruption scandal and had to resign in October 1973. With Watergate hearings looming over him, Nixon deliberately sought a replacement unsuitable for the presidency. This led him to Representative Gerald Ford. As biographer Evan Thomas notes, "with the poor political judgment that increasingly afflicted him, Nixon believed that Ford provided him with a layer of protection against impeachment."[64] At one point, Nixon remarked that Ford was a "good insurance policy."

As it turned out, Nixon was wrong. Ford was a seasoned and well-liked legislator with a base of support in Congress. Fear of elevating him would not stymie the impeachment proceedings. When Nixon finally resigned in August 1974, the nation breathed a sigh of relief at the thought of his "insurance policy" occupying the Oval Office. It's revealing, though, that Nixon sought to remain in power by poisoning the well. Although his effort failed, a president who would commit impeachable offenses is likely the kind of person willing to use such dastardly tactics.

* * *

The Framers made a profoundly important decision when they assigned impeachment to Congress. This power is inseparable from the institution that exercises it. Understanding how Congress assesses and undertakes impeachments is thus invaluable for anyone who would advance or oppose an effort to end a presidency. And it offers essential context for the colorful history of impeachment talk in the United States—a tale that stretches from political attacks on George Washington to the latest, greatest controversies surrounding Donald Trump.

5

IMPEACHMENT TALK

On January 25, 1809, Josiah Quincy of Massachusetts rose with solemn business for the House of Representatives. President Thomas Jefferson, he declared, had committed "a high misdemeanor . . . against this nation."[1] As his startled colleagues listened intently, Quincy made his case. General Benjamin Lincoln had served as Collector of the Port of Boston since the Washington administration. Hobbled by age, General Lincoln had repeatedly asked Jefferson for leave to resign the post. But Jefferson had ignored these requests. He didn't want the position to become vacant until his ally, Secretary of War Henry Dearborn, could be appointed to occupy it. As a result of Jefferson's deliberate inaction, General Lincoln—a hero of the Revolutionary War—was forced against his will to keep the position and endure brutal criticism from local papers. This misuse of the appointment power, Quincy reasoned, constituted an impeachable offense. The House had a moral and legal duty to investigate Jefferson's misconduct.

Quincy's peers knew that the Massachusetts Federalist was no fan of Jefferson's. Just months earlier, he had written to John Adams that Jefferson was a "dish of skim milk curdling at the head of our nation."[2] Elsewhere, Quincy dismissed Jefferson as a "snake in the grass"[3] and a "transparent fraud," supported only by "dupes or ruffians."[4] Even still, Quincy's call for impeachment hearings caused an immediate scandal in the House. Eighteen legislators took turns denouncing him. Representative James Gholson urged that the resolutions not be printed; they "had excited his astonishment more than anything which had occurred during the session."[5] Representative William Burwell remarked that he "knew of but one parallel to it, in the history of impeachments, and that would be found in Gulliver's Travels."[6] After a general pummeling, Quincy's proposal failed. The vote was 171 to 1.[7]

In Congress, though, success and failure are often more complex than they appear. Before the Senate adjourned that same day, Dearborn's nomination to serve as Collector of the Port of Boston was submitted to the Senate. Thanks to Quincy's aggressive maneuver, General Lincoln was soon relieved of his unwanted and tiresome duty. Further, as a biographer writes, Quincy's "political friends in Congress . . . approved of what he had done, and those in Boston were unanimous in their approbation." Decades later, after serving as president of Harvard University, Quincy fondly recalled his resolution to impeach Jefferson. "No public exertion of mine," he said, "has been more fully justified by the reflections of a long life."[8]

Until now, we've largely focused on credible attempts to end presidencies through impeachment. We've evaluated the reasoning, judgment calls, and decision makers involved in that process. We've also discussed the most important cases: John Tyler, Andrew Johnson, Richard Nixon, Ronald Reagan, and Bill Clinton. These stories anchor any history of the subject.

But the tale of impeachment is broader and more complex than is often appreciated. The vast majority of impeachment talk in US history hasn't ended with—or even sought to achieve—a House vote and Senate trial. To fully comprehend this constitutional power, we must therefore look beyond a single endgame. Impeachment has been invoked by many players, for many purposes, since the founding era. Exploring their tactics allows for a more sophisticated grasp of the use and abuse of impeachment talk—both historically and in our own time.

Taking the long view also confirms that we live in a strange new world. The culture of impeachment in the United States has ebbed and flowed over the years. For the most part, however, a study of our nation's past discloses a near-total absence of calls for impeachment. To be sure, there have always been radicals or outliers who favored expelling whoever happened to be president. But if we focus on mainstream opinion—even taking an expansive view of the term *mainstream*—the record is clear. Throughout most of US history, impeachment wasn't on anybody's agenda. As historian David Kyvig observed, "impeachment remained in the constitutional shadows." It was "occasionally called for by isolated voices but little remembered by the general public and seldom given serious consideration by public officials, journalists, or scholars."[9]

That world is over. Compared to the first two hundred years of the nation's history, impeachment now plays a drastically more important and disruptive role in US politics. Modern Americans live in the post-Clinton age of a permanent impeachment campaign.

We suspect this point will be intuitive. Who among us isn't frequently bombarded with tweets, Facebook messages, fundraising e-mails, newspaper editorials, and blog posts demanding (or opposing) impeachment? Although it's easy to take that background noise for granted, or to dismiss it as ordinary political rhetoric, that's a mistake. To borrow a phrase in widespread circulation under President Donald Trump, "this is not normal." In no other period has impeachment played the role it now occupies in the ordinary conduct of US politics. Here we're referring not only to the Trump administration but also to the presidencies of Bill Clinton, George W. Bush, and Barack Obama.

Efforts to end a presidency do not occur in a vacuum. They take place in a society with received norms and expectations about the use of this dangerous power. Understanding that culture is essential to any analysis of whether (and how best) to end a presidency. Without that context in mind, advocates of impeachment may discover that their plans tragically backfire.

* * *

George Washington was sworn in as president on April 30, 1789. As everyone knew, he was a living legend—an embodiment of republican virtue. Washington had led American forces to victory in the Revolutionary War. He had presided with dignity over the Constitutional Convention. He had been chosen unanimously by the Electoral College to serve as the nation's first president. And he was admirably self-conscious about making proper use of his powers: "I walk on untrodden ground. There is scarcely any part of my conduct which may not hereafter be drawn into precedent." [10]

Washington enjoyed a prolonged grace period. But leading a new nation is no easy task. Inevitably, forces of party and faction appeared on the scene. Criticism of Washington emerged. Then, in 1795, word leaked that Chief Justice John Jay—acting on Washington's orders—had secretly negotiated a treaty with Britain whose terms left most Americans aghast. Although the Jay Treaty passed the Senate by exactly two-thirds, James Madison and Thomas Jefferson whipped up a frenzied opposition. At the height of the political struggle, Jay bitterly remarked that he could travel the nation guided solely by the light of his own burning effigies.

As the tempest grew, calls to impeach Washington echoed in a few corners of the nation. In Virginia's *Petersburg Intelligencer,* for instance, an anonymous citizen wrote: "The constitution has given the mild punishment of impeachment for the greatest abuses. The people are not sanguinary—they only demand that those should be removed from the office who abuse power." [11] Even some who saw impeachment as futile still thought it worth the effort. As one commentator remarked in Philadelphia's *Aurora General Advertiser:* "There are important purposes to be gained by even a vote of impeachment . . . It would convince the world that we are free and that we are determined to remain so. It would be a solemn and awful lesson to future Presidents." [12]

In the 1790s, the idea of impeaching Washington amounted to political heresy and was never taken seriously. These editorials, however, suggest some early popular uncertainty about what exactly impeachment was for. This was a new power at the federal level, meant to limit a new kind of leader in a new form of government. The American people, having just fought a war against King George III of England, were excitable when they sensed tyranny. It wasn't clear at the very beginning what role impeachment would play in restraining the president. That instability in views of impeachment may explain why John Adams experienced such fear when his handling of the *Hermione* incident led opposition leaders to call for his ouster (as we saw in Chapter 4).

By the early 1800s, though, many Americans had come to see impeachment as a stillborn power. In 1820, for instance, Jefferson concluded that "impeachment is an impracticable thing, a mere scarecrow."[13] Although he made this remark in reference to judges, it was soon applied to presidents. Fourteen years later, expressing despair about President Andrew Jackson's many abuses of power, one senator wrote that impeachment had "ceased to be any effective protection to the purity of the Constitution." He added, "it has become but little better than a tale to amuse, like Utopia, or Swift's flying island."[14] In 1848, this understanding was treated as common sense. During the fight to censure James Polk for invading Mexico, a congressional Whig readily observed that "impeachment is almost a dead letter in the Constitution."[15]

The only serious impeachment effort in the antebellum period, which we discussed in Chapter 1, was the failed campaign against John Tyler. In that case, the outgoing House Whig majority was so infuriated by Tyler's aggressive use of vetoes that its political judgment temporarily short-circuited. Although we have not found evidence either way, we suspect that the Whigs' crushing defeat in the midterm elections in 1842 only encouraged perceptions that impeachment was virtually impossible.

On the heels of the Civil War, the House impeached a president for the very first time. But the Johnson proceedings hardly invited a more open attitude toward ending presidencies. To the contrary, the failure of this impeachment—and the widespread perception over the following decades that it was unjustified—encouraged skepticism about *any* use of the impeachment power. Rather than make impeachment seem more plausible, the Johnson acquittal durably tarnished this constitutional check on the presidency.

* * *

From 1868 through 1951, politicians and public intellectuals almost never raised the threat of impeachment. When they did so, it was usually to inflict political damage on the president and his party rather than to force actual removal from office. Moreover, those efforts at strategic use of impeachment talk usually fell flat. It wasn't until Harry Truman's administration that impeachment suddenly—albeit temporarily—roared back to life in US national politics.

Before jumping to the 1950s, we'll consider a handful of impeachment efforts in the long gap between Johnson and Truman. These examples offer a useful sense of impeachment's comparatively minor role in this period. They also show different purposes to which the impeachment power was put during a time when it was practically unavailable.

Let's begin with the presidential election of 1876. Eight months before Election Day, Democrats sensed opportunity. Republicans had held the White House since Abraham Lincoln replaced James Buchanan in 1861. But now Ulysses S. Grant was about to conclude his second term, and the nation had soured on Republicans and their Reconstruction program. In a foreboding twist, Democrats had scored crushing midterm victories two years earlier, bolstered by a weak economy and corruption in the executive branch. To Democrats' delight, the air of scandal around Grant had only intensified since then, ensnaring key cabinet members—including the secretary of war, who resigned in disgrace after the House opened impeachment proceedings against him. As biographer Ron Chernow notes, "a perfect torrent of scandal had swept over the administration and Grant seemed powerless to stem the rushing, foaming tide."[16] By April 1876, the president was widely perceived as a solitary beacon of innocence in the White House.

To build momentum before the election, Democrats wanted to change that perception. At first, they pursued charges that Grant had broken the law by using public funds for his campaign in 1872. This claim broke down, however, when a key witness was revealed as certifiably insane. Undeterred, Democrats stumbled toward charges that Grant had spent too much time away from the capital. Seeking to substantiate this theory, they demanded that Grant account for his whereabouts since March 1869. Commentators treated this step as laden with overtones of impeachment, and political cartoonists mocked Democrats for their flimsy accusations. Grant's response was suitably dismissive. The Constitution, he pointed out, nowhere empowers the House to make such a demand. Aware of the subtext, he added: "If this information be sought . . . in aid of the power of impeachment," then it violated his own right not to be "made a witness against himself."[17]

In fact, it isn't clear whether the right against self-incrimination applies to the president in an impeachment proceeding. Moreover, as discussed in Chapter 2, a president who unjustifiably decides to absent himself for lengthy periods might well be guilty of "high Crimes and Misdemeanors." Nonetheless, Grant's terse answer did the trick. Congressional Democrats' halfhearted effort to precipitate an impeachment ended almost immediately. They ultimately let the question die when Congress reconvened in December 1876. By then, legislators had more pressing business: breaking a tie vote in the Electoral College that had unleashed political bedlam. (This was resolved by the infamous Compromise of 1877, which awarded the election to Republican Rutherford B. Hayes in exchange for a promise to withdraw federal troops from the South and end Reconstruction.)

In Grant's case, Democrats took barely a step in the direction of impeachment and gave up as soon as they hit resistance. They never had any serious intention of impeaching the president; they knew it, and Grant knew it. Their only goal was to make Grant look bad. They failed at that, too. All said and done, this was not an especially effective use of the impeachment power.

Yet the Democrats' efforts to embarrass Grant were still far more productive than Congressman Milford Howard's quixotic bid to impeach Grover Cleveland twenty years later. As a dedicated Alabama Populist, Howard vehemently disdained Cleveland, an establishment Democrat serving his second (nonconsecutive) term. Indeed, Howard disdained most American politicians, whom he saw as mere servants of the wealthy: "All the plutocrats have a perfect understanding among themselves . . . they care not whether the Democratic or Republican party wins, so long as both parties favor the money power."[18] On June 6, 1896, with only a few months left in Cleveland's tenure, Howard filed an impeachment resolution. True to his populist roots, Howard charged Cleveland with mishandling federal bonds and funds, failing to enforce antitrust laws, corrupting politics, and deploying troops to crush the infamous Pullman Strike.

Howard's colleagues had no patience for these political antics. His populist *cri de coeur* flashed, then fizzled, on the House floor. *The Illustrated American* remarked that "under many conditions [Howard's call] would create a sensation in Congress," but in this case "it seemed grotesque."[19] As soon as Howard finished reading his resolution, Representative Nelson Dingley Jr.—a Republican—raised a procedural objection. On a full vote, and without discussion, the House refused to consider the resolution on the merits. It was never seen again, and there is no evidence that Howard's impeachment call had any notable effect.

In late 1919, Republicans took their turn at bat. Woodrow Wilson, a Democrat, had just seen the nation through World War I. Determined to reshape the international order, Wilson personally headed the US delegation to a peace conference in Paris. This gathering redrew the world map, breaking empires and devising countries. Throughout the negotiations, Wilson pushed hard to form a League of Nations. He accurately foresaw that "there will be another world war if the nations of the world do not concert the method by which to prevent it."[20] In his view, the League of Nations was that method. It would resolve disputes, nurture cooperation, and avert conflict. While the Paris Peace Conference produced a deeply flawed treaty, it established a version of the League of Nations. Wilson therefore signed the agreement at Versailles on June 28, 1919.

In early July, Wilson returned home to a divided nation. Many Democrats supported him, but Republicans controlled the Senate. Fourteen members of that majority were especially hostile to the treaty and called themselves "Irreconcilables." As historian George Herring recounts, they "launched a nationwide campaign, sending out thousands of pamphlets denouncing the 'Evil Thing with a Holy Name' and making hundreds of speeches, many of them appealing to the racial and nationalist prejudices of Americans."[21] The Irreconcilables were led by Senator Henry Cabot Lodge, who once confided that he "never expected to hate anyone in politics with the hatred I feel towards Wilson."[22]

To press his case with the public, Wilson embarked on a ten thousand–mile PR campaign. Not to be outdone, the Irreconcilables launched their own tour—which soon became a movable feast of impeachment talk. On September 11, 1919, Senator William Borah took the stage in Chicago and denounced Wilson's plan to "hand American destiny over to the secret councils of Europe." A furious crowd responded, "Impeach him!" and "Take the power out of his hands!"[23] That scene repeated itself days later in Kansas City. When Senator Hiram Johnson warned that Wilson could not guarantee "secret treaties" with "the blood of American boys," hundreds cried out, "Impeach Wilson!"[24] These rallies weren't isolated instances. The *Congressional Record* from 1919 and 1920 reveals a spike in citizen petitions urging the president's impeachment.

These accounts of the anti-treaty movement reveal a rare display of mass, popular impeachment talk before the 1950s. If newspaper accounts are to be trusted, it was the crowds—not only the senators—who called for Wilson's removal. According to press reports, they feared America would "give back to George V what it took away from George III."[25]

Although impeachment never seriously jeopardized Wilson's presidency, that didn't stop him from threatening those who supported it. This was wholly in character for Wilson, who had little respect for civil liberty. Citizens who called for impeachment at Republican rallies were generally safe. Promoting impeachment elsewhere, however, was risky—especially for political outliers. After Wilson returned from Versailles, the *New York Times* reported that the FBI had opened an investigation into a six-page petition urging Wilson's impeachment. According to the *Times*, "these charges are so worded as to give comfort to the Bolsheviki, the pro-Germans, the Sinn Feiners, and to other elements that oppose . . . the League of Nations." The FBI had already detained the pamphlet's publisher and was now seeking its author "to determine whether or not the petition is a part of the enemy propaganda which has since the armistice gained new life in this country." As part of that effort, "the names of the persons signed to such petitions as reach Washington will be investigated."[26] Looking back, Wilson's conflation of impeachment with disloyalty was disgraceful. If a modern president tried to persecute citizens for supporting his removal, that position would constitute powerful evidence that he probably *should* be ousted.

As far as we can tell, the FBI investigation of Wilson's critics ultimately came to naught. Ultimately, so did the president's crusade for the League of Nations. In November 1919, after Wilson suffered a crippling stroke, his treaty was put to a vote. Wilson's dream died that day on the Senate floor. Impeachment, though, had played only a bit part in its demise.

This isn't to say impeachment *never* destroyed a political agenda. In December 1932, after Franklin D. Roosevelt was elected but before his inauguration, Representative Louis McFadden sought the impeachment of Herbert Hoover. McFadden was a repulsive anti-Semite. He was also a conspiracy theorist and radical foe of the Federal Reserve. Most of his colleagues found him entirely unbearable. In calling for Hoover's removal, McFadden offered a bizarre grab bag of accusations, ranging from bad personnel decisions and mistreating protesters to increasing unemployment and usurping Congress's role in treaty negotiation.

As the *Washington Post* reported, McFadden's baseless resolution was "promptly and emphatically smothered . . . by a startled House of Representatives." With no debate, the chamber voted to table McFadden's motion by a vote of 361 to 8. House Republican leader Bertrand Snell deemed this "as hard a spanking as a grown man could get." The eight votes in McFadden's favor were met with loud hisses.[27]

McFadden suffered lasting consequences for submitting this baseless impeachment resolution. The Pennsylvania Republican delegation requested his resignation as its chair.[28] Senator David Reed, a fellow Pennsylvania Republican, stated that "we intend to act [for] all practical purposes as though McFadden had died."[29] And back home, the *Philadelphia Inquirer* asked whether McFadden "belongs not in the House of Representatives but in some other institution."[30] McFadden never recovered from this blunder. In the 1934 election, he was defeated by a Democrat—the only time between 1912 and 1950 that his district didn't vote Republican. He then tried to run for president on an avowedly anti-Jewish platform, but that effort went nowhere. In 1936, exiled from national politics, McFadden died at the age of 60.

The stories recounted in this section are fairly representative of the limited role that impeachment played from 1868 to 1951. If anything, they overstate it, since we sought out those unusual cases where the word *impeachment* was mentioned in national political disputes. This period thus marked the long slumber of the impeachment power in American life and politics.

* * *

In 1951, after a century of near-total inactivity, the nation experienced a wave of impeachment fever exponentially more intense than anything since Johnson. A second wave followed one year later, this time accompanied by impeachment resolutions in the House. Each bout of impeachment talk lasted only a couple of months, and neither produced durable public interest in presidential impeachment. In fact, that subject largely disappeared from public discourse from 1952 until 1974. Nonetheless, it's under Truman—a Democrat—that we can first locate a harbinger of the popular, partisan impeachment dynamic that now shapes our politics.

The first round of impeachment talk occurred in April 1951, after Truman relieved General Douglas MacArthur of command during the Korean War. MacArthur was flamboyant, egotistical, and mercurial. He was also a national hero and occasional genius. The combination of these traits led him to defy the rule that civilians, not generals, control our military and foreign policy. Although hugely unpopular at the time, Truman's decision to fire MacArthur is now recognized as a vindication of the Constitution. In a fine display of irony, his contemporaries rewarded him not with praise, but with impassioned calls for his removal.

This chain of events began in September 1950. After US troops were deployed to South Korea, they struggled to establish and hold a position. When all seemed lost, MacArthur saved the day by launching an amphibious assault at Inchon, deep behind enemy lines. MacArthur recaptured Seoul and then advanced past the 38th Parallel, which divided Korea as part of the settlement of World War II. Assuring Truman that he would "get the boys home by Christmas," MacArthur split his forces in late November and pushed to the Yalu River, which borders China.[31] That's when things fell apart. MacArthur had severely underestimated the strength and motivation of Chinese forces. On November 25, several hundred thousand Chinese troops attacked the US army, inflicting heavy casualties. MacArthur was forced to undertake a chaotic and embarrassing retreat to South Korea in subzero weather. It wasn't until General Matthew Ridgway arrived weeks later that US soldiers rallied.

At this fateful juncture, Truman and MacArthur reached a breaking point. The president wanted a limited war to stabilize the 38th Parallel and avoid a broader conflagration. MacArthur had grown obsessed with expanding the battlefield into China. Over time, their positions drifted further apart. Truman had no interest in starting World War III, while MacArthur fantasized about a grand struggle in the Far East that would forever obliterate communism.

Unwilling to limit his martial ambition, MacArthur railed against Truman and his advisors at the State Department. In public interviews, he accused them of appeasement, incompetence, and stupidity. MacArthur kept up his criticism even after Truman ordered all military commanders to use "extreme caution in public statements."[32] Then, in March 1951, MacArthur deliberately sabotaged Truman's effort to negotiate a cease-fire with China and North Korea. As Truman later concluded, his general had acted "in open defiance of my orders as President and as Commander in Chief."[33] Yet Truman responded only with a stronger gag order. This was his final effort to restrain MacArthur.

Secure in his own hubris and shielded by a wall of public support, MacArthur refused to stand down. People loved his message of American power and were dazzled by his military demeanor. His famous triumphs in World War II reminded them of total victory. Truman, in contrast, seemed weak and ineffectual. With his approval ratings barely clearing 25 percent, the president held a precarious position.

But at last the general went too far. On April 5, 1951, House Republican leader Joseph Martin took the floor and read a private letter in which MacArthur excoriated Truman's oversight of the Korean War. MacArthur's meddling in politics was inexcusable. Further, Truman's advisors believed that MacArthur's strategy "would involve us in the wrong war, at the wrong place, at the wrong time, and with the wrong enemy."[34] After consulting with the secretaries of state and defense, and with support from the

Joint Chiefs of Staff, Truman relieved MacArthur of his command. That way, he publicly explained, "there would be no doubt or confusion as to the real purpose and aim of our policy."[35]

Truman's announcement went off like a grenade. As historian David McCullough writes, "Truman had known he would have to face a storm, but however dark his premonitions, he could not possibly have measured what was coming."[36] Within forty-eight hours, more than two hundred thousand telegrams flooded the White House and Congress—many of them calling for impeachment. "IMPEACH THE IMBECILE" and "IMPEACH THE LITTLE WARD POLITICIAN FROM KANSAS CITY" were typical. Cars were plastered with signs and stickers reading, "Oust President Truman." The president was burned in effigy and damned as a traitor. Several state legislatures formally condemned him. Across the nation, flags were flown upside down and at half-mast. Petitions demanding Truman's removal circulated widely. The *Chicago Tribune* even ran a front-page editorial entitled "Impeach Truman." Blasting the president, it concluded: "The American nation has never been in greater danger. It is led by a fool who is surrounded by knaves. Impeachment is the only remedy."[37]

Meanwhile, the full Republican leadership in Congress met to discuss impeachment. House Minority Leader Joseph Martin made clear that he didn't plan to stop with Truman: "We might want the impeachments of 1 or 50."[38] In the Senate, Republican William E. Jenner thundered that "this country today is in the hands of a secret inner coterie which is directed by agents of the Soviet Union." "Our only choice," he implored, "is to impeach President Truman and find out who is the secret invisible government which has so cleverly led our country down the road to destruction."[39]

National outrage burned even brighter when MacArthur arrived home the next week. He was met at the airport by a crowd of ten thousand. More than 30 million Americans then watched his spellbinding address to a joint session of Congress on April 19, 1951. Millions turned out in New York City for a parade in his honor, and MacArthur was overwhelmed with invitations from every corner of the country. All the while, the general's adoring fans seethed at Truman and urged impeachment.

Within a few months, however, the uproar faded. From the outset, Democrats controlled Congress and refused to consider the idea of impeachment. As one Democratic senator noted, "there is nothing whatever to do in this instance except to stand with Truman. It is simply a question of whether civil government is to be maintained."[40] Calls for impeachment also faced another obstacle: opposition from influential newspapers, which blamed MacArthur for insubordination and grasped his threat to civilian control of the military. That feeling was fortified by seven weeks of Senate hearings, which revealed MacArthur as an extremist and let Pentagon leaders dissect his faulty reasoning. By late May 1951, popular support for MacArthur had plummeted. But there wasn't a corresponding boost for Truman. His handling of the situation, and his failure to make an effective case to the public, took a heavy toll on the president. Repeated calls for impeachment had reflected and reinforced a perception that Truman was fundamentally inadequate to the task.

* * *

One year later, Truman sparked another constitutional crisis. After labor disputes threatened to shut down many of the nation's steel mills, he decided to seize the mills as federal property. Truman justified his decision as necessary to preserve the war effort and the national economy. Since no statute authorized this massive taking of private property, Truman purported to rely on his inherent authority as president and commander in chief. When pushed to defend his position, Truman reasoned that "the President has the power to keep the country from going to hell."[41] This was a remarkable and limitless claim, but Truman had been privately reassured by Chief Justice Fred Vinson that the law was on his side.

Truman announced the seizure on April 8, 1952. His position was met with a furious, unrelenting outcry. The president's asserted

TO END A PRESIDENCY

power to seize private property in the name of national security reeked of tyranny. Congressional Democrats saw little reason to defend Truman, whose term in office was nearly over. Meanwhile, Republicans came out swinging.

Unlike a year earlier, impeachment was not the principal goal of their criticism. Republicans recognized that Democrats in Congress would shut down any removal proceedings. Still, they laced their public remarks with impeachment talk. Echoing his Republican colleagues, Senator Bourke Hickenlooper opined that Truman's action "constitutes *prima facie* grounds for impeachment proceedings."[42] In the House, many Republicans argued that Truman "should be impeached today."[43] Impeachment resolutions were introduced on April 22, 23, and 28. In addition, several congressional Republicans formally urged the House to create a bipartisan committee to investigate Truman's impeachable offenses.

Truman was untroubled. The *New York Times* reported on the president's casually dismissive attitude when he was asked about impeachment: "Oh, Mr. Truman replied, that is a political proposition. They have a right to do that if they want to. He said he had a pretty good defense. (Laughter)."[44]

Truman had little to fear in Congress, where his party controlled both houses and buried the impeachment resolutions. But in court, his own lawyers invoked impeachment to disastrous effect. On April 24, US District Judge David Pine held argument on a motion to block the president's order. There, defending Truman, Assistant Attorney General Holmes Baldridge cast his client's position in an extremely unnerving light:

THE COURT: So you contend the Executive has unlimited power in time of an emergency?

MR. BALDRIDGE: He has the power to take such action as is necessary to meet the emergency.

THE COURT: If the emergency is great, it is unlimited, is it?

MR. BALDRIDGE: I suppose if you carry it to its logical conclusion, that is true. But I do want to point out that there are two limitations on the Executive power. One is the ballot box and the other is impeachment.[45]

Judge Pine was incredulous. He asked Baldridge, "Is it your concept of Government that the Constitution limits Congress and it limits the Judiciary but does not limit the Executive?" When Baldridge stated "that's our conception," Judge Pine bluntly responded, "I have never heard that expressed in any authoritative case before."[46]

This wasn't the first time—and it wouldn't be the last—that impeachment was invoked in court to favor the president. In cases about the pardon power, the interpretation of treaties, and the president's legal immunity for his official acts, the Supreme Court has relied on the possibility of impeachment to reject the need for other constraints.[47] Most of the time, however, such arguments are wrong and dangerous. Impeachment is not meant to function as an all-purpose tool for enforcing the Constitution. Accepting that position would create perverse effects. On the one hand, given how hard it is to remove a president, this rule would allow an extraordinary amount of unconstitutional conduct. At the same time, it would warp the role of impeachment, which is meant exclusively for "high Crimes and Misdemeanors." Accordingly, when the president violates individual rights, there's an overwhelming presumption in favor of judicial review—not impeachment—as the appropriate response. If the president follows a court order directing him to cease an unlawful act, only in a rare case would impeachment also be justified. It gets things entirely backward to rely on the theoretical availability of impeachment as a reason for courts not to protect personal liberty. That is the core judicial role.

Baldridge's contrary argument was slammed in the court of public opinion. One of the president's aides described it as the "legal blunder of the century."[48] Truman himself disavowed that position, as did the Department of Justice. But the damage was done. In suggesting that the president had unlimited power—bounded only by elections and impeachment—Truman's lawyer confirmed the public's worst fears. Judge Pine blocked the seizure order, and the Supreme Court later affirmed by a vote of six to three. In a famous concurring opinion, Justice Robert Jackson reminded Truman that "the purpose of the Constitution was not only to grant power, but to keep it from getting out of hand."[49] Reassured by the Court's decisive repudiation of Truman's unlawful order—and by Truman's prompt compliance with the Court's decision—Republicans in Congress dropped their calls for impeachment.

At this point, the nation had seen two surges of impeachment talk in a single year. Both of them shared three notable characteristics. First, they ran hot and burned out fast. Neither emerged from—or turned into—an extended opposition campaign to remove the president from office. Indeed, given Democratic control of Congress, the odds of an actual removal always hovered near zero. The impeachment rhetoric instead reflected a high level of frustration with the Truman presidency and the Korean War. Viewed this way, impeachment talk was used primarily as an intensity booster to convey just how strongly some parts of the public disagreed with Truman.

Second, both impeachment fights of the early 1950s broke down along partisan lines. Despite Truman's deep unpopularity, Democrats in Congress stood by him. Nearly all calls for impeachment came from Republicans, though with some division in the ranks. Impeachment politics were thus continuous with preexisting partisan differences.

Finally, these developments were extraordinary. No president since Johnson had faced such prominent calls for his impeachment. While the Gilded Age and Progressive Era saw plenty of political turmoil, impeachment talk had been confined to socialists, extremists, and partisan outliers. Under Truman, it briefly returned to the heartland of national debates and took on renewed importance. In that respect, it offered a glimpse into the future of American politics.

* * *

After the tempests of the early 1950s, presidential impeachment returned to the political hinterlands. There were no substantial calls to impeach Dwight Eisenhower, John F. Kennedy, or Lyndon B. Johnson. The nation's experiences under Truman didn't generalize into a more robust conception of the role that impeachment should play. That held true even amid the pitched social battles of the 1960s.

Rather, impeachment talk in this period focused squarely on the Supreme Court. Led by Chief Justice Earl Warren, the Court decided *Brown v. Board of Education* in 1954. It then spent decades expanding and creating rules to safeguard civil rights. Southern backlash led to a flurry of "Impeach Earl Warren" billboards. Richard Nixon capitalized on that anger in his law-and-order presidential campaign, and then set out to impeach Justice William O. Douglas in 1970 (as we saw in Chapter 2). Although that particular effort failed, Nixon later succeeded beyond his wildest dreams—or nightmares—in reinvigorating the impeachment power.

In fact, some scholars have suggested that Watergate and its aftermath inaugurated an "age of impeachment" that continues to the present day.[50] There's no denying that the Nixon administration produced a new awareness of impeachment in American thought and politics. It also magnified and entrenched cynicism about our democratic institutions—especially the presidency. After 1974, to speak of impeachment was to speak of Nixon.

But Watergate was exceptionally traumatic. Nothing about the experience left Americans eager to reprise it. For that reason, among others, credible presidential impeachment talk almost completely abated for several decades after Nixon resigned from office in August 1974. This historical perspective cuts against heavy reliance on Watergate as the fountainhead of modern impeachment politics. The story is much more convoluted than that.

During Gerald Ford's tenure, talk of presidential impeachment emerged only once: after he decided to pardon Nixon. But this discussion was short lived. Although many Americans viewed the pardon as outrageous—and Ford paid a steep political price for it—there was no proof that he had entered into a corrupt bargain with Nixon. Instead, Ford consistently maintained that he had pardoned his predecessor to help the country move on, which would have been impossible during a drawn-out criminal trial. When challenged by skeptical Democrats, Ford effectively preempted impeachment talk by agreeing to testify before the House Subcommittee on Criminal Justice. This gave Ford a perfect opportunity to address and defuse accusations that the pardon was part of a *quid pro quo* arrangement. After his testimony, the issue quickly drifted away. The nation was exhausted. It had no interest in prosecuting yet another president without clear proof of grievous offenses.

Jimmy Carter succeeded Ford in January 1977. There was no serious impeachment talk on his watch. For all his many failings, Carter was neither corrupt nor abusive. To the contrary, Carter's modest view of the presidency led him to devalue and diminish rather than aggrandize the powers at his disposal. Torn by indecision and unable to lift the national mood, the main threat Carter posed was weakness.

Responding to Carter's perceived inadequacy, the nation overwhelmingly chose Ronald Reagan in 1980 as a leader who would restore strength to the White House. Too much strength, it turned out. At home and abroad, Reagan took a stunningly expansive view of his executive authority. This led to a minor uptick in impeachment talk during his first term. Then, on November 10, 1983, Representative Ted Weiss introduced a resolution in the House urging that Reagan be impeached for abuse of power.[51]

Weiss's resolution wasn't a bolt from the blue. Weeks earlier, and without consulting Congress, Reagan had invaded the Caribbean nation of Grenada. He justified the invasion by referring to a leftist coup on the island, which supposedly endangered US students and risked further chaos in the region. More fundamentally, though, Reagan aimed to intimidate Soviet-aligned forces in Latin America. He also hoped to break the post-Vietnam paralysis that made Americans wary of military intervention. While Reagan's covert invasion of Grenada drew international sanction, most Americans viewed it as a justified and successful operation.

But Ted Weiss was a die-hard Manhattan Democrat and he saw things differently. Reagan had violated the Constitution by deploying troops for combat in a foreign nation without congressional approval. That was the end of the matter. As Mayor Edward Koch later said about Weiss, "Whatever room he entered, a living room or the halls of Congress, he was the conscience of that room. There were times I thought he would impeach God, but the fact is, even then you knew he would be intellectually honest. You knew he thought God should be impeached."[52]

Weiss never got around to impeaching God; instead, he had to settle for Reagan. As Weiss explained, "by his actions in Grenada, the President has usurped the warmaking powers of Congress, contrary to the very constitutional framework of our Government." Weiss knew that his proposal did "not fit the current mood of most Americans." Nevertheless, he insisted on it because "the Constitution of the United States was not meant to apply only when its provisions enjoy majority support."[53]

Weiss didn't stand alone. His resolution attracted seven cosponsors. But it was still sent to the House Judiciary Committee for a slow, invisible death. Even if Reagan had exceeded his powers—and that's a murky legal issue—there was no political appetite for an impeachment. Consequently, Weiss and his allies were isolated. Even most Democrats looked away. Reagan thereby established an important precedent supporting executive control over the use of force abroad.

In Reagan's second term, impeachment talk swirled around the Iran-Contra Affair, which we explored in Chapter 3. Here was a case where impeachment might well have been justified, yet the president's opponents foreswore it. They did so for many reasons, including the absence of a smoking gun, Reagan's cooperation with investigators, and their fear of destabilizing the nation. Reagan emerged from Iran-Contra bruised and bloody but not beaten. His relatively gentle treatment suggested that Watergate had left Congress temporarily trigger-shy on impeachments.

Apart from Iran-Contra, Reagan had little reason to worry about serving out his full term in office. Four years later, however, George H. W. Bush couldn't stop thinking about impeachment. By November 1990, he already had decided on invading Iraq and Kuwait to thwart Saddam Hussein. Although many leaders in Congress favored more time for diplomacy and sanctions, Bush was confident that he possessed the raw constitutional authority to strike without requesting congressional approval (or to proceed even if Congress rejected his plan). But he also knew that he could suffer massive blowback if he invaded the Persian Gulf and his strategy went awry. Bush's biographer reports that the president wrote about impeachment in his diary five times during this period. That fear wasn't entirely of his own creation. "If you're wrong about this," Hawaii Senator Dan Inouye warned Bush, "you are going to be impeached by the Congress."[54]

That wasn't enough to stop him. "If I don't get the votes," Bush told Robert Gates, "I'm going to do it anyway. And if I get impeached, so be it."[55] Fortunately for Bush, he never had to cross that particular bridge. After days of eloquent debate in Congress, he won a resolution authorizing the deployment of troops. Between that victory and effective presidential diplomacy at the United Nations, the whole world now supported his plan. Bush was relieved. He wrote in his journal, "The big burden, lifted from my shoulders, is this Constitutional burden—the threat of impeachment."[56]

As if he had read Bush's mind (or diary), Representative Henry B. Gonzalez filed an impeachment resolution three days later, on January 16, 1991. Gonzalez was a famously combative, independent, and populist legislator. In 1961, he had become the first

Mexican American elected from Texas to the House of Representatives. Since then, he had established himself as ferocious defender of the poor and powerless. He was also known as an iconoclast, especially on matters of impeachment. He joined Weiss's call to impeach Reagan over Grenada, and then pushed to impeach Reagan again for Iran-Contra. Most legislators *never* draft or support a call for impeachment; when Gonzalez moved to impeach Bush in 1991, he reached a hat trick within a single decade.[57]

The main obstacle for Gonzalez was that Congress had squarely authorized Bush's use of force. Undeterred, he based his January 16 resolution on three alleged abuses: planning for war; intimidating the UN Security Council to support the war; and committing to war without legislative approval.[58] Five weeks later, on February 21, 1991, Gonzalez introduced another call for impeachment. It was similar to the first one, but added a new charge: that Bush had violated equal protection "by putting U.S. soldiers in the Middle East who are overwhelmingly poor white, black, and Mexican-American, as well as basing their military service on the coercion of a system that denies viable economic opportunities to these classes of citizens."[59]

Gonzalez's resolutions rested on general objections to the Persian Gulf War—and to structures of racial and economic injustice. Although framed as accusations against Bush, they went far past his presidency and his particular use of military force. Gonzalez drew no support for this societal critique. Both of his resolutions were quietly entombed in the Judiciary Committee. Thereafter, Bush didn't face any noteworthy impeachment chatter.

*　*　*

Before continuing, let's pause and review the story from 1950 to 1992. In this period, mainstream interest in presidential impeachment spiked four times: Truman (1951 and 1952), Nixon (1974), and Reagan (1986). There were also two minor calls to impeach, both meant to protest military action: Reagan (1983) and Bush (1991).

Compared with US history until 1951, this represented a marked increase in formal impeachment activity. Four presidents faced impeachment resolutions in the House across this forty-one-year period, as compared with five presidents in the preceding one hundred sixty-two years. And apart from those raw numbers, impeachment talk played a comparatively more substantial role in US politics in the late twentieth century. Indeed, if one were to compile a list of high-salience political disputes involving credible calls for impeachment, the lead examples before 1992 would be Jackson, Tyler, Johnson, Truman, Nixon, and Reagan. It's striking that half these examples come from before 1868 and the other half occurred after 1950.

This isn't to say that post–World War II America went on an impeachment bender. Demands to impeach the president remained extraordinary and intermittent before 1992. Most presidents to serve in this period never faced a mainstream impeachment threat (Dwight D. Eisenhower, John F. Kennedy, Lyndon B. Johnson, Ford, Carter, and Bush). While three did, two of them deserved it (Nixon for Watergate and Reagan for Iran-Contra). Truman didn't deserve it—at least not for firing MacArthur—but in that regard the wave of impeachment mania in 1951 was unusual and is best seen as a reflection of Truman's severe unpopularity.

More fundamentally, impeachment talk did not become an ordinary, recurring aspect of political disagreement across these decades. With only a few exceptions, Americans with strong objections to the president's conduct or temperament criticized him on those grounds. It was not seen as normal to demand impeachment every time the president made a bad decision. By and large, politicians and public intellectuals appreciated that calls to end a presidency should be reserved for truly extraordinary circumstances. While an undercurrent of impeachment talk persisted in popular discussion of politics, it played a minor role. That was partly because political elites usually avoided strategies built around inflaming their base to demand the president's forced exit.

In that spirit, the House generally acted responsibly in handling matters of impeachment. This was certainly true of Watergate, where the House Judiciary Committee did a first-rate job. To a lesser extent, it was also true of Iran-Contra. Equally revealing is how Congress handled meritless cases. When Weiss and Gonzalez submitted antiwar impeachment resolutions, the House shunted them aside with little fanfare. For the most part, other legislators didn't use them as a chance to grandstand, fund-raise, or debate the president's policy. The press, in turn, gave them relatively little attention. Impeachment was recognized as serious business, not as an opportunity to score points or engage in partisan gamesmanship.

Of course, we don't mean to overromanticize these tumultuous decades or to suggest that they offered a study in civility. With the fate of the world at stake, Cold War politics were not for the faint of heart. The 1960s birthed a radical and revolutionary ethos—and a conservative counterrevolution—that bolstered partisan differences. The noble struggles of the civil rights movement shook and reordered the foundations of our society. Presidents in this period faced no shortage of tough critics and motivated opponents, who at times resorted to extreme and bloody measures.

In some respects, that makes the limited role of impeachment talk even more noteworthy. Considering this period as a whole, and focusing only on the question of presidential impeachment, it was a time of comparative moderation. Even as impeachment talk achieved a new prominence in American life, it largely stood apart from the daily grind of partisan politics. Surveying the scene in 1992, one could say that most of the time, on most issues, presidential impeachment had little to do with the conduct and rhetoric of national politics. By the end of the decade, that would no longer be true.

* * *

Bill Clinton ran for president in 1992. He won, but never stopped running. Even after he was inaugurated, Clinton stuck to scripts and tactics from the campaign trail. Relying on polls to decide seemingly banal questions, like where to vacation, he sought an electoral edge at every turn. While this approach wasn't new, Clinton pursued it on a different level. So did the Republican majority that rose to power in Congress on his watch. Thus began the age of the permanent campaign, which has since expanded to dominate American politics. That context is crucial to understanding impeachment in the post-Clinton era.

Let's start with an uncontroversial claim: when US voters elect leaders, we hope that they will appreciate and fulfill their duty to govern the nation. In most cases, that requires a measure of deliberation, collaboration, and bipartisanship. Responsible officials should take a long view of the challenges facing the country and strive to improve the national welfare. They should also respect norms that facilitate workable government. In our diverse society, effective administration often depends on cooperation with political opponents and openness to compromise.

Accordingly, governing requires a different mentality than campaigning for office. Campaigns are built around winning and retaining power. Officials focused on campaigning are therefore more likely to adopt an adversarial and short-sighted approach. They may aim for quick, high-profile victories even at the expense of norms such as civility and comity. Further, many campaigns seek to build support by condemning opponents and issuing bold statements of principle. Although voters claim to prefer bipartisanship, they often reward officials who thwart compromise and make flashy statements of commitment to the right causes. Aware of that, campaigners frequently care less about concrete achievements than about symbolically pandering to a defined set of donors and demographics. If necessary, outrage and victimization can always be manufactured to fire up the base. As Professor Hugh Heclo wrote, the consultants, pollsters, and politicos who comprise the permanent campaign seek to "transform[] politics and public affairs into a twenty-four-hour campaign cycle of pseudo-events for citizen consumption."[60]

Politicians have always blurred governing and campaigning. But it's now conventional wisdom that American politics have veered sharply toward permanent campaign footing, at the near-total expense of actual governance. It's also generally accepted that this is a bad thing. The permanent campaign is blamed for exacerbating cynicism, paralysis, partisanship, obsessive fund-raising, and many other democratic dysfunctions that we'll explore in far greater detail in Chapter 6. As political scientist Norm Ornstein has remarked, "when politics is driven by the need to turn out your base and policy is dominated by the desire to cater to that base, our baser instincts come to the fore."[61]

Impeachment hasn't escaped that dynamic. Starting in the mid-1990s and continuing through the present, we've seen the creeping emergence of a permanent impeachment campaign. While demands to impeach the president were once extraordinary, they've become increasingly common in the nation's partisan civil war, where nothing is sacred and everything can be weaponized. The result has been a degradation of presidential impeachment—with potentially troubling consequences.

There are many causes for that development. But none looms larger than the Clinton proceedings. Born of partisan spite and rejected on partisan lines, they energized many of the most pernicious trends in our political system. At the same time, they dragged impeachment down into the mud. A whole generation came of age with Clinton's as the only impeachment they had ever seen. Even though many Americans rejected the Republicans' anti-Clinton campaign, it was too late. The same broken politics that led Republicans to impeach in the first place also guaranteed that the shockwaves would ripple far and wide.

To this day, Clinton's case is still cited as precedent to support aggressive deployments of impeachment. For an especially clear example, consider this argument by Michelle Goldberg in the *New York Times*: "Some commentators fear 'normalizing' impeachment as a tool of routine political warfare. But Bill Clinton's impeachment already normalized its use against Democrats on the flimsiest of pretexts . . . Democrats may wish to return to a less destructive brand of politics, but that's not an option while Trump sits in the White House."[62]

Goldberg's column makes a move that's currently popular in impeachment talk: jumping straight from Republican attacks on Clinton to a case against Trump. This eye-for-an-eye reasoning is part of a cycle that impels the permanent impeachment campaign forward. As related by Goldberg, though, the story is incomplete. Nearly twenty years elapsed between Clinton and Trump. During that period, Republicans and Democrats alike contributed to the normalization of impeachment talk.

After Clinton came George W. Bush. During Bush's first term, which was defined largely by his response to 9/11 and the invasion of Iraq and Afghanistan, there was little discussion of impeachment. That changed shortly after his reelection in 2004. Americans soured on the deteriorating situation in Iraq, especially when it became clear that Bush had built his case for war on faulty intelligence. Bush's popularity also declined amid revelations of torture, black sites, extraordinary rendition, and illegal surveillance. His gross mishandling of Hurricane Katrina and its aftermath inflicted further political damage. While Bush began his second term with roughly 50 percent approval ratings, that figure dropped to the mid-30 percent range in 2006 and fell below 30 percent in 2008.

As early as December 2005, impeachment talk picked up. That month, Democratic Representative John Conyers urged the creation of a select committee to make recommendations on possible grounds for Bush's impeachment. According to a contemporary Rasmussen poll, 32 percent of Americans agreed that Bush should be impeached and removed from office.[63] Impeachment sentiment held steady through the rest of Bush's second term, with polls noting support at 33 percent in April 2006 and 36 percent in July 2007. Predictably, the 2007 poll disclosed a stark partisan divide on impeaching Bush: Republicans were 9 percent in favor and 91 percent opposed, while Democrats were 58 percent in favor, 39 percent opposed (3 percent didn't answer).[64]

Those figures revealed that impeachment was a classic wedge issue: it split Democrats but unified Republicans. This may explain why many conservatives were thrilled in March 2006 when Democratic Senator Russell Feingold proposed censuring Bush for warrantless domestic surveillance. At that point, the president's public approval ratings had collapsed. With midterm elections on the horizon, Republicans feared losing control of Congress. What better way to fire up the base than to warn that Democrats would impeach Bush if they prevailed? "This is such a gift," Rush Limbaugh told listeners.[65] The *Wall Street Journal* ran an op-ed entitled "The Impeachment Agenda," which the Republican National Committee shared with 15 million supporters.[66] Other Republican operatives spread the word: "Impeachment, coming your way if there are changes in who controls the House."[67] This theme permeated Republican messaging throughout the midterm campaign.

As reporter David Kirkpatrick observed at the time, "in playing up the impeachment threat, conservatives have forged an alliance of sorts with the most liberal wing of the Democratic Party."[68] Indeed, the "liberal wing" had been hard at work building support for removing Bush immediately. Reflecting a majority view among Democrats, liberal stalwarts had already championed Bush's impeachment in *Harper's* and *The Nation*. Their cause received support from movie stars, some local governments and state legislatures, and a coalition of activists organized through ImpeachPAC.

By May 2006, Democratic Minority Leader Nancy Pelosi was sick of it. At a party meeting, she made clear that "impeachment is off the table"—a commitment she had to repeat many times over the next six months.[69] This decision triggered heated debates within the political left, but she stood by it as sound electoral strategy. One day after Democrats won control of Congress, Pelosi confirmed that impeachment remained out of bounds.[70] As she later explained, impeachment would have divided the country and allowed Republicans to portray Democrats as obstructionists. Further, an impeachment would almost certainly have failed in the Senate, unlike some of the domestic policy legislation that Pelosi hoped to pass with her new House majority.

From 2006 through 2008, liberal Democrats pushed Pelosi to impeach and she refused. This tension peaked on June 12, 2008, when Representative Dennis Kucinich introduced thirty-five articles of impeachment against Bush. These accusations covered the waterfront: abuses relating to the Iraq War, torture, rendition, unlawful surveillance, corrupting elections, an inadequate response to Katrina, and much more. The House voted 251 to 166 to send this resolution to the Judiciary Committee, where it would never see the light of day. In a stark departure from historical practice, the 166 "no" votes came from Republicans who hoped to embarrass Democrats by forcing a public debate on whether to impeach Bush. Speaking for Democrats, Howard Dean responded that "the American people sent us [to Congress] to get things done . . . [not] to impeach the President."[71]

Even then, the issue didn't die. When Pelosi launched a book tour two months later, reporter Carl Hulse described it in the *New York Times* as "The Why-Haven't-You-Impeached-the-President Tour."[72] According to Hulse, "Pelosi found herself under siege by people unhappy that she has not been motivated to try to throw President Bush out of office." Pelosi had to explain that "the proceedings would be too divisive and be a distraction from advancing the policy agenda of the new Democratic majority."

This response did not assuage her critics—including Donald J. Trump. In October 2008, Trump told Wolf Blitzer, "I was surprised that [Pelosi] didn't do more in terms of Bush and going after Bush. It just seemed like she was really going to look to impeach Bush and get him out of office. Which personally I think would have been a wonderful thing." Blizter asked, "To impeach him?" And Trump replied, "For the war. For the war! Well, he lied! He got us into the war with lies!"[73]

In some ways, George W. Bush's experience with impeachment was ordinary. Impeachment talk peaked as his popularity plummeted. It was confined largely to margins of the opposition political party. And it formally manifested only in a single resolution, introduced by a single representative, which was buried in the Judiciary Committee.

The underlying dynamics, however, were very different from those of any prior case. It's not unusual for the president's most zealous opponents to focus attention on impeachment. It was unprecedented, however, for the president's own allies to rely so heavily on impeachment threats to turn out their own base. It was also unprecedented for the president's party in the House to vote *against* killing an impeachment resolution just so that they could embarrass their opponents. This unholy alliance of interest between Rush Limbaugh and Dennis Kucinich reflected a deeply cynical calculus by Republican operatives about the political benefits of anti-Bush impeachment talk.

That calculus, in turn, rested on assumptions that wouldn't have held true in an earlier era. Here we see a post-Clinton shift in awareness of impeachment and expectations regarding its use. Republican voters could be incited by impeachment talk because they actually feared an impeachment effort and didn't see it as an unthinkable possibility. Democrats largely supported impeachment, though polls showed wide variation in their reasons for doing so. Most important, to both groups impeachment was salient in a way that it simply hadn't been to previous generations. Indeed, never before had a Speaker of the House traveled the country explaining why she *didn't* impeach the president. By 2006, however, many Americans viewed impeachment less as a last resort and more as a standard feature of partisan warfare. Political strategists on both sides of the aisle were more than happy to encourage this view, at least when doing so suited a short-term need for their latest campaign.

* * *

The normalization of impeachment in our politics proceeded apace under Barack Obama. Immediately after his election, millions of Americans—including Trump—seemed unwilling or unable to accept the idea that Barack Hussein Obama was a legitimate president. Many others didn't feel that way but simply had strong disagreements with Obama's vision for the country. The Republican Party offered both groups a home, branding itself as the scorched-earth opposition. Throughout Obama's eight years in office, Republicans stuck to that script, working at every turn to stymie the president and paralyze government. Obama eventually responded by making expanded and adventurous use of his executive powers to address immigration, the environment, LGBT rights, gun regulation, health care, and many other issues. These actions provoked more Republican hostility—as well as charges that Obama was a lawless tyrant with no respect for the Constitution. The Tea Party, a right-wing social movement, took the lead in attacking him. Eventually it urged impeachment with overpass protests across the nation.

Like Bush, Obama enjoyed a lull in impeachment talk during his first term. The idea was floated by a few congressional Republicans, including Darrell Issa, Michael Burgess, and John Kyl, but it never took off. That changed in Obama's second term. By 2013, impeachment was a common refrain in conservative circles. Senator Tom Coburn told constituents that Obama was "perilously close."[74] Representative Blake Farenthold believed that "the whole birth certificate issue" justified removal.[75] Representative Jason Chaffetz declined to rule out impeachment over Benghazi,[76] and Representative Dana Rohrabacher would have impeached for "unconstitutional approaches" to immigration reform.[77] After the massacre at Sandy Hook Elementary School, Representative Steve Stockman threatened to impeach Obama for any new gun regulations.[78] In Michigan, Representative Kerry Bentivolio admitted that impeaching Obama "would be a dream come true."[79] And when asked by conservative broadcaster Rusty Humphries, Representative Michele Bachmann said that Obama should be impeached for unspecified "thuggery."[80]

Through 2013 and 2014, these calls were echoed by prominent ring-wing figures. On Fox News, for instance, Jeanine Pirro demanded Obama's impeachment for "not protecting and defending Americans in the bloodbath known as Benghazi."[81] Sarah Palin later piled on, declaring that "the many impeachable offenses of Barack Obama can no longer be ignored."[82] By June 2014, *National Review* writer Andrew McCarthy had published *Faithless Execution: Building the Political Case for Obama's Impeachment*. In a sweeping indictment, he concluded that Obama could be impeached for nearly everything he had said or done since taking office. The only question, in McCarthy's view, was whether we wish to remain a "self-determining people."[83]

According to pollsters, a majority of the public didn't share McCarthy's view—though support for impeaching Obama was still relatively high. In July 2014, 35 percent of Americans favored impeachment; roughly 44 percent opposed it and 21 percent weren't sure. Much like under Bush, these divisions reflected partisan affiliation. Depending on which poll you believed, 57–68 percent of Republicans supported impeaching Obama, compared to 8–13 percent of Democrats and 35 percent of self-described "independents."[84]

In July 2014, with midterm elections months away, the events of 2006 repeated themselves—this time with the political parties flipped. On July 29, Nick Corasaniti reported that "Democrats cannot get enough of Republicans talking about impeaching President Obama." Those impeachment threats, he noted, had a "catalytic effect on [their] fund-raising."[85] Over the following months, Dan Pfeiffer—a senior advisor to Obama—highlighted the impeachment narrative. He was joined by Senator Harry Reid, who wrote a fund-raising letter claiming that a "Republican House and Senate could go beyond shutting down the government—they could waste months of our lives on impeachment."[86]

All the while, Republican leaders in Congress strenuously denied that there was a secret plot to impeach Obama. In frustration, Speaker of the House John Boehner responded: "This whole talk about impeachment is coming from the president's own staff and coming from Democrats on Capitol Hill. Why? Because they're trying to rally their people to give money and to show up in this year's elections. We have no plans to impeach the president."[87] Boehner stuck to this position all year long, even as members of his own party gravitated in a more radical direction.

By August 2014, *New York Times* reporter Neil Irwin had picked up on an "odd symbiosis" in the midterm campaign. As he observed, "unelected voices on the right and elected Democrats both want to keep impeachment buzz going, while Republicans who actually hold power dismiss the idea out of hand and grumble about the Democrats' use of the 'threat' for fund-raising purposes."[88]

Republicans ultimately retained control of the House. True to their word, they never sought to impeach Obama. In fact, nobody did. Instead, as was true under Bush, impeachment talk under Obama was little more than a manifestation of the permanent campaign. Democrats used it to scare their base into voting. Right-wing Republicans used it to agitate supporters while signaling loyalty to the anti-Obama movement. Both groups used it to fundraise and add new supporters. Meanwhile, Republican leaders worked hard to avoid the issue—which risked alienating independents—even as their attacks on "King Obama" were riddled with impeachment-caliber language. Throughout Obama's second term, impeachment was unavoidable everywhere except in the halls of Congress, where no one dared propose it.

* * *

By early 2016, the architecture of a permanent impeachment campaign was in place. Through the Clinton, Bush, and Obama presidencies, impeachment had become an accepted, predictable tool of partisan combat. This was true for liberals *and* conservatives. To their credit, most legislators still acted responsibly and avoided promiscuous use of the "i-word." But on both sides of the political aisle, a coterie of journalists, operatives, and officials had spent decades mastering the strategy and rhetoric of impeachment talk. In that same period, the American people had grown accustomed to it. Calls for impeachment—and denouncements of those calls—were now firmly established in the political dialogue. When the president did something outrageous or controversial, an angry public knew how to respond.

And then along came Donald Trump and Hillary Clinton (to whom we'll refer as Hillary). We suppose it's possible that a talented fiction writer could imagine two candidates better calculated to trigger impeachment alarms. We doubt it, though. Hillary was weighted down by decades of Republican animus, a horde of conspiracy theories, questions about her "missing e-mails," and a weakness for sketchy dealings. Trump, in turn, had a web of disturbing entanglements with Russia, open disdain for democratic norms, decades of racist and sexist conduct, a history of fraudulent business practices, and a temperament that many viewed as disqualifying. From the very outset, commentators warned that this would be an exceptionally ugly campaign.

They were right. And it only got uglier as 2016 wore on. Presented with escalating charges of criminality and corruption, the American public swiftly defaulted to impeachment talk. This was now a conditioned response. It had become so natural that many Americans barely hesitated before debating the impeachment of people who didn't yet hold office. When impeachment talk is inevitable, why wait?

To our knowledge, 2016 was the first campaign between two non-incumbents marked by open threats of impeachment for whoever won. As early as April 2016, before he had secured his party's nomination, *Politico* reported on speculation about the likely impeachment of a hypothetical President Trump.[89] That belief simmered throughout the campaign—sometimes encouraged by conservatives who saw it as a creative path to installing Mike Pence as president. Generally, though, Democratic officials avoided pre-election impeachment talk. The same couldn't be said for Republicans. On November 3, 2016, the *Washington Post* reported that "senior Republican lawmakers are openly discussing the prospect of impeaching Hillary Clinton should she win the presidency."[90] *New York* magazine and the *New York Times* separately confirmed statements by top Republicans that Hillary would face impeachment if she were elected.[91] Trump joined the fray at his rallies, reminding crowds of Bill's trial and asking, "Folks, do we want to go through this again?"[92] Republicans used these threats to achieve two goals: (1) increasing their odds of winning the election, and (2) laying groundwork for their siege of a likely Clinton administration.

After Trump's surprise victory, many Democrats fell into a state of grief and despair. The sheer enormity of the disaster left them too stunned to plan their next steps. Within weeks of the election, though, early sparks of impeachment talk appeared in liberal blogs and Twitter feeds. Like so much else about the 2016 election, the wave of impeachment sentiment that built from November through January was unprecedented. But so were Trump's flagrant violations of the Emoluments Clauses, which made it conceivable that he would commit an impeachable offense on his very first day.[93] As winter gripped the nation, calls for Trump's swift ouster appeared in *Huffington Post*, *Vanity Fair*, and other liberal outlets.[94] Then, on Inauguration Day, the impeachment campaign launched in earnest. ImpeachDonaldTrumpNow.org went live and received so many hits that it crashed. In *GQ*, commentator Jay Willis explained "How to Impeach a U.S. President (Say, Donald Trump)."[95] And in Ireland, the online bookmaker Paddy Power cheerfully reported that 90 percent of all relevant bets wagered against Trump lasting a full four-year term.[96]

Through the rest of 2017, impeachment remained a dominant motif of Trump's presidency. Indeed, just two weeks after Trump's inauguration, nearly one-third of the American public supported impeaching him. Even in a world gone topsy-turvy, this was a truly extraordinary data point. As the year progressed, Trump's approval ratings started low and trended lower—impelled downward by legislative failures, outrageous public statements, and a thick haze of malice, incompetence, and kleptocracy. At the end of 2017, 41 percent of Americans favored impeachment proceedings, including 70 percent of Democrats and 40 percent of independents.[97] An unceasing parade of dismal polls confirmed that Trump was the most unpopular first-year president since the advent of polling. Quinnipiac University reported that "idiot," "liar," and "incompetent" were the most common words used to describe Trump in a December 2017 survey.[98] And real-money prediction websites offered 20 percent odds that Trump would be impeached by the end of 2018.[99]

Of course, impeachment talk during Trump's first year resulted from more than his unpopularity. Time and again, Trump violated basic norms of presidential behavior and personal decency. It soon became clear that no major issue would escape his unparalleled capacity for mayhem, dishonesty, and vulgarity. This realization cast a pall over American democracy. As journalist Masha Gessen wrote in November 2017, "the sun still rises every morning, but an [early] barrage of Trump's tweets might obscure it . . . we have settled into constant low-level dread."[100] Ultimately, many people concluded that Trump threatened the rule of law, national security, and global peace. This threat was so great, they believed, that only his immediate removal could stop it.

Support for impeachment drew strength from plausible claims that Trump may have committed "high Crimes and Misdemeanors." His alleged offenses included grave abuse of the pardon power and illegal financial entanglements with foreign countries. Some experts also invoked impeachment as a remedy for Trump's assault on the news media, his attacks on free speech and religious pluralism, and his chilling demands that federal prosecutors target his political opponents.

But nothing loomed so large as Russia. Too many officials close to Trump had lied about meeting and dealing with Russians, and had then lied about the circumstances and context of those meetings. By December 2017, pollsters reported that over half of American voters believed that members of the Trump campaign had colluded with Russia to interfere in the 2016 presidential election.[101] An increasing number of Americans also suspected that Trump himself had played a role in such collusion. Trump stoked these suspicions by pandering to Vladimir Putin, bragging to the Russian Ambassador about firing FBI Director James Comey, denying Russian interference despite clear evidence, and sabotaging efforts to protect the nation from Russian cyberattacks.

At the same time, many of the calls to remove Trump were based on conduct that is not properly impeachable. For instance, some Americans appeared to support impeaching him for withdrawing from the Paris Agreement on Climate Change, for having abused women before taking office, for gutting the US Foreign Service, or for lending comfort to the neo-Nazi thugs who terrorized Charlottesville, Virginia. Others pushed impeachment as a response to Trump's many illegal executive orders—including his anti-Muslim entry bans, his ban on military service by transgender persons, his threats to punish sanctuary cities, and his mistreatment of undocumented migrants brought here as children ("Dreamers"). Still others favored removing Trump due to his erratic nuclear brinksmanship with North Korean Leader Kim Jong-un. As many experts pointed out, Trump risked disaster by publishing tweets bragging that his "nuclear button" is "much bigger & more powerful than his, and my Button works!"[102] (Obviously, Trump suffers from severe insecurity about size.)

As 2017 wore on, the bill of particulars against Trump grew longer and more detailed. So did the bizarre reports swirling around him. Rumors spread that Trump's mental capacity had deteriorated—as

evidenced by a noticeably smaller vocabulary, a near-total unwillingness to read, and increasingly frequent repetition of the same point.
Reporters claimed that Trump spent four to eight hours per day obsessively watching (and sometimes live-tweeting) cable news, mainly
Fox and CNN. Cabinet officials were overheard describing him as
an idiot, a moron, and a dope—but were also forced to attend meetings where they fawned over him and offered obsequious thanks
for his leadership. Trump got into weird Twitter fights, including an
exchange in which he said that he should have left three UCLA bas-
ketball players in Chinese prison because one of their parents was
not grateful enough for his son's release. Trump also falsely accused
Barack Obama of wiretapping Trump Tower; endorsed an alleged
pedophile to win a Senate race in Alabama; claimed credit for the
lack of any commercial airplane crashes worldwide in 2017; and
continued to favor eating food from McDonald's due to a nonspecific fear that somebody would try to poison him.[103]

To many Americans who supported Trump's removal, there
was little need for fine-grained analysis of whether particular misdeeds qualified as "high Crimes and Misdemeanors." Rather, a
generalized assessment of Trump's conduct led them to a single
conclusion: Trump was unfit to serve as president and had proved
it by committing a bevy of impeachable (or at least despicable)
acts. Channeling that mindset and urging an expansive view of
when impeachment is justified, political commentator Ezra Klein
made a sharp case for Trump's ouster:

Sometimes I imagine this era going catastrophically wrong—a
nuclear exchange with North Korea, perhaps, or a genuine
crisis in American democracy—and historians writing about
it in the future. They will go back and read Trump's tweets
and his words and read what we were saying, and they will
wonder what the hell was wrong with us. *You knew*, they'll
say. *You knew everything you needed to know to stop this.*
And what will we say in response?[104]

Even as Trump's base largely stood by him, dismissing attacks on their hero as elitist hokum, millions of Americans concluded that Trump posed too great a threat if left in power.

That rise in impeachment sentiment was accompanied by large and creative public displays. When a US science envoy submitted his resignation to the State Department, he spelled "IMPEACH" with the first letter of each paragraph (needless to say, it went viral).[105] On October 15, Larry Flynt and Hustler Magazine took out a full-page ad in the *Washington Post*, offering $10 million for information leading to Trump's impeachment. Five days later, a billionaire philanthropist named Tom Steyer launched an eight-figure television ad campaign laying out the case for impeaching Trump. In a stroke of genius, Steyer made sure to purchase airtime during *Fox & Friends*, one of Trump's favorite shows. True to form, Trump responded almost immediately: "Wacky & totally unhinged Tom Steyer, who has been fighting me and my Make America Great Again agenda from beginning, never wins elections!"[106] Thanks in part to free publicity from Trump, Steyer's impeachment petition boasted more than 3.6 million signatures by the end of the year.[107]

Steyer's national campaign crystallized a dynamic familiar from 2006 and 2014. Once again, a strong majority of the opposition party supported impeaching the president. Once again, an alliance of wealthy donors, grassroots campaigners, and ideological House members called for impeachment. Once again, allies of the president publicly emphasized the threat of impeachment to inflame and unify his base. And once again, leaders of the opposition party in Congress repeatedly discouraged impeachment talk—explaining that the best way to win the next midterm election was to offer an attractive governance agenda.

This time, however, the stakes were higher and the possibility of impeachment less remote. The White House was beset by scandals, resignations, investigations, and indictments. Attempts at damage control faced crushing external pressure and intermittent bouts of presidential sabotage. Even though Republicans in

Congress generally stood by Trump's side, especially after they passed a major tax cut, impeachment came to feel like a plausible endgame. That seemed to excite right-wing talk show hosts and agitators, who rallied Trump's base with warnings of a coup. At the same time, it energized the anti-Trump *#resistance* movement. Buoyed by a wave of popular outrage, aggressive Democratic legislators formally proposed articles of impeachment against Trump in November and December 2017. House Democrats then chose Representative Jerrold Nadler—an expert on impeachment—as their ranking member for the Judiciary Committee.

These developments reflected extraordinary public opposition to Trump, but they also put Democratic leaders in an awkward position. *Vanity Fair* nicely captured their dilemma with the headline "Will Impeachment Mania Doom the Democrats?"[108] Political pundits filled the air with warnings that Democrats risked losing the midterm elections if they stood for nothing more than impeaching Trump. In response, other pundits insisted with equal certainty that dodging this issue would alienate the Democratic base and demonstrate unforgivable cowardice.

Deploying strategies that she had honed a decade earlier, House Minority Leader Pelosi came down in favor of muzzling impeachment talk. As *Politico* reported in November 2017, "Pelosi is eager to show her party can govern—in contrast to the chaos surrounding Trump—and she believes that a reputation as the 'no drama' Democrats is key to taking back the House in 2018."[109] Senate Minority Leader Chuck Schumer echoed Pelosi in urging caution. But he pointedly left the door open: "There may be a time. It is premature. And to call for [impeachment] now you might blow your shot when it has a better chance of happening. It is serious, serious, serious. And so . . . you wait."[110]

As we finish this book in mid-March 2018, the American people are still waiting. Thanks to heroic efforts by investigative journalists, the public has become intimately acquainted with the tawdry affairs of Trump's inner circle. Americans have been flooded with accounts of Trump's highly irregular conduct in office, as well as his financial dealings in foreign nations. They have come to anticipate that his latest tweet might range from a snarky putdown of CNN to blustery threats of a nuclear holocaust. And they have taken a keen interest in Special Counsel Robert Mueller.

Mueller was appointed by Deputy Attorney General Rod Rosenstein in May 2017 to investigate ties between Russia and the Trump campaign. For good reason, his selection was initially received with bipartisan acclaim. Trump, however, spent much of 2017 desperately trying to demonize and discredit Mueller. He was joined in that effort by a gaggle of right-wing hacks and ambitious congressional Republicans. Their partisan criticism ultimately expanded to encompass the FBI and the entire Justice Department, which Trump denounced as part of the "deep state" (even though he had appointed its senior leadership). As part of this strategy, Trump and his allies sought to distract the public by demanding federal investigations of Hillary Clinton, her associates, and private groups that had found evidence of Trump's shady conduct.

Many Democrats now hope—and many Republicans now fear—that Mueller will produce incontrovertible evidence of "high Crimes and Misdemeanors." We don't know if these expectations will be met. Even if Trump engaged in misconduct, it's very difficult to find a smoking gun in these sorts of cases. But we do believe that the nation needs definitive, credible answers to important questions about the 2016 presidential election. At this point, Mueller may be the only person capable of delivering them. We therefore hope that Trump's cynical strategy will not succeed. Firing Mueller, subjecting him to improper political control, or turning half the country against him would forever condemn an anxious public to disruptive uncertainty. The people of this nation deserve better.

Given the pace of recent events, we can't begin to imagine what will happen next. Trump has repeatedly matched law and order with chaos and nihilism. At least until the 2018 midterm elections, his political destiny will be determined by Republicans, who have yet to find a principle they won't sacrifice at his altar. For the time being, it is solely by virtue of continuing support from congressional Republicans that Trump remains in office. But even if Congress ultimately declines to act against him, it's clear that impeachment will remain a defining theme of Trump's presidency— and likely of many more presidencies to come.

*   *   *

There are numerous compelling explanations for the surge of impeachment talk under Trump. Most of them involve the unique circumstances of his presidency. But this development also reflects dynamics with deeper historical roots and more enduring significance. Since 1998, impeachment has become a weapon of first resort in partisan combat. The post-Clinton normalization of impeachment talk is a dramatic and underappreciated departure from past practice. While it's too soon to grasp the full implications of this change, we suspect that it will ultimately cause more harm than good.

To be sure, impeachment talk can sometimes play a valuable role in our constitutional scheme. When a president approaches the outer limits of his power, inspires doubt concerning his mental fitness, or adopts bizarre positions on important issues, demands for his removal may function as an early warning system. In that respect, they might help the American people signal in a peaceful way that opposition to the president has escalated beyond ordinary political disagreement. Such warnings may convince the president to turn back or change tactics. In the alternative, they may invigorate other checks and balances by creating an atmosphere of constitutional crisis. If nothing else, a burst of impeachment talk can allow an outraged segment of the public to blow off steam.

Impeachment talk is also essential when there is credible proof that the president committed "high Crimes and Misdemeanors." As we've seen, impeachment doesn't automatically fall from the sky when a president veers toward tyranny. Instead, it's a fundamentally political process that should involve extensive public deliberation. When a president's conduct lands him in impeachment territory, the nation must decide how to respond. In those circumstances, it would be irresponsible for the American people not to debate whether removal is warranted.

But impeachment talk can fulfill its worthy functions only if it is taken seriously. When calls to impeach the president are played on repeat for years at a time, they lose their punch. And two full decades after the Clinton saga, that is where we find ourselves. The normalization of impeachment has trapped the American people in a massive "boy-who-cried-wolf" dilemma. Panicked warnings that the public must impeach or face extinction have dulled our senses and encouraged skepticism. A nation over-saturated with impeachment talk may find it especially difficult to remove a president from office when it's really, truly necessary.

Rising partisanship exacerbates this concern. To succeed, an impeachment must transcend party conflict. Since the 1990s, however, impeachment has become increasingly entangled with the daily grind of partisan politics. As a result, the president's political opponents are quick to frame their major disagreements in terms of impeachment. The president's supporters, in turn, are quick to dismiss even legitimate impeachment talk as a partisan conspiracy to nullify the last election. This state of affairs is unfortunate. In principle, calls for impeachment should seek to vindicate the constitutional foundations on which all other political debate transpires. In practice, impeachment talk has been degraded in ways that may prevent it from achieving that purpose.

Even as partisanship has subverted the impeachment power, an overdose of impeachment talk has pushed our politics toward extremes. This dynamic should now sound familiar. When political conflict unfolds in the constant company of impeachment threats, it can feel more existential and all-encompassing. That's true even when the odds of a successful impeachment are low. Committed to an impeachment mindset, some of the president's opponents may come to view every skirmish as a battle in their larger war to depose a tyrant. Some of the president's allies, in turn, may see every challenge as a threat to their leader's survival and legitimacy. Public fixation on impeachment can thus reinforce tribal tendencies on both sides of the aisle, undercutting compromise and bipartisanship. It can also divert valuable time, energy, and resources from the ordinary business of politics and policy. When the major question on TV and Twitter is whether to impeach, other issues may fail to attract the attention they deserve.

Perversely, the normalization of impeachment talk can actually leave presidents *freer* to commit abuses. That's true for three reasons. First, removal from office becomes less likely when a president's supporters presumptively view impeachment talk as a tired partisan ploy. Second, as threats of impeachment motivate a president's base to rally around him, he may worry less about political pushback from within his own party. Finally, the public may punish a president's opponents at the polls if they're seen as standing only for the negative step of impeachment.

This is why recent presidents and their political advisors have deliberately stirred the pot around midterm elections. It's why Pelosi resisted calls to support impeaching Bush and Boehner did the same with Obama. And it's why anyone publicly urging impeachment should think strategically about what they're trying to achieve—especially if their party doesn't control enough seats in the House to initiate impeachment hearings.

There are circumstances in which impeachment talk is necessary. There are circumstances in which full-blown impeachment proceedings are necessary. It's possible that Trump has created those circumstances. But we must proceed with caution. When impeachment talk overtakes our politics, it can cause a lot of harm without doing any good. Since the late 1990s, that dynamic has increasingly afflicted our democracy. If we are going to spend the Trump presidency immersed in impeachment talk, we must reflect carefully on the use and abuse of such potent rhetoric.

6

IMPEACHMENT, INCAPACITY, AND BROKEN POLITICS

More than any other enemy, a rogue president can threaten our freedom, democracy, and very survival. Impeachment ensures that we aren't left defenseless against abuse and corruption in the Oval Office. Given the risks involved, responsible use of this emergency measure requires political judgment of the first order. But these days, the public is bitterly divided and virtuous statecraft is a lost art. We'll thus conclude by exploring whether the impeachment power can still protect American democracy in an age of broken politics.

Popular writing about impeachment often floats free of such real-world considerations. Instead, many commentators focus all their attention on whether particular acts qualify as "high Crimes and Misdemeanors." At its worst, this perspective flattens the inquiry into a two-step analysis: *Would James Madison have viewed the president's misconduct as impeachable? If so, will the public honor Madison's wise decision or will "politics" interfere?* Approached that way, the political judgments surrounding impeachment are little more than a distraction from the only decision that really matters (which was made for us at the Constitutional Convention).

Over the last five chapters, we've presented a radically different vision of attempts to end a presidency. As we've emphasized, impeachments unfold over months or years, through citizen activism, public deliberation, investigations, committee hearings, floor votes in the House, and a Senate trial. They encompass debates over what the president did, whether he poses a continuing danger if he remains in office, and what the consequences of removing him might be. They involve a host of decision makers in Congress, the White House, the Department of Justice, and the news media—not to mention the broader American public. And these judgments can be shaped by a diverse array of political, personal, and policy considerations, many of which have little to do with the president's guilt or innocence of the alleged abuses. To a conscientious citizen or legislator, this decision encompasses all the risks of impeaching and not impeaching, as well as the adequacy of alternatives. It also involves an assessment of how to pursue impeachment in a manner that pulls the nation together to the greatest extent possible.

Simply put, an impeachment is a dynamic undertaking deeply enmeshed in the politics of the moment. The Constitution guides and structures the process but rarely tells us exactly what to do.

Of course, that doesn't mean we're wholly at sea. This book has identified some of the most important recurring questions and offerred a historically grounded framework for how to think about them. While impeachments involve many tough decisions, and will often generate strong disagreements, at least those discussions can occur on common ground.

Public agreement on foundational principles is unusually important here. Without it, the impeachment power cannot function properly. The Constitution denies any fleeting political majority the ability to end a presidency. No matter how compelling the case against a president may seem in the abstract, it can prevail only if 218 representatives and 67 senators are convinced. Ordinarily that means a bipartisan consensus is required—not only in the Senate but also in the electorate. Our constitutional design thus ensures that presidents will be removed only for conduct so appalling that neither political party can abide it.

In this respect, the Constitution places a life-or-death bet on the American people and their representatives. It gambles that presidential misconduct risking grave harm to the nation will arouse unified popular opposition so strong that it prevails over partisanship, personal loyalty, and political inertia. This is a noble wager. If the public won't resist tyrants and defend its form of government, the game is already lost. Democracy has never been a spectator sport. Although impeachment exists to save our political system from tyranny, it can do so only if that same political system rises to the occasion in times of constitutional crisis.

Accordingly, the impeachment power may fail in its essential purpose if an abusive or corrupt president successfully undermines the political preconditions for exercising it. It isn't hard to imagine how that might occur. There are many ways in which a dangerous president could disorient, divide, or appeal to the American public. Even freedom-loving people have their moments of weakness. And tyranny rarely announces itself by name. Often it creeps up slowly and craftily, pushed by charismatic demagogues who insist that they alone can save us from the challenges we face. The democratic decline that they engineer may seem invisible at first—or may provoke only scattered resistance—until suddenly it's terrifying and inescapable.

Moreover, even if a decisive majority of the American electorate *does* awaken to the onset of tyranny, all it takes to block impeachment is enough support to sway thirty-four senators. Particularly in light of the Senate's unrepresentative composition, which gives small states an outsized voice in government, a president backed by less than 20 percent of registered voters can become practically immune to removal. For an impeachment threat to be credible, either it must be supported by an overwhelming majority of Americans, or a block of legislators must prioritize their conscience over their prospects for reelection. Neither of these conditions is likely to materialize unless citizens (and their representatives) agree on the principles that limit chief executives—and are willing to take action against presidents who violate them.

Understanding the practical preconditions for impeaching a tyrant naturally directs attention to the current state of US politics.

It may seem quaint in 2018 to invoke the ideal of good-faith, bipartisan consensus—or to suggest that legislators could prioritize constitutional principle over electoral self-interest. Even a casual observer will appreciate that the nation's politics are brutal, divisive, and shockingly superficial. Warring partisan tribes now define a dysfunctional system. They typically seem less interested in actually governing than in battling for power through flashy, symbolic gestures. That has become especially true of the Republican Party under Trump, who secures extraordinary loyalty from his base by instigating culture war disputes, railing against the system he now heads, and toppling foundational norms of American governance.

In Chapter 5, we saw the rise and normalization of a permanent impeachment campaign unlike anything in US history. Here we continue that story. We begin with a deep dive into the unhealthy dynamics that have weakened democracy in the United States. With that picture in place, we speculate about the future (and possible failure) of the impeachment power. We also consider a surge of interest in using Section 4 of the Twenty-Fifth Amendment to disempower Trump on the basis of his alleged mental incapacity. Be warned: This is an unsettling and unhappy story about a democracy in distress. But it's a story whose end we can still rewrite.

* * *

US politics is in a terrible state. That isn't just a claim about elected officials and party operatives; it's a claim about our society as a whole. Intense polarization has thwarted consensus on many run-of-the-mill issues—and has defeated most attempts to address clear public policy failures. In this poisonous environment, mustering the national will to restrain a tyrant would be a daunting effort.

Let's start with some data. Recent studies from the Pew Research Center reveal the troubling outlines of partisan polarization in the US electorate. In 2017, Pew found that the divisions between Republicans and Democrats on "fundamental political values" had reached record levels, dwarfing divisions along lines of gender, race, religious observance, and education.[1] These differences, moreover, were matched by high levels of interparty hostility:

- Fifty-five percent of Democrats and 49 percent of Republicans said that the other party makes them feel "afraid." Those numbers jump to 70 percent of Democrats and 62 percent of Republicans if we consider "highly engaged" citizens.
- Forty-seven percent of Democrats and 46 percent of Republicans said that the other party makes them feel "angry."
- Eighty-one percent of both Democrats and Republicans have an unfavorable view of the other party; 44 percent of Democrats and 45 percent of Republicans have a *very* unfavorable view (those figures have doubled since 1994).
- Forty-one percent of Democrats and 45 percent of Republicans said that the other party's policies are a threat to the nation's well-being (an increase of 10 percent over the past ten years).

In other words, respectful disagreement has become passé in our conception of politics. Fear and loathing now shape how members of each party view the opposition.

This polarization extends beyond the political realm. Strong majorities of both parties believe that someone's political opinions say a lot "about the kind of person they are." Americans thus presume the worst of people who affiliate differently. Republicans generally view Democrats as close-minded (52 percent), immoral (47 percent), lazy (46 percent), and dishonest (45 percent).[2] Democrats reciprocate the malice. Republicans, they say, are close-minded (70 percent), dishonest (52 percent), immoral (35 percent), and unintelligent (33 percent). Although having friends from the other party tends to mitigate these cold feelings, cross-party friendships are increasingly rare. In 2016, 55 percent of Republicans and 64 percent of Democrats reported that few or none of their friends belonged to the other party. At a gut level, Republicans and Democrats don't understand (or like) each other.

There are many explanations for the rise of intense partisanship throughout American life. It would be impossible to address them all here. Most scholars agree that conflicting views on racial and economic inequality are a crucial aspect of that story. The parties are now sharply split along lines of race and class—both in membership and in core values. Geographic differences are also highly relevant. In *The Big Sort*, scholar Bill Bishop demonstrates that Americans "have clustered in communities of sameness, among people with similar ways of life, beliefs, and, in the end, politics."[3] This residential sorting, he contends, has caused not only an "increase in political partisanship, but a more fundamental kind of self-perpetuating, self-reinforcing social division." Nowhere is that chasm more apparent than along the rural–urban axis, which now plays a central role in defining (and dividing) the parties—leaving the suburbs as the only place left to compete for dominance.

The upshot of these trends is that partisan affiliation has become increasingly central to personal identity and social relationships. In 2018, the political is personal. When people say how they vote, they reveal more than what policies they favor. They also suggest the likely contours of their lifestyle, moral outlook, and beliefs about what it means to be American. On this basis, membership in the other party is often taken as a character flaw, or even as a ground for discrimination. Indeed, it's socially acceptable to stereotype people for their political commitments in ways that would be unthinkable for almost any other characteristic. As Professor Cass Sunstein astutely observes, "partyism now exceeds racism."[4]

The polarization of the American electorate has contributed to rampant tribalism, in which reflexive loyalty to a party—and hostility to its foes—is assigned overriding importance. That mindset can lead people to support or trivialize conduct within their own political party that they would elsewhere consider morally repulsive. This usually happens unconsciously, as a tribal worldview overcomes individual moral commitments. But sometimes it results from utilitarian logic: when the world hangs in the balance, and one's enemies are indisputably evil, they must be denied access to power at any cost. Over time, commentator Ross Douthat explains, this tribal reasoning can transform "otherwise decent people into defenders of the indefensible."[5]

In 2013, for instance, a poll found that 13 percent of US voters believed that President Barack Obama was *literally* the Antichrist.[6] With Lucifer in the White House, why quibble over any bad acts by Republicans? Under Trump, that mindset has grown deeper roots on both sides of the aisle: he must always be supported or opposed, no matter the cost. As former right-wing radio host Charlie Sykes notes, "in this political universe, voters accept that they must tolerate bizarre behavior, dishonesty, crudity and cruelty, because the other side is always worse; the stakes are such that no qualms can get in the way of the greater cause."[7]

This manichean mentality in the electorate creates enormous pressure on elected officials to reject any kind of political compromise. Political scientist Lee Drutman has explained the dynamic: "When division involves purity and impurity, when it devolves into a pure contest between 'us' and 'them'—then there is no bargaining, because there are no negotiable principles, just team loyalties. 'We' are good and pure, while 'they' are evil and corrupt. And, of course, you cannot compromise with evil and corrupt."[8]

Forces of partisan polarization in American society have been amplified by changes in the information environment. We've recently seen the rapid proliferation of new media sources, many of which are defined by a specific, carefully cultivated viewpoint. We've also seen old-media stalwarts tilt in a more partisan direction. Like never before, it's now possible to personalize the subject matter and ideological perspective of the information we consume. On social media platforms, this is often done automatically by elaborate algorithms that create individualized "filter bubbles."

These developments have democratized and diversified political discourse. But they've also had more nefarious effects. Human psychology comes equipped with a strong confirmation bias. Now people can satisfy that bias at all times. Political analyst Char-lie Cook thus warns that "a large proportion of Americans have moved into ideological echo chambers," where "everything they read or hear reinforces their predispositions and makes them more intolerant of opposing views."[9] Studies have shown that people tend to prefer, click, and share content in tune with their existing beliefs.[10] All too easily, we immerse ourselves in news streams that never challenge our views, correct our errors, or expose us to com-peting narratives. Mindless repetition can thereby replace thought-ful reflection in the marketplace of ideas, eroding the foundations of deliberative democracy and informed self-government.

When people do make an effort to engage with different opin-ions on social media, it rarely ends well. The architecture of sites like Facebook and Twitter isn't conducive to meaningful dialogue. Instead, it tends to promote snarky, uncharitable, and cruel interac-tions. Most Americans describe these platforms as "uniquely angry and disrespectful venues for engaging in political debate"—and yet they're where much of that debate occurs.[11]

As if this weren't bad enough, screens are now flooded with realistic-seeming "fake news." Much of it comes from radical right-wing sites, including *Breitbart*, *Infowars*, *The Daily Caller*, and *Truthfeed*. Those sources mix conspiracy theories and white su-premacy with tales of media betrayal and government corruption. Fake news is also an established weapon of choice for Russian agents, who use it to weaken American influence by inflaming do-mestic instability. Unleashed into social media echo chambers, dis-information can appear from nowhere and instantly reach millions of people strongly inclined to believe it. This undoubtedly affects our politics. As *BuzzFeed* has shown, in the final months of the 2016 presidential race, the top-performing fake election news sto-ries on Facebook generated higher engagement than the top stories from mainstream outlets.[12] The most read fake stories in this period included "Pope Francis Shocks World, Endorses Donald Trump for

President, Releases Statement," and "FBI Agent Suspected in Hillary Email Leaks Found Dead in Apparent Murder-Suicide."

In light of all these developments, Professor Sunstein concludes, "we are living in different political universes—something like science fiction's parallel worlds."[13] Unlike in the mid-twentieth century, when most people relied on a small number of trusted sources for basic data, we can no longer assume that Americans share a common (or even similar) set of facts. Republicans and Democrats understand the nation's history and current events in *very* different ways, and get their news from increasingly non-overlapping sources. This enhances polarization, fragmentation, and mutual misunderstanding in ways that are hard to combat.

These trends also discourage politicians from doing anything at odds with the party line. As Professors Jonathan Haidt and Sam Abrams reason, when politicians show signs of independence, "the partisan media on their own side will say awful things about them to their own side's voters, whereas a few words of praise from the other side's media will not sway voters or donors to support the maverick."[14] Commentator David Frum has decried this perverse outcome: "Republicans originally thought that Fox worked for us. Now we're discovering we work for Fox."[15]

* * *

In this era of polarization and echo chambers, it is harder than ever before to generate political consensus—even on fundamental precepts of our constitutional order. These developments have gone a long way toward undermining the preconditions for a prudent, successful exercise of the impeachment power. At the same time, partisanship at all levels of government has whirled into overdrive. The center has been hollowed out, and moderates have become an endangered species. As political observers Thomas Mann and Norman Ornstein write, "parties today are more internally unified and ideologically distinctive than they have been in over a century."

This pattern, they report, "is most evident in the Congress, state legislatures, and other bastions of elite politics, where . . . abiding partisan conflict is the norm."[16] The unrelenting acceleration and acceptance of bitter political divisions have only enhanced the structural difficulty of impeaching a president.

At times like this, it's important to recall that the political parties, for all their failings, play an important role in US democracy—one that the Framers almost completely failed to anticipate. The parties help to organize and engage the electorate, and to maintain balance between groups with different interests. In moderation, party competition is usually a good thing. A government with only one party stands on the brink of fascism.

But recently the parties' internecine warfare has gotten out of hand. This is partly the consequence of changes we've already covered. It's also an effect of partisan gerrymandering. Party officials have grown exceptionally talented at using computer software to draw districts that maximize the number of seats they can easily win.[17] In more and more congressional districts, the only competition that matters is therefore *within* rather than *between* political parties. This competition mainly occurs in primaries. And studies have shown that party primaries are almost always dominated by the most intensely partisan voters—a group that grows more polarized with each passing year.[18] Elected officials are therefore motivated to appeal to an extreme wing of their own political tribe, leaving moderates voiceless even when they comprise a majority. Political scientist Darrell West accurately observes that this regime "discourages deliberation, distorts the policy making process, [and] encourages the two parties to compete rather than to cooperate."[19]

Three other converging trends have encouraged these destructive consequences. First, daily life for members of Congress has changed in ways that undermine compromise. Some of the most notable changes began in 1994, after Republicans captured the House and Senate. Speaker of the House Newt Gingrich urged newly elected members to spend only a few days each week in the capital, keeping their primary residence in their home districts. This practice disrupted many of the social bonds and evening happy hours that once brought members of the parties closer together. Around the same time, many congressional customs that facilitated civility and comity were abandoned. As Ornstein and Mann recount, "regular order in the legislative process—the set of rules, practices, and norms designed to ensure a reasonable level of deliberation and fair play in committee, on the floor, and in conference—was often sacrificed for political expediency."[20] These developments set in motion a cycle of partisan payback that remains with us today. It's hard to negotiate in good faith when you think the other side is fighting dirty.

Second, the role of money in politics has expanded in ways that empower ideological outliers and weaken party institutions. Following a series of Supreme Court cases invalidating campaign finance rules, it's widely understood that unprecedented sums of money have flowed into political campaigns. Less appreciated is the fact that many of the largest donors are far more ideological and partisan than the average American. Further, the vast majority of them don't live in the districts whose elections they seek to influence. According to Professor David Fontana, "donors in five percent of the nation's zip codes—concentrated in the nation's major metropolitan areas—contribute more than three times as much in itemized contributions to federal elections than the rest of the country combined."[21] In addition to highly partisan primary voters in their own districts, members of Congress must prioritize highly partisan donors at the national level—many of whom insist on purity and principle at the expense of deal making.

Critically, these donors funnel hundreds of millions of dollars through super PACs, 501(c)(4) entities, and other private vehicles rather than through the parties. In so doing, they undercut the influence of political parties as a restraining and organizing force in US politics. There are major downsides to that trend. While party insiders can be secretive, corrupt, and high-handed, they typically embrace a long-term perspective and institutionalist outlook. As journalist Jonathan Rauch writes, historically this led the parties to hold politicians "accountable to one another," thus preventing "everyone in the system from pursuing naked self-interest all the time."[22] Moreover, to borrow Dean Heather Gerken's insight, political parties have long answered to a committed network of "party faithful."[23] By serving as a "bridge between the elites and the voter," this group provided an "institutional check on the bargains that elites can make, some brake on how many principles will get compromised along the way." As recent experience confirms, the replacement of political parties with a dispersed network of dark money groups has empowered wealthy elites and extremists, while diminishing interdependency and mutual accountability.

Finally, partisanship has been exacerbated by an expansion of executive power that dramatically raised the stakes of presidential elections. Although it didn't use to be this way, the executive branch now has a major effect on every hot-button issue in American life. The difference between Republican and Democratic policies, moreover, is often the difference between night and day. Control of the presidency is therefore the Holy Grail for both parties. In October 2010, for instance, Republican Senator Mitch McConnell made clear that "the single most important thing we want to achieve is for President Obama to be a one-term president."[24] When he decided this was best accomplished through a campaign of merciless obstruction, McConnell brought the government to a halt. Here we see how the emergence of an extremely powerful presidency encouraged destructive forms of political warfare.

The result of all these dynamics is unprecedented hyperpartisanship. That development has already caused severe dysfunction and paralysis. But the long-term consequences are even worse. Drutman calls them the *trust-doom loop*: "Political gridlock follows. Institutions don't function. Trust declines. Anger grows. Somebody needs to be blamed. That somebody is always the other side. They cannot be trusted. They must be crushed."[25] In that discordant world, it may seem all the more necessary—but all the more impossible—to invoke impeachment as a final constraint on abuse of power by the president.

*   *   *

With politics trapped in a vicious cycle, bipartisan consensus has become little more than a mirage—and faith in democratic government has faltered. Based on their analysis of survey data, political scientists Roberto Foa and Yascha Mounk report that Americans assign "less and less importance to living in a democracy," hold "increasingly negative views about key democratic institutions," and are "more open to illiberal alternatives."[26] Young Americans, in particular, are less inclined to say that "living in a democracy is essential," and are more likely to say that "having a democratic political system" is a "very bad" way to run America. Other studies confirm disenchantment with the government, including one poll of registered voters in which 40 percent of participants said they have "lost faith in American democracy."[27]

These survey results partly reflect a response to disastrous politics. Many Americans have concluded that their government isn't capable of addressing the serious problems they face. No matter whom they support, and no matter what reforms are promised, nothing ever seems to change. That experience has led to profound cynicism about the whole enterprise. It has also led some voters to favor outsiders, populists, and wild-card candidates (including Trump).

Diminishing faith in democracy is linked to a more general decline of confidence in the nation's major public institutions. In the 1970s, most Americans trusted government to do the right thing. Now, a strong majority believes that the nation is heading in the wrong direction and that officials don't have our best interests at heart. Less than 40 percent of the country has confidence in public schools, banks, organized religion, organized labor, the medical system, big business, the Supreme Court, or the presidency. Congress ranks last, with 12 percent support as of June 2017. Only the military, the police, and small business enjoy broad national trust—and public trust of the police is hardly uniform across lines of race and class.[28]

We suspect that this collapse of confidence in institutions helps to explain trends toward partisan polarization. People gravitate to tribal extremes when they feel threatened. A world controlled by powerful institutions that we don't trust is a scary and disorienting place. It can be especially scary for people who feel threatened by forces of cultural and technological change outside their control. Whereas America's major institutions once played a major role in anchoring people and shaping their self-understanding, they increasingly seem alien, threatening, and unreliable.

This loss of trust has extended to institutions' gatekeeping role as arbiters of fact and fiction. Nowhere is that more apparent than in the world of journalism. According to Gallup, American trust in mass media to report the news "fully, accurately and fairly" fell from 53 percent in 1997 to 32 percent in 2015.[29] Further, as of June 2016, only about 20 percent of Americans had confidence in newspapers and TV news. These figures reflect a massive drop in public respect for the news media as a reliable source of information about the world. Intriguingly, that trend reversed itself—at least temporarily—after Trump's election. By September 2017, Gallup saw trust in mass media jump from 32 percent to 41 percent.[30] But this reflected a sharp partisan split: trust among Democrats had risen from 51 percent to 72 percent, whereas trust among Republicans stood unchanged at 14 percent. Trump's relentless criticism of the news media had polarized opinion on whom to trust when weighing truth and falsity.

Trump's attacks succeeded not only because they resonated with the partisan zeitgeist, but also because they evoked Americans' complex relationship with the concept of truth. That story began long before Trump arrived—indeed, long before postmodernism, deconstruction, and all the other theories that birthed an "age of fracture."[31] In some ways, it's a tale as old as the nation.

As Kurt Anderson recounts in *Fantasyland*: "From the start, our ultra-individualism was attached to epic dreams, sometimes epic fantasies—every American one of God's chosen people building a custom-made utopia, each of us free to reinvent himself by imagination and will. In America those more exciting parts of the Enlightenment idea have swamped the sober, rational, empirical parts."[32] Over time, Anderson explains, Americans' impulse toward supernatural and conspiratorial explanations—coupled with our faith that every individual has the right to believe whatever he wants—has produced a society in which "reality and fantasy are weirdly and dangerously blurred and commingled."[33] Especially in the age of Trump, he warns, "factual truth is just one option, the *consensus* reality, and Americans feel entitled to their own facts."[34]

Ironically, while conservatives spent the late twentieth century berating liberals for abandoning truth and embracing relativism, this sentiment is now most clearly pronounced among Republicans. Charlie Sykes, a "Never Trump" conservative, has offered an explanation and *mea culpa* for how this came about:

> One staple of every radio talk show was, of course, the bias of the mainstream media. This was, indeed, a target-rich environment. But as we learned [in 2017], we had succeeded in persuading our audiences to ignore and discount *any* information from the mainstream media. Over time, we'd succeeded in delegitimizing the media altogether—all the normal guideposts were down, the referees discredited.
>
> That left a void that we conservatives failed to fill . . . We destroyed our own immunity to fake news, while empowering the worst and most reckless voices on the right.[35]

The result, Sykes concludes, is that right-wing echo chambers— like *Fox News* and *Breitbart*—have "morphed into a full-blown alternate reality silo of conspiracy theories, fake news and propaganda." In that world, truth is always tribal. Information is evaluated not against standards of consistency or evidence, but rather with an eye to whether it supports the party's short-term objectives and is espoused by party leaders. This tribal mentality explains why a Republican congressman would say in 2017 that it's "better to get your news directly from the president. In fact, it might be the only way to get the unvarnished truth."[36]

American democracy faces many looming threats, but the rejection of truth as a limit on power is the most dangerous. And this trend has accelerated exponentially since Trump took office. Like no president before him, Trump lies constantly, surrounds himself with liars, and exults in bullshit. The lies are large and small, strategic and chaotic, plausible and comically unbelievable. Alone, many of them are harmless. But in the aggregate, they can crush a person's spirit. Why bother with politics when it's reduced to an endless play of falsehoods and half-truths where nothing matters, everyone is angry, and the powerful always seem to get their way?

As journalist Masha Gessen warns, Trump's endless firehose of lies has a still more menacing aspect. Whether by design or by instinct, Trump seeks to "assert power over truth itself"—or, rather, to displace objective truth and falsity as relevant criteria for evaluating his conduct.[37] The same pattern emerges from Trump's frequent complaints about US libel law. Here is a man who blasts the courts for protecting falsehoods, but claims that Barack Obama isn't a citizen and that Ted Cruz's father was behind the JFK assassination. At bottom, truth and falsity are beside the point. Trump wants to silence his critics—and he resents anything, including the law, the courts, and the free press, that prevents him from using wealth and power to exercise total control over the marketplace of ideas.

In many respects, Trump's approach to political conduct is essentially autocratic in character. It thus calls to mind Alexander Hamilton's prescient warning:

When a man unprincipled in private life desperate in his fortune, bold in his temper, possessed of considerable talents, having the advantage of military habits—despotic in his ordinary demeanour—known to have scoffed in private at the principles of liberty—when such a man is seen to mount the hobby horse of popularity—to join in the cry of danger to liberty—to take every opportunity of embarrassing the General Government & bringing it under suspicion—to flatter and fall in with all the non sense of the zealots of the day—It may justly be suspected that his object is to throw things into confusion that he may ride the storm and direct the whirlwind.[38]

While Trump declined to serve his country, and thus lacks "the advantage of military habits," the rest of this description is unnervingly accurate. With a showman's flair, Trump creates and capitalizes on chaos—often with little apparent concern for the inconvenient constraint of factual information.

History offers an unnerving lesson on this point: without the ideal of objective truth, democracy is doomed. As Professor Timothy Snyder warns in his influential pamphlet, *On Tyranny*, "to abandon facts is to abandon freedom. If nothing is true, then no one can criticize power, because there is no basis upon which to do so."[39] Authoritarian leaders who cannot destroy a free press instead disable and delegitimize it. Inducing a nihilistic view of facts—and disbelief in the institutions that support them—goes a long way toward achieving that goal. Hannah Arendt described the final consequences of this strategy in *The Origins of Totalitarianism*: "In an ever-changing, incomprehensible world the masses had reached the point where they could, at the same time, believe everything and nothing, think that everything was possible and that nothing was true."[40] We're not there yet, indeed we're far from it, but that's the direction in which we're trending.

Stepping back, we can now see how the various ailments of the US political system reinforce one another. As Americans lose faith in institutions, including the media, they start trusting only a handful of sources for truthful information. Because many of these sources are balkanized along partisan lines, and because people can now filter out the sources that they don't agree with, Democrats and Republicans increasingly feel they inhabit different realities. In some respects, they *do*. The other party comes to seem dangerous and delusional—a view encouraged by friends and leaders in one's own echo chamber. This increases tribalism, polarization, and partisanship, which in turn enhance dysfunction, which in turn leads Americans to continue losing faith in democratic institutions. It's a terrible cycle that we have thus far been unable to stop.

*　*　*

Taken together, what does all this mean for impeachment? Although prediction is tricky business, we're confident in three forecasts. First, the nation's broken politics will generate high levels of harmful, hyperpartisan impeachment talk. Second, removing a president by impeachment will remain exceptionally difficult and may become an even heavier lift (due to partisan dysfunction in Congress). Finally, it will become increasingly important for impeachment analysis to assign substantial weight to the risk of long-term democratic decline. These three predictions capture trends that will be relevant not only to Trump but also to his successors—though we certainly recognize that if Trump is impeached, the arc of history may bend along a very different path.

1. *Impeachment talk*. Modern Americans are quick on the draw when it comes to demanding impeachment. The history recounted in Chapter 5 shows how unusual that makes us. Only in the post-Clinton era has impeachment talk become a routine aspect of partisan strife. As we've emphasized, Trump's irregular conduct is the most important explanation for the current fixation on impeachment. Some of his sketchy dealings and abuses of power might well constitute "high Crimes and Misdemeanors," and it's wholly appropriate to insist that Congress investigate these subjects. But there's also a much bigger picture to consider. The broken political dynamics that we've described provide crucial

context for calls to impeach Trump. They also help to explain why frequent resort to impeachment talk likely will outlast him.

We now live in a society where many voters believe that the other political party threatens national security and is controlled by bad people with terrible values. For Republicans and Democrats alike, the resulting feelings of distrust and animosity make it increasingly unbearable to imagine leaving their opponents in control of the White House for four years. Reduced confidence in other institutions that might check the president, and daily reminders of expanded executive power, enhance that anxiety. So do opposition echo chambers, which usually cast the president's conduct in a menacing and conspiratorial light.

The resulting tendency is toward an existential dread that makes mere political opposition seem insufficient. Because every president uses power in controversial ways, it isn't hard for motivated operatives to identify plausible "high Crimes and Misdemeanors." Almost inevitably—and at times immediately—many electoral losers become impeachers-in-waiting. Even if party leaders in Congress disclaim any intent to impeach, outlier party officials (and echo chamber participants) will cater to the base and give credence to their demands. That's especially true if one or more billionaires decide to throw their formidable muscle behind the cause. When Tom Steyer spent tens of millions of dollars on impeachment ads in 2017, and then insisted that Democratic candidates support that position, he offered an unusually raw display of money's power to redefine the political terrain.[41]

Impeachment talk is thus here to stay. In a polarized and partisan climate, vocal members of the opposition party will almost always go there. Following tactics used under George W. Bush and Barack Obama, the president's allies will then seek to exploit that rhetoric for their own benefit.

The result is a variant on Godwin's law. In 1990, Mike Godwin noticed that nearly every debate on the Internet somehow ended in the same place. He therefore proposed the most famous theory of cyber-argumentation: "As an online discussion continues, the probability of a reference or comparison to Hitler or Nazis approaches 1."[42] A similar rule now applies to our political system. Call it the Tribe/Matz Hypothesis: *As a discussion of US politics continues in the early twenty-first century, the probability that someone references presidential impeachment approaches 1.0.* Sometimes discussion of impeachment is right and reasonable. Most of the time, though, it's needless and harmful. As we saw in Chapter 5, a superabundance of impeachment talk can encourage political extremism and partisanship while undermining the availability of impeachment when it's truly needed.

2. *Impeachment will remain difficult.* Impeachment talk has now become so common—and so casual—that it's easy to forget the United States has never actually removed a president from office this way. By design, impeachment has always been an exceptionally difficult power to invoke. Polarization and hyperpartisanship have made that truer now than ever before.

First consider the House of Representatives. As explained in Chapter 4, when the House majority and the president belong to the same party, impeachment is a virtual nonstarter. Recent changes in the political system have only entrenched that rule. For many House members, key decisions are now driven by highly partisan donors and primary voters. Those groups are the most strongly inclined to dismiss, tolerate, or rationalize evidence of wrongdoing within their party. Although it's not unimaginable that they could be convinced to support impeachment, the evidence would have to be overwhelming and the president's conduct would have to be almost unimaginably evil. Otherwise, a House controlled by the president's party might refuse to act even if national public support for impeachment shot well above 50 percent. Voters who favored removal would have to wait until the next election to make their voices heard in Congress.

In contrast, when the House majority and the president belong to different parties, the House will face substantial pressure to impeach. Modern political dynamics all but guarantee it. That's true regardless of whether the president has actually committed an impeachable offense, as we learned under Bush and Obama. Even though neither of those presidents deserved impeachment, over 30 percent of the electorate—including a clear majority of the opposition party—came to feel otherwise. These opinions were based less on any single misdeed than on a general view that the president was a lawless tyrant. And promoting that view has now become a standard tactic in opposition politics. We can therefore expect a general increase in the number of impeachment resolutions filed in the House. We can also expect that opposition leaders will be pushed to impeach, and will suffer internal blowback if they don't. The key question is whether they will cave to this pressure. One risk of our broken politics is that the House will undertake additional, doomed partisan impeachments—a development that would be disastrous for the nation as a whole.

If the House does impeach the president, we arrive in the Senate. There have been moments in US history when the Senate lived up to its reputation as the world's greatest deliberative body. But this isn't one of them. In a dramatic speech on July 25, 2017, shortly after he was diagnosed with brain cancer, Senator John McCain mourned the Senate's decline:

> Our deliberations . . . are often lively and interesting. They can be sincere and principled. But they are more partisan, more tribal more of the time than any other time I remember. Our deliberations can still be important and useful, but I think we'd all agree they haven't been overburdened by greatness lately. And right now they aren't producing much for the American people.

McCain exhorted his colleagues to look past partisan allegiance and reflexive loyalties. "We are an important check on the powers of the Executive," he reminded them. "Whether or not we are of the same party, we are not the President's subordinates. We are his equal!"[43]

This was a timely and important warning. Sadly, it fell flat. As Norm Ornstein writes, the Senate is now a "bastion of tribalism" in which "mass obstruction remain[s] the modus operandi."[44] The ranks of moderates, mavericks, and independents have thinned at an alarming rate, while partisan warriors on both sides have descended into legislative trench warfare.

In this climate, finding sixty-seven votes to convict a president would be a Herculean task. There are more than thirty-four senators at any given point from deep blue or deep red states. And as compared to the Clinton or Nixon eras, the most partisan votes in the Senate today are considerably *more* partisan. Some of the president's most committed political allies would therefore have to support his removal for an impeachment to succeed. This isn't to say that nothing could sway them, especially if the president is deeply unpopular. But the force of evidence and argument necessary to overcome resistance in the Senate is at a historical zenith.

3. *Increased risk associated with impeachment decisions.* In Chapter 3, we identified the most important risks of impeaching—and not impeaching—when the president is suspected of "high Crimes and Misdemeanors." Although any serious impeachment decision is fraught with peril, the stakes of these political judgments have reached unnerving heights in recent years.

That's partly because legislative alternatives to impeachment are now particularly feeble. A steady expansion of executive authority has reduced Congress's ability to restrain the president when he is determined to abuse the powers of his office. Further, intensified partisan animosity, the rise of ideological echo chambers, and a breakdown in legislative process make it less plausible that Congress could stand firm in superintending the White House. Finally, the reduction of politics to spectacle and hyperbole has weakened the relevance of honor, integrity, and shame as considerations that would lead a president to dread censure.

The most unique feature of the modern era, however, is that impeachment decisions must now assign overriding significance to the threat posed by democratic decline. In our view, that is the single most important context for impeachment analysis in the twenty-first century. This may sound hyperbolic. But over the past decade, scholars who study failed democracies have sounded alarms in the United States. Indeed, the broken politics that we've described in this chapter include many well-recognized symptoms of an ailing democracy. And while those dysfunctions did not emerge overnight, they've worsened significantly under Trump. His open admiration for third-world strongmen is increasingly matched by rhetoric and conduct lifted straight from banana republics. In his first year alone, Trump infected the US government with additional signs of democratic decline. These include self-enrichment from public office; appointment of family members to high-level positions; claims that the press is an "enemy of the American people;" relentless efforts to establish favored news outlets as his personal equivalent of state TV; calls to imprison political opponents and critics; tacit support for armed extremists and private militias; assaults on the independent judiciary; and apparent comfort with hostile powers meddling in elections to his advantage.[45]

In the US system of government, the powers of the presidency are vast. Wielded to their fullest, and deployed maliciously or recklessly, they can corrode the very fabric of democracy. As polarization, partisanship, and tribalism have weakened external checks on the executive branch, Americans have come to rely increasingly on the president's good faith and self-restraint. That's a precarious position for any democracy—especially since our nation's warped politics also make it more likely that voters will favor populist demagogues who pander to their darkest instincts.

The immediate danger isn't a sudden declaration of martial law. Rather, it's that the norms, institutions, and culture that support democracy will erode, allowing a president with autocratic tendencies to consolidate power. As analyst David Frum cautions, liberty in a "modern bureaucratic state" is threatened "not by diktat and violence, but by the slow, demoralizing process of corruption and deceit."[46] The nation's descent into authoritarian governance may be invisible—or even welcome—to most voters. Democracies don't fail overnight. Instead, they fade before our eyes, dying in halls of power and in the hearts of their citizens.

Accordingly, decisions about whether to impeach must now account for the pressing threat of democratic decline. Like so many other considerations we've discussed in this book, that concern can cut both ways. Its significance in any particular case turns on a sensitive political judgment.

In some circumstances, a desire to protect democracy may ultimately cut *against* promoting or pursuing impeachment. As we've seen, even a well-justified impeachment poses grave risks. The main long-term threat is that it turbocharges forces of dysfunction and despair in our democracy. The main short-term threat is that an embittered minority refuses to accept the result and uses unlawful means to resist a perceived coup. A cross-cutting threat is that the impeachment fails when it should succeed, leaving the country with a corrupt tyrant and his angry, vengeful supporters. All of those risks are now at a historical high point. The public's capacity to build and maintain political consensus in favor of removal—and to absorb any damaging aftershocks—is open to serious doubt. This isn't to say that a tyrannical president and his committed loyalists deserve a terrorist's veto. But in assessing whether (and when) to impeach, we all must reckon with broader risks to the democratic system we're trying to save.

Of course, those risks may ultimately cut *in favor* of impeachment. Allowing abuse, corruption, or betrayal in the White House is always a dangerous proposition. Amid democratic decline, however, deciding not to impeach for "high Crimes and Misdemeanors" is *exceptionally* risky. Now more than ever, we must defend our constitutional order and resist authoritarian drift. That means refusing to tolerate or normalize presidential conduct that chips away at the foundation of US democracy. Invoked successfully, the impeachment power can save us from tyranny, repudiate dangerous precedents, and re-establish norms essential to a free society. It can also remind future presidents that nobody is above the law. In contrast, if we sit on our hands, an abusive leader might accelerate and benefit from preexisting elements of democratic decline. We may eventually find that our politics are too broken and too divisive for impeachment—or any other power—to stop a president who threatens all we hold dear.

* * *

Until 2017, discussions about lawfully removing the president began and ended with impeachment. Since Donald Trump took office, however, we've all been treated to a crash course in the Constitution's latent and dormant powers. Many Americans have grown particularly interested in the Twenty-Fifth Amendment, which creates a procedure for benching the president when he is "unable to discharge the powers and duties of his office." The idea of ousting Trump this way appeals to those who believe that he is mentally unsound. As they see things, it's more important to depose an unhinged commander in chief than to agonize over which of his crazy deeds might also qualify as "high Crimes and Misdemeanors."

Calls to invoke the Twenty-Fifth Amendment are often laced with hints that this approach would be easier, savvier, or more clearly justified than invoking the impeachment power. It wouldn't be. As compared to the Impeachment Clause, the Twenty-Fifth Amendment erects a far more daunting barrier against politically motivated efforts to end a presidency. And in the event of a genuine dispute, the Twenty-Fifth Amendment process could inflict significantly more damage on American democracy. Especially in our polarized partisan climate, the Twenty-Fifth Amendment could be legitimately employed only if the president were manifestly incapable—physically or mentally—of performing the core requirements of his job.

This high threshold is consistent with original understanding. The Twenty-Fifth Amendment was not enacted as an off-ramp for citizens who regret selecting an unfit or unqualified president.

Rather, it was ratified in 1967, following the assassination of John F. Kennedy, to address enduring confusion about three discrete issues in presidential succession. Section 1 of the amendment clarified that when a president dies, resigns, or is removed, the vice president "shall become President." This provision resolved uncertainty about whether the vice president fully became president or merely held the powers of that office in an acting capacity. Section 2 authorized the president to nominate a new vice president "whenever there is a vacancy in [that] office." This part of the Twenty-Fifth Amendment altered the historical practice of leaving such vacancies unfilled until the next presidential election.

Finally, Sections 3 and 4 addressed cases of presidential incapacity. In so doing, they brought order and transparency to a problem once handled through irregular, secretive, and sketchy practices. During the War of 1812, for example, James Madison went AWOL for a full month while suffering a high fever; Daniel Webster subsequently reported that Madison had been too weak to read. Nearly seventy years later, after James Garfield was wounded by an assassin in July 1881, the nation lacked a functioning head of state for eighty days until the president finally expired. In 1893, when Grover Cleveland developed a malignant oral tumor, his advisors kept everyone in the dark by arranging for secret surgery on a friend's private yacht. Even Vice President Adlai E. Stevenson didn't know Cleveland's whereabouts. From September 1919 through March 1921, Woodrow Wilson's formidable wife—Edith Wilson—effectively ran the White House while he was immobilized by a stroke. And following a heart attack, an intestinal obstruction, and a mild stroke, Dwight Eisenhower entered into a public agreement with Vice President Richard Nixon to transfer power in the event of his own disability.

The architects of the Twenty-Fifth Amendment had examples like these in mind when they crafted rules for presidential incapacity. Section 3 of the amendment applies when the president anticipates that he will be incapacitated. It allows him to temporarily transfer authority to the vice president by submitting a written declaration that he is "unable to discharge the powers and duties of his office." The president can later reclaim control by submitting a second declaration "to the contrary," which automatically restores his constitutional power.

In contrast, Section 4 covers situations in which the president cannot or will not declare his own incapacity. It creates a three-step process. First, the vice president and a majority of the cabinet must declare that the president is "unable to discharge the powers and duties of his office." At that time, the vice president "shall immediately assume the powers and duties of the office as Acting President." Second, if and when the president declares that "no inability exists," he regains his authority four days later—unless the vice president and a majority of the cabinet formally declare within this period that he remains incapacitated. If that occurs, the third and final step of Section 4 is triggered: Congress must assemble within forty-eight hours and then decide, within twenty-one days, whether the president is truly incapacitated. The vice president remains "Acting President" while Congress deliberates. In order to keep the president out of power, two-thirds majorities in both the House and the Senate must separately conclude that he is incapacitated. If either chamber of Congress does not do so within the constitutionally-prescribed period, the president's power is automatically restored.

As if that weren't complicated enough, there are a few more quirks to Section 4's process for resolving disputes over presidential incapacity:

• Section 4 can never be used without the vice president's concurrence. But Congress can swap out the cabinet and instead require the concurrence of a majority of any other body. Moreover, Congress can do this at any time—including in the middle of an incapacity dispute, if it loses faith in the cabinet. To make this change, however, Congress might have to overcome a veto from whoever is serving as president.

- If Congress leaves concurrence authority with the cabinet, it is unclear whether acting agency heads may vote. This would matter a great deal if the allegedly incapacitated president has fired the Senate-confirmed heads of any cabinet departments.
- The legislative record shows that the framers of the Twenty-Fifth Amendment believed it would be appropriate to impeach the vice president if he abused his powers—or acted in bad faith—during a Twenty-Fifth Amendment proceeding.
- In deciding whether the president is incapacitated, Congress is free to use any procedures that it deems necessary. In principle, it could require the president to undergo medical tests, or could require that he submit to questioning in a public forum.
- If Congress upholds a finding of incapacity, the president may contest it repeatedly. Each contest would require the House and Senate to vote within twenty-one days; if the president mustered over one-third support in either chamber on any vote, his power would be restored.

Finally, it's important to recognize that Section 4—unlike conviction on articles of impeachment—doesn't formally remove the president from office. He remains the president, which is why he may continue to contest the incapacity finding. But he doesn't possess "the executive Power," which devolves on the vice president during a period of incapacity.

The constitutional mechanism established by Section 4 thus has a distinct Rube Goldberg quality, with gears and levers and complex procedures for bouncing the ball back and forth among branches of government. In the face of a contested incapacity finding, it could run continuously for years until the allegedly incapacitated president's original four-year term comes to an end.

It is this extraordinary process that some political commentators would now deploy to banish Trump from the White House. In their view, his post-inauguration conduct demonstrates that he is "unable" (in all relevant senses) to discharge the powers and duties of his office.

That conclusion draws some support from statements by senior officials who are well positioned to assess Trump's state of mind. Former Secretary of State Rex Tillerson reportedly remarked that Trump is a "fucking moron."[47] Multiple sources claim that National Security Advisor H. R. McMaster blasted Trump as an "idiot" and a "dope," with the mind of a "kindergartner."[48] Republican Senator Bob Corker mocked the Trump White House as an "adult day care center."[49] And former Director of National Intelligence James R. Clapper, Jr. has stated, "I really question his ability to be—his fitness to be—in office."[50]

Other executive branch insiders appear to share this assessment. In May 2017, conservative *New York Times* columnist Ross Douthat painted a grim picture of Trump's interactions with White House staff: "They have no respect for him, indeed they seem to palpitate with contempt for him, and to regard their mission as equivalent to being stewards for a syphilitic emperor."[51] Seven months later, Joe Scarborough of MSNBC echoed Douthat's assessment: "Many who move through his orbit believe Trump is not well. That is a verdict that was reached long ago by many of the president's own staff."[52] Elsewhere, Scarborough claimed that "one of [the] people closest to Donald Trump during the campaign [says] he's got early stage dementia."[53]

These statements are consistent with unattributed quotes in national newspapers warning that Trump is unstable, unhinged, and unraveling. Anonymous reports from the White House describe a leader who erupts at subordinates without rhyme or reason, blithely dashes out world-shaking tweets, seems unable to read lengthy memos, espouses insane conspiracy theories, and obsessively watches cable news. Based on such accounts, some armchair psychologists have purported to diagnose Trump with a host of mental ailments, including a severe case of narcissistic personality disorder.[54]

In January 2018, following a series of especially shocking leaks, criticism of Trump's mental capacity reached a boiling point. Trump responded by tweeting that he's "like, really smart" and "a very stable genius."[55] Trump also requested that his physician administer a cognitive test designed to assess his mental reflexes. (Although Trump got a perfect score on this exam, many medical experts noted that it was limited in scope and couldn't detect an array of neurological and psychological disorders.[56])

These developments have fueled unprecedented interest in Section 4 of the Twenty-Fifth Amendment. In an op-ed that helped to jump-start public discussion of the issue, Douthat argued that Trump should be ousted because he can't perform basic duties of the presidency:

> One does not need to be a Marvel superhero or Nietzschean Übermensch to rise to this responsibility. But one needs some basic attributes: a reasonable level of intellectual curiosity, a certain seriousness of purpose, a basic level of managerial competence, a decent attention span, a functional moral compass, a measure of restraint and self-control. And if a president is deficient in one or more of them, you can be sure it will be exposed. Trump is seemingly deficient in them all.[57]

Douthat's conservative colleague David Brooks has rendered a similar verdict on Trump: "We've got this perverse situation in which the vast analytic powers of the entire world are being spent trying to understand a guy whose thoughts are often just six fireflies beeping randomly in a jar."[58]

Although these criticisms of Trump's temperament and intelligence are amply justified, they don't (yet) show "inability." Senator Birch Bayh, the main architect of the Twenty-Fifth Amendment, explained that "inability" means the president "is unable either to make or communicate his decisions as to his own competency to execute the powers and duties of his office."[59] According to an authoritative historical study by Professor John D. Feerick, "cases involving a mental inability were generally referred to as falling within [Section 4], as were situations in which the President is kidnapped or captured, under an oxygen tent at a time of enemy attack, or bereft of speech or sight."[60]

Simply put, the president must in fact be mentally or physically *unable* to carry out his constitutional functions. This is a high bar that requires objective proof of genuine incapacity. If the president is capable of doing his job, the Constitution doesn't authorize a transfer of power merely because he can't do it well. Professor Feerick's treatise confirms that "unpopularity, incompetence, impeachable conduct, poor judgment, and laziness do not constitute an 'inability' within the meaning of the Amendment."[61]

Efforts to give the Twenty-Fifth Amendment a much broader scope are not only historically unjustified; they also risk political illegitimacy and instability. Commentator Ezra Klein has convincingly explained the perils of ending Trump's presidency this way:

> To many of Trump's supporters—and perhaps many of his opponents—this would look like nothing less than a coup; the swamp swallowing the man who sought to drain it. Imagine the Breitbart headlines, the Fox News chyrons. And would they truly be wrong? Whatever Trump is today, he was that man when he was elected too. The same speech patterns were in evidence; the same distractibility was present. The tweets, the conspiracy theories, the chaos: It was all there. The American people, mediated by the Electoral College, delivered their verdict; mustn't it now be respected?[62]

To be sure, it's possible for a president to rapidly degenerate *after* taking office. But that isn't the real basis for most calls to depose Trump.

As a result, there's no avoiding the fact that Trump's basic mental defects were known to voters and he was elected anyway.

The Twenty-Fifth Amendment was designed for presidents who unexpectedly become mentally or physically incapacitated while in office; it isn't properly (or legitimately) applied to a president who was temperamentally unfit from the very outset. As Professor Keith Whittington has emphasized, "empowering a set of political elites to overturn the judgment of the people on the question of the general fitness of an elected official takes a large step toward autocracy."[63] Particularly in an era of democratic decline, that is not a step we should take unless there is an unmistakable national consensus in favor of doing so.

For all these reasons, we're not persuaded—as of mid-March 2018—that Trump has manifested "inability" in the relevant sense of the term. Instead, we agree with *Washington Post* columnist Jennifer Rubin: the Twenty-Fifth Amendment "is not meant for a situation in which the president is so stupid as to raise questions about whether he is a danger to the country."[64]

*   *   *

As Trump's case highlights, allegations of mental incapacity in the Oval Office may present uniquely difficult questions. Anticipating those difficulties, the Twenty-Fifth Amendment—much like the Impeachment Clause—establishes a multi-layer decision making process. An examination of how this political process is structured, and how it likely would work in practice, confirms that it would be imprudent to try to sideline a president whose mental incapacity is open to reasonable debate.

In thinking about that issue, it's important to recall that the Constitution doesn't strip the American people of their right to elect leaders with mental illnesses. Nor does it require presidents who suffer depression, anxiety, or other mental ailments to step aside. Indeed, as Professor Jeannie Suk Gersen reports, "[m]any Presidents in our history appear to have served while managing various forms of mental illness."[65] That all said, there surely comes a point at which Alzheimer's disease, crippling depression, a psychotic break, or other mental problems can render a president incapacitated within the meaning of the Constitution. When signs and symptoms of such presidential disability become evident, the vice president and cabinet have an inescapable duty to act. They needn't hold back until disaster befalls.

Responding to the subjectivity and potential illegitimacy inherent in such mental health determinations, advocates of sidelining Trump through the Twenty-Fifth Amendment often frame their argument in clinical terms. Citing prominent psychiatrists from elite schools, they offer detailed accounts of Trump's diagnosable mental illnesses. The overall effect is to give their criticism an objective, scientific air: *It's not that we disagree with him or dislike him; it's that he's certifiably crazy.* But the Twenty-Fifth Amendment does not enact the *Diagnostic and Statistical Manual of Mental Disorders* into law. Nor does it vest psychiatrists with control over the presidency. In a democracy, political decisions of this magnitude can never be reduced wholly to clinical assessments. When a finding of presidential "inability" requires reasonably debatable judgment, medical science can only get us so far.

Recognizing that fact, the Constitution protects the requirement of genuine "inability" by creating an extraordinary decision-making process. The vice president always must concur. Unless Congress says otherwise, so must a majority of the cabinet, whose members have been hand-picked by the president and work closely with him in many contexts. Usually, most of these men and women will belong to the same political party as the president and will feel intense personal loyalty to him. Vesting initial control in this group reduces the odds of unsavory political shenanigans. As Professor Cass Sunstein points out, "the real risk is not that the Twenty-Fifth Amendment will be invoked when it shouldn't, but that it won't be invoked when it should."[66] Of course, even if the president's inner circle decides that he lacks the capacity to govern, the president can still prevail by persuading one third of either house of Congress that he can do his job. Here, too, Section 4 of the Twenty-Fifth Amendment is weighted overwhelmingly in favor of allowing the duly elected president of the United States to exercise the powers of his office.

These constitutional procedures are well-suited to cases where the president is in a coma, has suffered a devastating stroke, or has been kidnapped. In those situations, the president hasn't done anything impeachable but clearly can't perform his constitutional functions. It should be uncontroversial to declare that the vice president will serve as acting president.

In contrast, it makes little practical sense to attempt a Twenty-Fifth Amendment ouster of someone like Trump, who is lucid and capable of using his executive powers. As Professor Brian Kalt notes, "a president who is competent enough to read public musings about Section 4 can preemptively fire Cabinet members he suspects of plotting against him. This would serve a double purpose: showing that he is able to discharge the powers and duties of his office; and stacking the Section 4 decision-making deck."[67] Further, if the vice president and the cabinet took action against Trump by submitting a declaration to Congress, the aggrieved president could rally his base and wage a spectacular legislative battle. In that fight, Trump would have many opportunities to publicly address the claim that he is mentally incapacitated. And even if Congress did find him disabled, Trump could keep the dispute alive by repeatedly declaring his own competence to govern—thus forcing new votes in Congress every few weeks.

In the interim, the nation would remain trapped in a divisive, disruptive, and profoundly traumatic cycle of contested presidential legitimacy. No matter how firmly one believes that Trump's mental deficiencies threaten our democracy, this isn't a responsible way to address the problem.

The main exception that comes to mind is a circumstance in which Trump gives a truly insane, destructive order—for example, to secretly launch a nuclear first strike. In that event, the vice president and the cabinet should invoke Section 4 to immediately dispossess him of power. Once the crisis has been contained, Section 4 can keep Trump under control while Congress conducts full impeachment proceedings to permanently remove him from office.

Apart from such an emergency, the Twenty-Fifth Amendment should be reserved for cases of clear presidential inability. And as of mid-March 2018, Trump does not meet that standard under a good faith reading of the Constitution. More fundamentally, it is a grave mistake to view the Twenty-Fifth Amendment as little more than a medicalized version of impeachment. This provision wasn't meant to function as an all-purpose remedy for buyer's remorse at having elected a terrible president. Efforts to use it that way invite confusion and conflict that would harm democracy. They also confront steeper political obstacles than an impeachment: whereas the Impeachment Clause requires half the House and two-thirds of the Senate (each for a single vote), Section 4 requires the vice president, a majority of the cabinet, and two-thirds majorities of both chambers (potentially on a continuing basis). And instead of removing the president, the payoff of a Twenty-Fifth Amendment intervention is months or years of continued controversy.

Given Trump's disturbing conduct, it is understandable that some critics have shifted their focus from tyrannical acts to the tyrant himself. But in this fragile political moment, using the Twenty-Fifth Amendment to sideline Trump for who he is—instead of debating whether to impeach him for what he's done—would be misguided.

* * *

As we finish this book, a majority of the American public believes that Donald J. Trump is unfit to serve as president. Many have concluded that Trump threatens American democracy, freedom, and global leadership. Calls to remove him from office are now standard fare in Democratic and "Never Trump" conservative circles. It appears inevitable that demands for Trump's ouster—and furious denunciations of those demands—will persist so long as he occupies the White House. It's therefore essential for the public to develop a clear-eyed view of impeachment as a constitutional power inextricable from the political process. Only then can citizens and elected officials properly judge what role, if any, impeachment should play in addressing the myriad challenges that bedevil our democracy.

In our experience, one of the main obstacles to even-keeled analysis of impeachment under Trump is the fear and fury that he inspires in many of his political opponents. This raw emotion is partly a consequence of broader societal trends toward polarization and hyperpartisanship. But it is also a direct response to Trump's conduct in office, which has mixed a hard-right agenda with swaggering disregard for the rules and culture of our constitutional order. As journalist Michael Grunwald notes, Trump has repeatedly shattered bipartisan norms of "honesty, decency, diversity, strategy, diplomacy and democracy."[68] Along the way, he has embraced a cruel, reckless, and autocratic approach to exercising power.

Trump's antidemocratic vision of the presidency has already led 40 percent of the public to support his immediate impeachment. For many Americans who feel that way, this isn't any ordinary political preference. It's an overriding moral and political imperative. They fear that Trump poses an existential threat to our Constitution and the free society it establishes. Moreover, given his access to the nuclear codes and reckless approach to Twitter, Trump could all too easily instigate global war.

Within that worldview, deposing Trump can assume extraordinary psychological importance. Every additional day of the Trump presidency is cause for anxiety, depression, and fear. This has led some Americans to support a Twenty-Fifth Amendment Hail Mary, which would turn Trump's mental health into a ground for removal. And it has led many more to preserve their own mental health by resolving that an impeachment *will* happen, *will* succeed, and *will* set everything straight. Consider this parody advertisement, posted online in March 2017, for a fake drug named *Impeachara*:

> Do you find yourself feeling depressed? Hopeless? Having trouble sleeping? Struggling with frequent panic attacks? Irritability? Constant arguments with family? Friends? Or even friends of friends on Facebook? Yelling at your phone or computer screen? And that constant urge to pull out your hair . . .
>
> You may be suffering from T.I.A.D., "Trump Induced Anxiety Disorder." *Impeachara* may help . . .
>
> *Impeachara* works on your brain's neurotransmitters and optical receptors convincing you that Donald Trump has already been impeached. Not all patients have the same reactions. Results may vary. Side effects may include elation, the ability to focus on work and family again, and reconnecting with people you called ignorant fuckfaces on social media.[69]

For some Americans, when it feels too awful to imagine Trump remaining in power until January 2021, impeachment offers the glowing promise of a better, saner world. After the orange-faced lunatic is (inevitably) displaced, everything will go back to normal. Even Facebook. Maybe even Twitter.

Such fantastical thinking about impeachment's potential has become increasingly common in anti-Trump political circles. We suspect that many people now see impeachment as far more than a political process that would replace Trump with Vice President Michael Pence. Instead, they see it as a general "reset" button to undo the chaos and disruption of the recent past.

While writing this book, we've been asked repeatedly whether impeaching Trump would trigger an immediate special election between Trump and a Democrat, or would prohibit Pence from running in 2020, or would reverse the results of the 2016 election and install Hillary Clinton as president. We've also been asked whether a successful impeachment would remove Trump's life-tenured appointments, including Supreme Court Justice Neil Gorsuch, and whether it would erase all of his executive orders, regulatory actions, and foreign affairs decisions. More than once, we've been pushed to explain whether it would be possible to simultaneously impeach Trump, Pence, Speaker of the House Paul Ryan, and Senate Majority Leader Mitch McConnell.

By now, it should be clear that our response to all of these questions is "absolutely not." As we saw in Chapter 1, the Framers deliberately chose to limit the consequences of ending a presidency through impeachment. (Moreover, as legislators rather than executive or judicial officers, neither Paul Ryan nor Mitch McConnell is even subject to the impeachment power.) It's nonetheless intriguing that we've received a steady flood of such imaginative, adventurous questions. Some of the inquiries we've fielded would make excellent plot lines for *House of Cards* or *Veep*, but would be disastrous if attempted in the real world. Others transcend any basis in the Constitution and compose their own genre of escapist political fantasy. All of these questions, however, are unified by an earnest hope that stripping Trump of power would turn back time and mend a broken nation.

This is a scary moment. We recognize that many Americans are afraid of where the country and the world are heading. We understand that Trump has played (and will continue to play) a substantial role in making things worse. Moreover, we agree that a thorough investigation might well reveal that Trump has committed one or more impeachable acts. But we worry that a large part of the American public has invested too much of its capacity for hope in a supposed impeachment miracle.

There is no *Deus Ex Machina* Clause in the Constitution. The impeachment power acts on the world as it is—not as it once was, or as it could have been. Under most circumstances, removing the president from office this way is bound to be divisive and disheartening. Even when taking that step is fully justified, the price may be higher and the benefits more modest than some would envision.

In an era that presents weighty challenges to American democracy—few of which will vanish if Trump is expelled—the impeachment power has been burdened with impossible expectations.

Miraculous thinking about impeachment isn't an abstract issue. It can cause concrete harms. Too many of our friends and colleagues have succumbed to the nihilistic view that everything is terrible, nothing matters, and only impeachment can fix our problems. (In early 2018, that belief lurks behind claims that Special Counsel Robert Mueller is the only hope for American democracy.) This isn't to say that support for impeachment precludes political engagement. Millions of Americans who support impeaching Trump have turned out to vote, protest, organize, knock on doors, sign petitions, serve as plaintiffs, and call legislators. But others may give up as they wait for a white knight to arrive with irrefutable proof of "high Crimes and Misdemeanors."

An all-or-nothing mindset, in which impeachment alone can save the world, is depressing and enervating. It relegates most citizens to the sidelines, leaving a handful of secretive insiders in control of the only politics that really matter. As *Slate*'s Dahlia Lithwick writes, such "magical thinking" can thereby "numb us, and lead to a declining sense of agency or ownership."[70] It can also falsely devalue other ways of defending democracy, including popular activism, local and state political engagement, filing lawsuits, donating to civil rights groups, and undertaking private ventures in the public interest.

In addition, fetishizing impeachment as a political cure-all can be self-defeating. Trump will not be removed from power unless a large number of Republicans and independents, along with Democrats, agree that he has to go. But the truth is that most of those voters don't believe the sky is falling. Nor are they automatically inclined to view impeachment as an appropriate sanction for Trump—even when they disagree with him or find him embarrassing. In engaging with those voters, urging impeachment and suggesting that it will undo all of his major decisions could prove counter-persuasive. They may be pleased with some of Trump's appointments and policies since taking office. They may look skeptically on Democrats who favored impeachment on Inauguration Day. And they may be especially wary of joining an impeachment crusade led by a party they otherwise disdain.

History teaches that the ways in which people think and talk about impeachment can significantly affect the odds that an impeachment effort will succeed. It is hard enough to persuade the president's supporters under any circumstances that he should be removed for "high Crimes and Misdemeanors." We doubt the wisdom of making it harder still by describing that effort as the first shot of a revolution—or, even less realistically, as a revolution in itself.

Of course, fantastical thinking isn't confined to those who *support* removing the president from office. Just as Trump has evoked an unyielding political opposition, so has he instilled intense loyalty within his base. Many Americans who voted for Trump view themselves as belonging to a victimized, disenfranchised class that has finally discovered its champion. For some of them, Trump's appeal is less what he will accomplish programmatically than whom he will attack personally. Were Trump removed from office by political elites in Washington, DC—even based on clear evidence that he had grossly abused power—some of his supporters would surely view the decision as an illegitimate coup. Indeed, some right-wing leaders have already denounced the campaign to unseat Trump as a prelude to civil war. This rhetoric, too, escapes reality and indulges pernicious tendencies toward apocalyptic thinking about the impeachment power.

* * *

In calling for a clear-eyed view of impeachment, we have emphasized realism over fantasy. Impeachment is neither a magic wand nor a doomsday device. Instead, it is an imperfect and unwieldy constitutional power that exists to defend democracy from tyrannical presidents. Deploying this emergency measure always requires extensive national deliberation, as well as agreement from many Americans who originally supported the disastrous leader. Further, even when successfully invoked, impeachment serves only to end a presidency. It doesn't fix the democratic decline that brought a tyrant to power. It doesn't undo the havoc he wreaked while in office. And it doesn't forestall the trauma of expelling him through such extraordinary means. In the wake of an impeachment proceeding, "We the People" must set our world aright.

Maintaining a realistic mindset is important because the Impeachment Clause demands that we exercise sound political judgment—especially at times of crisis. That isn't possible when the public ascribes miraculous powers to impeachment; treats it as a weapon of partisan warfare; or seeks to shift responsibility to the Framers, the pollsters, or the criminal code. Facing the impeachment power head on, with all its complexity and limitations, can be frustrating. But as Andrew Shepherd warned in *The American President* (an Aaron Sorkin film), "America ain't easy. America is advanced citizenship." There are no small mistakes when it comes to ousting a president. It's crucial to get these decisions right.

And as we've seen, impeachment-related judgments are not limited to final votes in the House and Senate. They encompass innumerable choices that arise before, during, and after any hearings on Capitol Hill. On many of these issues, the Constitution says little—or nothing at all. The public must therefore rely upon its general understanding of politics and democracy, sharpened by an appreciation of impeachment's history and purpose.

To see what that means in practice, consider this question, which millions of Americans have asked about Bush, Obama, and now Trump: *What should I do if I believe the president must be impeached, but a majority of the public doesn't (yet) agree?* The answer to that inquiry may look very different depending upon who has asked it and when they've done so. Still, drawing on the framework set forth in this book, we can identify some of the most important considerations that should structure the analysis.

Let's start with first principles: when faced with an aspiring tyrant, it is essential to call evil by its name. Presidents who abuse their power, betray the nation, or corrupt their office must be confronted and constrained. There are many checks and balances within our system that can be activated in defense of freedom. There are also many forms of political engagement through which to resist an autocrat. Yet sometimes only the extreme remedy of impeachment will suffice. And the option of expelling an alleged tyrant doesn't just appear out of nowhere. Ending a presidency requires months or years of concerted political and investigative activity. It also requires substantial public deliberation over the factual, legal, and political case against the chief executive. In other words, removing a tyrant requires impeachment talk—and lots of it. Forcefully advocating in favor of the president's ouster, and building the infrastructure to support that agenda, is imperative in the lead-up to a successful impeachment.

But as legislators and presidential advisors have long recognized, and as we explained in Chapter 5, aggressive calls for removal can backfire. Most immediately, they may shore up the president's support within his own party by intensifying tribalism and partisan polarization. Further, people who voted for a president might simply shut down, rather than change their minds, when faced with such extreme rhetoric. In addition, if the president's congressional opponents put all their chips on impeachment, they may suffer in midterm elections—unless there is a deep reservoir of voter interest in removal. And if they ultimately prevail in the midterms, those legislators may suffer from a lack of credibility in the impeachment process because they've already publicly committed to a particular outcome. Finally, an endless stream of impeachment chatter risks desensitizing the public to abuse—and may thus ironically allow the president more leeway to test the limits of his office.

Accordingly, there will be circumstances in which the best way to combat an out-of-control executive is to resist frequent public use of the "i-word." History teaches that views on presidential wrongdoing can be shaped by a wide range of logical and emotional pleas. An all-or-nothing appeal based on impeachment talk is the rhetorical equivalent of a battering ram: direct and forceful. Sometimes that is just what the situation calls for. But at other times building political consensus against a tyrant requires thoughtful, nuanced engagement with his supporters. This is particularly true when an unrelenting barrage of hostility may only increase their sense of political alienation, victimhood, and tribal loyalty. As economist Andrés Miguel Rondón has insightfully observed, it can be vital to avoid "playing into the polarization game instead of defeating it."[71]

The Constitution wisely declines to specify any single approach to combating tyranny. These judgments are always context-dependent. When a president's opponents conclude that he threatens ruin, they must carefully and tactically gauge what forms of political rhetoric and activity will most effectively safeguard American democracy. It can't be taken for granted that impeachment talk (or a full-blown impeachment) will best advance this strategic objective. That decision, too, is context-dependent.

This analysis leads us to a deeper truth about impeachment's role in American politics. In the first instance, the impeachment power is a constraint on the president and a check against abuse of executive authority. But its most fundamental purpose is greater still: the preservation of American democracy under the Constitution.

Invoking impeachment in ways that *destabilize* democracy is thus perverse and profoundly irresponsible. This is most obviously true of impeachment proceedings, like those against Bill Clinton, motivated by partisan animus and doomed by lack of public consensus. Yet it can also be true of promiscuous, hyperpartisan, and implausible calls for impeachment that reinforce (and accelerate) a cycle of broken politics. To ensure that the impeachment power supports democracy, rather than erodes it, Americans must rehabilitate the distinction between opposing a president and supporting his removal. This will require unlearning bad lessons of the recent past and adopting a saner, more discerning mindset. Impeachment must be treated as a last resort in times of crisis—not as a knee-jerk response to hints of misconduct.

Admittedly, achieving these goals while Trump remains in office will not be easy. He has abused power in so many ways—and committed so many potential "high Crimes and Misdemeanors"—that calls for impeachment are a foregone conclusion. But even in the short term, American democracy will fare better if we can nurture a more reflective and consensual view of impeachment. Promoting such even-tempered thinking would improve our shared perspective on when ousting the chief executive is *really* necessary.

This connection between impeachment and democracy runs both ways. As we've seen time and again, impeachment depends on the very same democracy that it exists to protect. The power to end a presidency will not keep us safe if American politics are so broken that the public cannot recognize and rally against a tyrant.

These days, however, our political system is sick and getting sicker. Polarization and partisanship are on the upswing, while extremists on all sides grow ever bolder. Younger Americans have started losing faith in our basic plan of government. And the last few years have offered a continuing lesson in the fragility of rules and norms long seen as essential to preserving democracy. These trends evoke the classic lines from W.B. Yeats: "Things fall apart; the centre cannot hold; mere anarchy is loosed upon the world."[72] Ultimately, our cycle of political dysfunction may well impel us toward tragedy. The same decline and dysfunction that beget a president who threatens democracy itself might also make impeaching that president all but impossible.

To avoid this dark trajectory, we must abandon fantasies that the impeachment power will swoop in and save us from destruction. It can't and it won't. When our democracy is threatened from within, we must save it ourselves. Maybe impeachment should play a role in that process; maybe it will only make things worse.

Either way, reversing the rot in our political system will require creative and heroic efforts throughout American life. And at the heart of those efforts will be the struggle to transcend our deepest divisions in search of common purpose and mutual understanding. We must draw together in defense of a constitutional system that binds our destinies and protects our freedom. As Abraham Lincoln once reminded a nation far more divided than ours, "We are not enemies, but friends. We must not be enemies."[73]

Transcending forces of decay, disinformation, and disunion will not be easy. This is the great national calling of our time—the North Star that must guide decisions about ending or enduring disastrous presidencies. There is no quick fix for the challenges we face. They are surmountable only if each of us resolves anew that America and democracy are well worth fighting for.

EPILOGUE TO THE PAPERBACK EDITION

As we reflect on the story of impeachment during President Donald J. Trump's first two years in office, a single number stands out: 40 percent. Plus or minus four percent, that figure reflected public support for impeaching Trump in May, August, and October 2017, as well as January, March, and November 2018. The available data thus suggests remarkable stability in public attitudes. For all the drama and tumult of Trump's presidency—and despite a slew of high-profile scandals—few Americans have changed their minds on this issue. While support for impeachment ticked up to 49 percent in August 2018, following Michael Cohen's guilty plea and the conviction of Paul Manafort, that number quickly returned to 40 percent. As we write this epilogue in December 2018, the polls have *never* shown a consensus (or even a majority) in favor of removing Trump from office. But they have indicated a high level of baseline support for doing so, largely among Democrats.

As a matter of political reality, a president cannot be ousted with only 40 percent of the public backing that result—no matter how compelling the legal case against him might be. That is particularly true when the president's party controls both houses of Congress. Throughout 2017 and 2018, these considerations supported an understanding that Trump was unlikely to face imminent impeachment.

At the same time, 40 percent is a breathtakingly high number by historical standards. It has served to make impeachment a mainstream issue and a credible political threat. Starting from this baseline, things could easily go south for Trump—especially given his high disapproval ratings, the persistence of multi-pronged investigations, trends toward economic recession and global instability, and a steady drip of unsavory revelations suggesting he may well have committed criminal and impeachable offenses.

The specter of impeachment has therefore exercised a strong gravitational pull over the past two years. This has been true, first and foremost, at the White House. News reports suggest that key figures in the administration, including Trump, saw themselves as acting in the shadow of potential impeachment proceedings. Trump has met with his lawyers on numerous occasions to discuss the risk of impeachment. He has hired senior lawyers with impeachment experience. And according to the *Washington Post*, Trump's aides have successfully "invoked the prospect of impeachment to persuade the president not to take actions or behave in ways that they believe would hurt him."[1] We don't know what Trump might have done in a world without the impeachment power, but there is strong circumstantial evidence that the mere existence of this eject button has influenced him.

Impeachment strategy has also shaped Trump's response to Special Counsel Robert Mueller. In a series of public statements, the president's legal team has asserted that Trump cannot be held liable under the criminal law, that Mueller would not dare to indict him, and that he could pardon himself if accused of federal crimes. As Rudy Giuliani observed, because this leaves impeachment as "the only thing that hangs out there," Trump would be crazy not to "attack the legitimacy of the investigation."[2] After all, the key question "is going to be impeach, not impeach," and that is a matter "for public opinion."[3] On this view, the facts will not be found—and the law will not be vindicated—in a courtroom or the Department of Justice. Instead, Trump's best defense to the Mueller investigation (and to the array of related criminal probes) is to convince, confuse, or polarize the public. Even if Mueller makes a devastating case that Trump committed high Crimes and Misdemeanors, it will fail in Congress if enough Americans see only a witch hunt.

This anti-Mueller strategy dovetailed nicely with Republicans' heavy emphasis on impeachment talk throughout the 2018 midterm elections. As we predicted in Chapter 5, Trump and his allies repeatedly used the risk of impeachment to rally Republican voters. On the campaign trail, Trump warned that if he was impeached, "it's your fault, 'cause you didn't go out to vote." He added, "I'll be the only President in history they'll say: 'What a job he's done! By the way, we're impeaching him.'"[4] Elsewhere, Trump insisted that markets would crash if he were impeached. He also asserted that Congress can't "impeach somebody that's doing a great job,"[5] and that "the people would revolt" if he were impeached.[6] Other Republicans joined the chorus, peppering campaign events, fundraising requests, stump speeches, and TV appearances with dire warnings of a Democratic plot against Trump.

Just as in 2006 and 2014, the result was a midterm in which the majority of impeachment talk came from the president's own party. In fact, most Democrats followed their leadership by denying plans to impeach, calling for additional investigation before reaching any conclusions, or avoiding the issue entirely. As *FiveThirtyEight* observed in August 2018, "Republicans are talking about impeachment way more than Democrats. . . . If the Democrats are planning to impeach Trump if they win control of the House, they are doing a really great job of hiding it."[7] After Election Day, the *Washington Post* confirmed that of the 52 newly-elected Democrats, only 11 had called for impeachment; 13 had opposed impeaching Trump and 17 had indicated their intent to wait on Mueller.[8] Many more Americans were keen to vote for particular Democrats than were keen to vote for impeachment—and savvy candidates acted accordingly.

This required considerable skill because so much of our political discourse had collapsed into relentless impeachment talk. The topic was unavoidable. Hardly any development in the federal government escaped the inevitable think piece opining that Trump's presidency had finally been doomed or saved. By late November 2018, the word "impeachment" had already been uttered on cable news 12,000 times that year. New books and articles arrived every week, accompanied by an endless stream of op-eds, essays, and Twitter tirades. Tom Steyer pumped tens of millions of dollars into his "Need to Impeach" campaign, and prominent liberal voices took up the cause. Their calls for Trump's removal echoed widely in #resistance circles—and also on *Fox* and *Breitbart*, which gleefully featured this "proof" of a liberal conspiracy waiting in the wings. The odds of impeachment hearings in the House remained relatively low in 2018, but even in this dormant state, impeachment shaped and structured public discourse.

Many people who participated in these debates did so in good faith, moved by genuine concern for the fate of the nation. Many scholars offered valuable explanations of complex legal and political questions. And there were exceedingly good reasons for this surge of impeachment talk. Trump's conduct during the 2016 election and since taking office had caused grave harm to our democracy—and may well have involved numerous "high Crimes and Misdemeanors." It would have been strange, even irresponsible, to avoid the issue entirely.

Still, it was hard to ignore a sense that the nation boasted a surplus of *impeachment entrepreneurs*: politicians and pundits looking to make a name for themselves by taking extreme, highly partisan, and often reckless positions on matters of impeachment. Offering a thin diet of soundbite impeachment talk, these figures treated impeachment as little more than partisan warfare by other means. In that respect, they contributed to the continuing post-Clinton degradation and weaponization of impeachment.

This trend was linked to another: the rise of a ceaseless death watch for the Trump presidency. In ways large and small, the supposed inevitability of impeachment hearings began to influence news coverage. Stories were judged, explained, and assigned significance by reference to their role in the anticipated narrative of Trump's impeachment. Rather than ask about the legality, morality, or wisdom of Trump's conduct, commentators focused only on whether we had finally hit midnight on the Impeachment Clock.

That outlook was understandable in a world where other checks and balances were in disrepair. But it was also pernicious. The president wins—and everyone else loses—when the main framework for evaluating his conduct is whether it will trigger impeachment. By battling on that terrain, he preemptively sets aside most standards by which a democracy should judge its leader. He also invigorates his base by turning every dispute into a referendum on his continued tenure in office.

As we explain in Chapters 5 and 6, an unyielding focus on impeachment can flatten and distort our politics. Many of Trump's worst policies—including those based on prejudice, contempt for science and expertise, and utter ignorance—can't properly be squeezed into an impeachment framework. The same might be said about many of Trump's scariest public statements and personnel decisions. When impeachment talk overtakes our politics, it directs attention toward some issues and away from others. It prompts us to ask about "high Crimes and Misdemeanors," rather than about adherence to the norms, rules, and sense of dignity that we rightly expect of the chief executive. It leads us to focus on a small set of elite political actors, and to elide other forms of political engagement that might mitigate or prevent harm to our society. And it raises the stakes in ways that favor polarization, tribalism, and a downward spiral of acrimony, while making compromise and moderation less likely.

Of course, this is all a question of degree. We certainly aren't saying that impeachment talk should cease, or that it's wrong to ask whether some of Trump's abuses might justify his removal. Given what we now know about Trump's conduct, a substantial measure of impeachment talk is fully appropriate. The trick is to strike a balance. And in doing so, it is helpful to reflect on the downsides, as well as the virtues, of seeing the world through an impeachment lens.

Maintaining such perspective will remain important for the foreseeable future. So long as Trump remains in office, the nation will continue to debate his impeachment. While we are wary of making predictions, that one seems safe enough.

So do a few more. First, we hope and expect that the new Democratic majority in the House will exercise its power responsibly. Despite strong support for impeachment within their base, party leaders have signaled their reluctance to take that extraordinary step without bipartisan support. This position would be commendable under any circumstances and makes particular sense given the composition of the Senate. Barring a major change in the state of play, both houses of Congress would be well served to focus on legislation, governance, oversight, and investigation. Of course, this includes investigations that might be relevant to assessing potential impeachable offenses.

Second, we anticipate that the sense of urgency around questions of impeachment will increase, not decrease. The House will now make full use of its subpoena power. The Mueller investigation—and the related array of state and separate federal criminal probes—will reach a boiling point. The press will make further headway in discovering the nature of Trump's familial and financial entanglements (or lack thereof) with Russia, Saudi Arabia, Qatar, Turkey, and other foreign powers. We doubt that Trump will respond well to these developments. He may take drastic steps. Indeed, he may feel especially motivated to do so now that prosecutors have openly implicated him in one or more felonies (more on that below). And all of these developments will unfold against the incendiary, partisan backdrop of the 2020 presidential race.

Finally, we predict a continued battle over the ground rules for impeachment. Over the past year, Trump and his allies have advanced a number of meritless claims that would render the

Impeachment Clause a lifeless husk. At the same time, some of Trump's opponents have gotten out over their skis in describing "high Crimes and Misdemeanors" and a supposed "duty" by the House to impeach—a "duty" we do our best to debunk in Chapter 3. In the heat of political combat, we can expect to hear many arguments born of convenience, not conviction. That makes it more important than ever to think critically about impeachment, and to follow the rules and principles set forth in the Constitution.

In the remaining sections of this epilogue, we will focus most of our attention on allegations that Trump has committed "high Crimes and Misdemeanors." We will also respond to criticism of our book by Alan Dershowitz. Finally, we will explore how several recent developments may affect Congress's risk calculus in deciding whether to end this particular presidency.

* * *

In Chapter 2, we explored the Constitution's limitation of impeachment to "Treason, Bribery, or other high Crimes and Misdemeanors." This led us to a careful study of the phrase "high Crimes and Misdemeanors." Drawing on text and structure, as well as original meaning and history, we identified key characteristics of impeachable offenses:

- They involve betrayal of the nation, corruption of the office, or grave abuse of power
- They pose a risk of serious harm to the nation and suggest that the president will remain a threat
- They involve deliberate, intentional wrongdoing, not mere incompetence or bad policy
- They render the president unviable as the leader of a democracy premised on the rule of law
- They involve misconduct so plainly wrong by current standards that no reasonable official could honestly profess surprise at being impeached

- They may well involve criminal conduct, but that is *not* a requirement under the Constitution
- They will often involve a pattern of closely related abuses, rather than a single dastardly deed

The ultimate inquiry is whether the president has done something so terrible that we must consider removing him *now*—instead of waiting for the next election and relying on ordinary checks in the interim. This necessity arises because the president's misconduct is so destructive in its own right, or so disturbing a sign for the future, that it could imperil our constitutional democracy to leave him in power.

Applying that standard to known facts in Chapters 2 and 5, we sought to separate the wheat from the chaff in demands to impeach Trump. This was a vital undertaking. Many calls for Trump's removal have targeted decisions or policies that do not actually satisfy the constitutional requirement of "high Crimes and Misdemeanors." Although we condemn Trump's conduct on many fronts—and have participated in multiple lawsuits against him—it is still important to recognize the difference between those disagreements and impeachable offenses.

Some examples may be helpful. Merely four months after Trump took office, Allan J. Litchman described as impeachable Trump's "war on the press," his "war on women," and his "crime against humanity" of failing to act on climate change.[9] In December 2017, Representative Al Greene proposed an article of impeachment for "associating the presidency and the people of the United States with bigotry."[10] Here he cited the travel ban, the ban on military service by transgender persons, and Trump's claim that migrants from "shithole" countries are less desirable than Norwegian migrants. More recently, the distinguished former legislator Elizabeth Holtzman has opined that Trump's pattern of lies, as well as his family separation policy, are impeachable.[11] Need to Impeach (Steyer's group) seeks Trump's ouster on nine grounds, including the reckless handling of foreign policy and failure to uphold the equal protection of the laws.[12] Finally, former White House Counsel Bob Bauer has argued that "[a] president who is a demagogue, whose demagoguery defines his style of political leadership, is subject for that reason to impeachment."[13]

It is unappetizing to defend Trump with respect to these issues. We will not minimize the gravity of his misconduct or imply that he has acted in accordance with the Constitution. Nor will we pretend that these judgments are cut-and-dried. As Gillian Metzger notes, "any effort to separate ordinary politics from the constitutional realm of impeachment" is "Herculean at best."[14] Still, considering the criteria for impeachment, as well as the facts now known to the public and all applicable law, we consider it doubtful that the offenses listed above presently qualify as impeachable.

We remain particularly wary of efforts to characterize Trump's rhetoric as a "high Crime and Misdemeanor." That is true even though we agree strongly with Bauer's warning against Trump's demagoguery. In fact, we would go further and join Michiko Kakutani in concluding that Trump has "exchanged the language of democracy and its ideals for the language of autocracy."[15] Trump's anti-constitutional vocabulary reveals itself in his reckless and potentially dangerous verbal assaults on journalists, prosecutors, courts, civil servants, election officials, and racial minorities. But as we explain in Chapter 2, this pattern of statements—considered on its own—does not rise to the level of an impeachable offense. Concluding otherwise would violate the rule against impeachment for maladministration. It would also create insurmountable line-drawing difficulties and risk chilling presidential speech on matters of public concern.

In our view, Trump's public statements could qualify as impeachable only if they were essential to the execution of—or intimately connected to—a broader pattern of conduct that itself justified impeachment. Our position is consistent with the first article of impeachment that the House Judiciary Committee approved against Richard Nixon on July 27, 1974. It is occasionally suggested that this article proves that presidential lies are impeachable in their own right. That's because the eighth paragraph of the article accused Nixon of "making or causing to be made false or misleading public statements for the purpose of deceiving the people of the United States." But read in context, this paragraph merely described one of nine separately-alleged "means" that Nixon "used to implement" the offense actually charged as impeachable: obstructing justice in the Watergate investigation. Nixon's lies were essential to the execution of that cover-up, and so they were properly included in the article of impeachment.

Thus, even if we treat the Nixon articles as carrying the weight of congressional precedent (and it's worth recalling that they were never voted on by the House or Senate), they don't suggest that a pattern of lies is removable. Rather, they show only that lies in furtherance of a broader plot against democracy may support the case for impeachment. This point is not true only of lies, but also applies to statements that undermine democratic values and institutions.

Ironically, one of the main reasons that Trump's public statements have avoided impeachment territory is that his own officials have ignored them. Since taking office, Trump has repeatedly urged the FBI and Justice Department to investigate and prosecute his political opponents, to show leniency to his allies and associates, and to support demonstrably false claims (e.g., that Barack Obama wiretapped him and that Russia never interfered in our elections). Trump has also declared that prosecutors should seek harsh sentences against those who cooperate with Mueller, and has criticized the Attorney General for bringing charges against "two very popular Republican Congressmen . . . just ahead of the Mid-Terms." In other contexts, Trump has called upon police to rough up suspects during arrests, expressed support for severe restrictions on the free press, and urged regulators to target his political critics.

In a normal administration, the president's word on such matters would carry decisive weight. He alone possesses "the Executive power" under Article II of the Constitution. But the "unitary executive" theory has fared poorly since Trump entered the White House. As Jack Goldsmith writes, "What is most remarkable is the extent to which his senior officials act as if Trump were not the chief executive. Never has a president been so regularly ignored or contradicted by his own officials."[16] This tendency, Goldsmith adds, is not confined to low-level bureaucrats or the "deep state": "I'm talking about senior officials in the Justice Department and the military and intelligence and foreign affairs agencies. And they are not just ignoring or contradicting him in private. They are doing so in public for all the world to see."

If Trump's tweets were actually implemented as policy, they would support multiple articles of impeachment. The widespread practice of ignoring his statements—or treating them as merely advisory—has thus saved Trump from potentially dire political consequences. Under normal circumstances, we wouldn't celebrate a president's inability to superintend his own branch of government. But these are hardly "normal" circumstances. All of us, arguably including Trump, should be thankful for this bout of intermittent insubordination.

* * *

Now that we've explored limits on impeachable offenses, we can turn to the other side of the ledger. In Chapter 2, we identified four allegations meriting further investigation: (1) improper dealings with Russia surrounding the 2016 presidential election; (2) obstruction of justice in Russia-related investigations; (3) abuse of the pardon power; and (4) implementing kleptocracy in the federal government. We stand by our original conclusions. Indeed, in many respects the facts have grown worse for Trump. The evidence of sketchy interactions with Russia during the election is now much stronger; his assaults on the Russia investigation have continued apace; and Trump's financial entanglements with the Saudis might well have affected his extremely weak response to the gruesome murder of a *Washington Post* journalist at the direction of Prince Mohammed bin Salman.

Based on more recent developments, we believe that two more potential "high Crimes and Misdemeanors" warrant investigation. But we also believe that both of them involve a number of under-appreciated complexities that require further reflection.

First, Trump should be investigated for corrupt failure to defend the United States—and its electoral system—against domestic operations launched by a hostile foreign power. As Bauer has written, "Trump is misleading the American people about the very fact of Russia's actions and, according to intelligence officials, Russia's plans to press [its] attacks in the future. He has declined to vigorously lead in defending against these assaults: He is virtually flaunting his unwillingness to do so."[17] One of the president's most basic responsibilities is to protect this nation from foreign attacks. Just as he is obliged to repel foreign armies, so must he guard against cyberattacks and intelligence operations designed to destabilize democracy and undermine our electoral system. In light of the overwhelming, terrifying evidence of ongoing Russian interference, Trump's ostentatious failure to defend the country—or even to recognize that we're under assault—is an unconscionable abdication of his duties as president.

It is possible to argue that Trump's inaction is, by itself, an impeachable offense. On this view, Trump is guilty of *nonfeasance*: a failure to act when action is required. In Chapter 2, we discussed Akhil Amar's argument that "gross dereliction of duty imperiling the national security . . . might well rise to the level of disqualifying misconduct."[18] That view is also supported by Charles L. Black, Jr.'s hypothetical about a president who moves to Saudi Arabia and seeks to conduct his job "by mail and wireless from there."[19] Or to offer a closer analogy, imagine if Franklin D. Roosevelt had done nothing on December 7, 1941; it seems hard to imagine that he wouldn't have been removed for inaction (and rightly so). Several commentators, including Holtzman, have relied on similar logic to contend that Trump's failure to act in response to Russian attacks on our democracy is inherently impeachable.[20]

Of course, as philosophers delight in pointing out, the line between "action" and "inaction" is slippery. That is most certainly true here. It appears as though Trump has not merely *forgotten* or *neglected* to act; rather, he has made a *considered decision* against doing so. Put differently, his chosen course of action is not to act. Viewed this way, the key question is *why* he has decided against defending the nation. Does he have a comprehensible, legitimate justification relating to foreign policy, domestic governance, or America's national security? In that case, his only offense may be maladministration. Or are his motives largely or entirely illegitimate? In our view, it would be appropriate to impeach a president who ignores a foreign nation's attacks on our democracy because he hopes that nation will help him at the polls or in future business endeavors; or because he fears compromising the legitimacy of his own election; or because that nation has some kind of actual or suspected leverage over him or his family. Trump's motives for adopting this policy of apparent inaction are therefore worthy of investigation.

Any such investigation should also encompass the other elements of "high Crimes and Misdemeanors." Many nations engage in intelligence and cyber operations directed at the United States. The president is not mandated to address every single one. Impeachment would be permissible only if Trump's failure to act in response to Russian inference was, in fact, likely to pose a grave risk of harm to the nation. Congress would also have to assess whether Trump's failure to act was so clearly wrong that he had fair notice of potential removal on this basis. To make these determinations, Congress would have to weigh Trump's motives for inaction, which might themselves signal a substantial risk of harm to the United States if he were to remain in office. Further, Congress would likely need to assess intelligence findings, prior counterintelligence activities, our relationship with Russia, and the state of global affairs. The complexity of these judgments might make it difficult to justify impeaching on this basis. But we believe that Trump's failure to defend the nation may qualify as impeachable.

The same is true of allegations that Trump broke the law during the 2016 presidential election. Here we have in mind Trump's personal involvement in directing payments to two women to suppress their allegations of sexual impropriety. Trump appears to have given this order not to protect his family or private reputation, but to benefit his presidential campaign.

That conduct, undertaken in concert with his lawyer Michael Cohen, violated federal law and deprived the public of facts that Trump evidently feared might turn voters against him. Here's how prosecutors described the nature and gravity of the offense in a sentencing memorandum for Cohen: "While many Americans who desired a particular outcome to the election knocked on doors, toiled at phone banks or found any number of other legal ways to make their voices heard, Cohen sought to influence the election from the shadows. He did so by orchestrating secret and illegal payments to silence two women who otherwise would have made public their alleged extramarital affairs with Individual-1 [a.k.a. Trump]. In the process, Cohen deceived the voting public by hiding alleged facts that he believed would have had a substantial effect on the election."[21] The Manhattan-based prosecutors who filed this memo are independent of Mueller. And they found that Cohen "acted in coordination with and at the direction of Indivudual-1."

Trump and his lawyers have desperately downplayed the seriousness of this allegation. They have also pretended that the campaign finance laws are endlessly confusing, or hopelessly ambiguous, on the legality of this conduct. Poppycock. It seems fairly clear that the president personally directed criminal conduct for the specific purpose of increasing his odds of winning the election. As Rick Hasen has observed, "these are serious criminal activities for which others have gone to jail."[22]

The main question that remains is whether Trump *willfully* broke the law when he directed Cohen's conduct. But given the nature, timing, and elaborate structuring of these hush payments, as well as Trump's participation in the meeting where this scheme was set up, it seems likely that the president willfully directed a crime in hopes of affecting the election outcome. This assessment of Trump's mental state is bolstered by his subsequent conduct: shifting from one lie to another as evidence came to light proving that he knew about the payments and helped orchestrate them. That isn't how an innocent man behaves. Viewing Trump's conduct as a whole, we see a sustained disregard for the law—and a willingness to use his wealth in illegal ways while buying silence from those who might harm his political fortunes with the truth.

As we explain in Chapter 2, pre-inauguration wrongdoing aimed at the corrupt acquisition of office is impeachable. So Trump's misconduct can't be set aside on the ground that it occurred before Election Day. This raises a question: how do we decide when pre-inauguration conduct is properly ranked as a "high Crime and Misdemeanor"? Philip Bobbitt has recently identified several principles to guide this analysis: "When a substantial attempt is made by a candidate to procure the presidency by corrupt means, we may presume that he at least thought this would make a difference in the outcome, and thus we should resolve any doubts as to the effects of his efforts against him. Yet we must confine the operation of such a rule to truly substantial [misconduct], lest we ensnare every successful campaign in an unending postmortem in search of [impeachable] misdeeds."[23]

As Bobbitt's formulation suggests, not every campaign misdeed—indeed, not every crime—will qualify as an impeachable offense. Before impeaching, we must ask all of the questions we ordinarily ask about alleged presidential wrongdoing. In that analysis, it may be relevant whether the candidate's misdeeds actually affected the election outcome. But in our view, that is not (and can't be) the determinative question. Campaigns are chaotic, contingent, and highly momentum-driven. Their outcomes invariably have many causes. Except where a candidate tampered with ballots or bribed members of the Electoral College, it will nearly always be impossible to assess in retrospect whether a specific misdeed affected the outcome. That is especially true when the misdeed involved stealing information or silencing accusers. As Bobbitt suggests, the more helpful question is whether a candidate *believed* his conduct would likely affect the outcome. We might also focus on factors including the scope and severity of the offense, whether it was linked to a broader pattern of misconduct, whether it is likely to recur in future political efforts, whether it may compromise the candidate once in office, and whether it involved creating and coordinating a multi-member criminal conspiracy.

We are not yet in a position to answer some of these questions with respect to Trump's hush money payments. What does seem clear is that Trump engaged in meaningful election-related misconduct—some of which involved contact with foreign powers, some of which involved violations of federal criminal law, and some of which might check both boxes. It is also clear that numerous senior figures around Trump, not to mention Trump himself, have lied about important facts relating to his campaign activities while seeking to discredit investigators. Given all this, there is a compelling basis for further investigation to assess whether Trump may have committed campaign-related impeachable offenses. Congress and federal prosecutors should therefore persist in their efforts to ascertain what happened. Congress must then decide whether further proceedings, including impeachment hearings, are proper.

*   *   *

Many of the potential "high Crimes and Misdemeanors" discussed above extend beyond violations of the criminal law. All of them turn on an assessment of whether the president acted with corrupt motives. There can be no doubt that these are permissible considerations in the law of impeachment. As we show in Chapter 2, that conclusion follows inevitably from the Constitution's text and structure, as well as original public meaning, historical practice, and the basic purpose of the impeachment power. In books published over the past two years, Phillip Bobbitt, Jeffrey

A. Engel, Michael Gerhardt, Elizabeth Holtzman, and Cass Sunstein—among others—have explored these issues anew.[24] They offer powerful arguments that confirm and complement our own.

The main outlier is Alan Dershowitz, a brilliant former Harvard Law professor who has appointed himself as Trump's pugnacious public defender. For all the flak he has received, Dershowitz raises important concerns about politicizing impeachment and criminalizing ordinary politics. But in *The Case Against Impeaching Trump*, Dershowitz overplays his hand. He starts by casting himself in the role of the hero—a lone, principled libertarian standing athwart the deranged anti-Trump horde. He then develops an account of the impeachment power that guts it of any substance. In his zeal to defend Trump, Dershowitz all but writes the Impeachment Clause out of the Constitution—and offers a lesson in how *not* to interpret our founding charter.

First consider Dershowitz's claim that *only* crimes are impeachable. This is a helpful starting point because he tries to support that assertion mainly by attacking our book.[25] His opening gambit is to frame the disagreement as a clash between originalism and living constitutionalism: "The question is whether the enumerated criteria for impeachment are *alive* or *dead*."[26] On that view, Dershowitz cares about the settled meaning of "high Crimes and Misdemeanors" in the 1780s, whereas we are happy to make things up willy-nilly. But here Dershowitz faces a big problem: in Chapter 2, we draw extensively on original public meaning and demonstrate that it supports our conclusions about impeachable offenses.

Perhaps for this reason, Dershowitz pivots almost immediately to a very different and quite radical claim: that we don't need to consider history—originalist or otherwise—because the text is unambiguous. Here's how he puts it:

When the Constitution speaks in clear terms, its plain meaning must prevail over other considerations. It's hard to imagine a clearer set of words than those governing impeachment:

"The President, Vice President, and all civil officers of the United States shall be removed from office on impeachment for, and conviction of, treason, bribery, and other high crimes and misdemeanors." The text speaks clearly of *crimes*, enumerating treason, bribery, and other high crimes and misdemeanors. It requires a trial in the Senate and *conviction* of one or more of those crimes.[27]

There's a lot happening in this paragraph—which comprises the crux of Dershowitz's argument—so let's break it down.

First, Dershowitz runs away from his flashy assertions about originalism. This is confirmed a few pages later, when he insists that "the plain meaning must prevail over all other interpretive mechanisms, since it was the word[s], not the intentions behind them, that were voted on and accepted."[28] Just look at the text, he insists. Never mind history, context, purpose, or practice. Isn't it *obvious* that this language requires proof of indictable crimes?

No, it isn't. For starters, Dershowitz's textual argument is unconvincing on its own terms. To be sure, "treason" and "bribery" are crimes. And as we explain in Chapter 2, the *ejusdem generis* principle suggests that a catch-all phrase like "other high Crimes and Misdemeanors" must capture misdeeds of the same kind as "treason" and "bribery." But this raises a question: *which* attributes of "treason" and "bribery" also apply to "high Crimes and Misdemeanors"? The text alone doesn't tell us. It is hardly self-evident that the defining characteristic of "treason" and "bribery" as impeachable offenses is that they are also punishable as crimes. Moreover, if the goal was to limit impeachment to violations of the criminal law, it seems odd that the Impeachment Clause uses a parliamentary term of art—"high Crimes and Misdemeanors"—that appears neither in the criminal law itself nor anywhere else in the Constitution (which *does* refer to "crimes" and "offenses"). It would have been easy to write a provision limiting the impeachment power to serious crimes—and yet the Framers didn't go that route. So on close inspection, the "plain meaning" of the text isn't as "plain" as Dershowitz insists.

This is why scholars have recognized for centuries that we must look beyond the "plain text." And once we do so, the problems with Dershowitz's position grow exponentially. We cover many of the key points in Chapter 2. To summarize:

- There is powerful historical evidence that the meaning of "high Crimes and Misdemeanors" extended past the criminal law to capture "great and dangerous offenses" against the nation
- The structure of the Constitution—including the Bill of Attainder Clause, *Ex Post Facto* Clause, and Pardon Clause—shows that the Framers separated criminality and impeachability
- There was no body of criminal law in the 1780s that would suffice: it would offend federalism to treat *state* crimes as impeachable, but Congress lacked the authority to enumerate many *federal* crimes
- Given the purposes of the impeachment power as described by those who created it, a categorical restriction to criminal law would be impractical and absurd

Dershowitz barely responds to these arguments. Instead, he dismisses the historical evidence as entirely irrelevant, and ignores the bulk of our structural and practical reasoning.

That said, Dershowitz does offer some structural claims of his own. The first rests on two premises: (1) the Senate must "try" impeachments; and (2) the result of the trial may be a "conviction." It follows, according to Dershowitz, that the impeachment trial process has a criminal quality.[29]

This argument presumes that any adjudication resulting in a conviction must be criminal in character—and so must the underlying offenses. But that presumption is wrong, both as a matter of common English usage and historical practice. Neither "try" nor "conviction" automatically implies a determination of *criminal* guilt. To the contrary, a president can be tried for (and convicted of) *political crimes*, including abuse of power and betraying the nation.

Moreover, as we show in Chapter 4, the Senate may "try" an impeachment case in a manner very different from what occurs in criminal court. Those differences flow from the Constitution itself. The Fifth and Sixth Amendments impose safeguards on criminal trials that, by their express terms, *cannot* apply to the Senate sitting as court of impeachment. For example, the Fifth Amendment requires that trial for "a capital, or otherwise infamous crime" be preceded by "a presentment or indictment of a Grand Jury." The Sixth Amendment, in turn, requires "a speedy and public trial, by an impartial jury of the State and district wherein the crime shall have been committed." Neither of these criminal law rules could possibly apply to the Senate in an impeachment case.

That is just the tip of the iceberg. As a matter of text and historical practice, the Senate is not required by the Fifth and Sixth Amendments to recognize rights to counsel, to confront accusers, to a public trial, to avoid self-incrimination, or to the full range of due process safeguards applicable in a criminal hearing. And on the flip side, Article I, § 3 mandates several rules unique to presidential impeachment trials: a special oath, a supermajority voting requirement, and the Chief Justice as presiding officer. (The Chief Justice presides not because the Senate is convened as a criminal court, but rather to lend solemnity and to prevent the conflict of interest that would arise if the Vice President presided.) With respect to all other procedural issues, Article I, § 5, empowers the Senate to "determine the Rules of its Proceedings." While there are some similarities between impeachments and criminal trials, there are also many fundamental differences.

Dershowitz's argument thus falls apart. The Senate's duty to "try" cases of impeachment says little or nothing about which offenses are impeachable. Instead, this rule speaks to the nature of impeachment trials as quasi-judicial: rather than *vote*, the Senate must *adjudicate*. Viewed this way, it's natural to treat a guilty verdict as a "conviction."

As part of his effort to show that only crimes are impeachable, Dershowitz also grasps at Article III, § 2, which provides: "the Trial of all Crimes, except in Cases of Impeachment, shall be by Jury."[30] Here the flaw is obvious. Some crimes *are* impeachable. Article III, § 2 simply confirms that even when a president (or another civil officer) is impeached for conduct involving crimes, the impeachment hearing shall occur in Congress, rather than before a jury.

Accordingly, there's no merit to Dershowitz's position. Every rule of constitutional interpretation cuts against it.

So does common sense. Near the end of his discussion, Dershowitz offers the following example to prove the depth of his conviction that only crimes are impeachable:

> Assume Putin decides to "retake" Alaska, the way he "retook" Crimea. Assume further that a president allows him to do it, because he believed that Russia has a legitimate claim to "its" original territory. That would be terrible, but would it be impeachable? Not under the text of the Constitution. (It would, of course, be different if he did it because he was paid or extorted.)[31]

Dershowitz prudently admits that such traitorous conduct would be disturbing. But in his view, we can't impeach a president for giving away swaths of American territory to a foreign adversary. And in his telling, this is *all* the Framers' fault—the only fix available to us is a constitutional amendment.

To borrow a line from Antonin Scalia, that is "pure applesauce."[32] It's also exactly the wrong way to interpret the Constitution. When we know what the Framers sought to achieve, we should to seek vindicate rather than torpedo their goals. In defiance of that principle, Dershowitz would leave the nation defenseless against presidential abuse, betrayal, and corruption that doesn't fall within the four corners of the criminal code. And he would do so on the basis of flimsy, results-oriented logic that collapses upon scrutiny.

* * *

Like any good defense lawyer, Dershowitz has more cards to play. In addition to limiting "high Crimes and Misdemeanors" to crimes in the federal statute books, he would impose another major caveat: The President's "motives or state of mind in taking constitutionally authorized actions [can't] be questioned as part of a criminal or impeachment investigation."[33] Put differently, if the president has the raw constitutional power to do what he did, we cannot consider why he did it. That rule covers granting pardons, firing senior officials, giving orders to the FBI and CIA, declassifying sensitive information, revoking security clearances, directing counter-intelligence (or failing to do so), and lots more.

Remarkably, Dershowitz does not deign to offer a legal argument for this conclusion. He conjures it out of thin air, referring vaguely to Article II, which vests the president with "the executive Power." Citing the Speech and Debate Clause, which applies only to legislators, Dershowitz adds that this (alleged) rule exists for "the same reasons members of Congress and the judiciary generally cannot be charged or questioned for their legislative or judicial actions."[34]

Dershowitz's analogy rests on rotten foundations. If a judge imposed a harsh sentence in exchange for a bribe, Congress would be free to impeach that judge—both for accepting the bribe and for corruptly imposing the sentence. As the Supreme Court has explained, "if in the exercise of the powers with which they are clothed as ministers of justice, [judges] act with partiality, or maliciously, or corruptly, or arbitrarily, or oppressively, they may be called to an account by impeachment."[35] Turning to Congress, it's simply untrue that legislators' motives are beyond inquiry; courts regularly consider "legislative intent" when reviewing laws.[36] Further, several legislators have been indicted and convicted for engaging in official action on the basis of corrupt or criminal motives.[37] And the Expulsion Clause, which permits each house of Congress to expel a member "with the Concurrence of two thirds," imposes no limit on assessing a member's motives for inappropriate conduct undertaken in an official capacity.[38]

Dershowitz's theory that impeachment hearings can't test a president's motives is also inconsistent with historical practice. In its first article of impeachment against Nixon, the House Judiciary Committee accused him of "endeavoring to misuse the Central Intelligence Agency," as well as "interfering or endeavoring to interfere with the conduct of investigations by the Department of Justice of the United States, the Federal Bureau of Investigation, the office of Watergate Special Prosecution Force, and Congressional Committees."[39] Each allegation encompassed conduct within Nixon's constitutional authority, but deemed it impeachable because Nixon's motives were abusive and corrupt.

That said, of all the problems with Dershowitz's claim, here's the biggest: it would mean that the president can almost never be impeached, under any circumstances, for how he uses—or abuses—his constitutional powers.

Generally speaking, impeachable offenses (criminal or not) require proof of deliberate, knowing wrongdoing. In *Cramer v. United States*, the Supreme Court held that treason requires proof of a "disloyal state of mind"; a person must "intend to betray his country by means of the act."[40] In *United States v. Sun-Diamond Growers of California*, the Court explained that bribery requires "a *quid pro quo*—a specific intent to give or receive something of value in exchange for an official act."[41] And as the Court noted in *Elonis v. United States*, "the general rule is that a guilty mind is a necessary element in the indictment and proof of every crime."[42] This rule applies fully to perjury, obstruction of justice, witness tampering, destruction of evidence, and most other crimes.

If Congress is forbidden to consider his "motives or state of mind," the president is practically immune from removal for abusing his powers. This seems clear, though Dershowitz denies it. For instance, in his "returning Alaska" example, Dershowitz allows for impeachment if the president "did it because he was paid or extorted."[43] But in that sentence, "because" refers to the president's motives—which Dershowitz tells us two pages earlier can't be "questioned as part of a criminal or impeachment investigation."[44]

Ultimately, in the name of defending Trump, Dershowitz destroys the impeachment power. We've covered only two of his unsupportable moves: limiting impeachment to crimes and preventing any analysis of motive. He also contorts key federal criminal laws into nothingness (including those that address conspiracy and coordination with foreign powers); demands an absurdly high burden of proof; suggests that the Chief Justice can unilaterally dismiss impeachment charges in the Senate; and contends that the Supreme Court may well be required to substantively review impeachment judgments. Then, after all this, Dershowitz comes shockingly close to implying that Trump might refuse to leave office if he were impeached and convicted on grounds—or with procedures—that Trump unilaterally deemed inadequate.[45]

The very fact that Trump's public advocate can credibly imagine him defying conviction on articles of impeachment is clear evidence of Trump's autocratic pretensions. Indeed, it is revealing that Dershowitz believes the best strategy here is a series of claims meant to confound and eviscerate the impeachment power. When "The Case Against Impeaching Trump" amounts to "The Case Against Impeaching Ever," it's hard to avoid the conclusion that Trump is in dangerous territory.

* * *

In the near future, the American people may well have to decide whether impeachment is an appropriate response to Trump's wrongdoing. This book has identified many of the most important considerations relevant to that decision. As we've made clear, impeachment always poses a grave risk of enduring national trauma. But in some circumstances, *not* impeaching would be much more dangerous. And in this age of broken politics, it is entirely possible that impeachment may be fully justified yet politically impossible. Navigating these treacherous waters will require top flight political judgment, as well as an abiding commitment to our democratic order. It will also require an appreciation of the fact that reasonable people can disagree in good faith on such difficult questions.

Recently, several scholars have sounded a distinctly sour note about impeachment. Jeffrey Engel, for instance, warns that impeachment "disrupts the American political landscape as few other events do, leaving scars for generations while dimming the political careers of all involved."[46] Surveying the Johnson, Nixon, and Clinton cases, he warns that using and talking about impeachment has caused much more harm than good. He adds that this will remain true in our "tribal political environment," which prevents agreement on "basic facts" and thwarts the "widespread moral outrage" necessary to muster sixty-seven senators.[47] The nation should therefore take a big step back from impeachment: "So long as there remains no doubt that the next election will occur (and its results trusted), we would all be less frustrated if we focused on winning the next rather than litigating the last."[48]

This outlook is shaped by anxiety about Americans' increased unwillingness to accept election results. In recent years, presidents have not only faced ordinary opposition, but also claims that they are somehow illegitimate. Needless to say, the Tea Party's animus-laden objections to Obama can be distinguished from more substantial criticism of Trump: there was never any hint that Obama obtained office through corrupt means. Still, it is unnerving that so many people on both sides of the aisle now view the opposing party as un-American—and are quick to contest the validity of any election they lose. As Jane Chong notes, "our faith in the presidency has become contingent on the identity of the party controlling it. It is no faith at all."[49] To the extent our nation's recent spike in impeachment talk partakes of that partisan worldview, in which the opposition is evil and can never legitimately exercise power, there are reasons to worry.

A final, related ground for hesitancy about impeachment shines through in Peter Baker's masterful account of the Clinton case. As Baker notes, Clinton's defense rested on a single strategy: "Consensus was their enemy; partisanship was the key to acquittal."[50] Democrats therefore "decided to turn every issue into a party-line struggle, regardless of the merits," since "the more partisan the impeachment effort looked, the less legitimate it would seem in the eyes of the public."[51] To be sure, Republicans were hardly innocent: the impeachment campaign rested at least as much on personal animus and partisan hostility as it did on any legitimate principles. As we make clear in Chapter 1, we do not believe the case against Clinton justified his removal. But there's no denying that Clinton and his allies took every opportunity to magnify partisanship throughout the impeachment process. And in the end, this tactic helped Clinton keep his job.

The lesson is clear: A president facing impeachment will be powerfully motivated to amplify partisan hostility, even as he sows doubt about the facts, attacks investigators and journalists, and discredits or minimizes the rules he's accused of violating. This defense strategy can *itself* inflict great harm on our polity—especially in an environment primed for polarization.

Of course, as we emphasize throughout the book, all these warnings about the risks of ending a presidency must be balanced against the dangers of *not* impeaching. There may come a point at which the scales tip. Some believe we are already there—and that the moment calls for courage, not caution. Holtzman exemplifies this outlook: "It's easy to find reasons to be anxious. I'm not afraid."[52] Holtzman invokes her own role in the Nixon hearings, whose "thorough, fair, and above all bipartisan proceedings" offer a "blueprint for how an impeachment can be successfully pursued today."[53]

Watergate is a powerful case study about the risks of not impeaching after revelations of grave presidential misconduct. Imagine a world where Nixon's involvement in the Watergate saga was never discovered. That should be easy: the Watergate story is riddled with contingencies that happened to break the right way at the right time. In that world, Nixon still would have committed "high Crimes and Misdemeanors." If historians subsequently discovered his crimes, they would be horrified. But the harm caused by his secret, undiscovered wrongdoing would be far less than in our own world. The public revelation of Nixon's abuses and crimes—along with Nixon's attempted cover-up and related obstruction of justice—*itself* amplified the damage. It also drastically increased the perils of not impeaching. Once enough people appreciated what Nixon had done, a decision to leave him in power would have created a precedent, and supported a perception of tolerable presidential conduct, that would have undermined our democracy far more than the actual Watergate break-in. In this peculiar sense, one of Nixon's most egregious impeachable offenses arising from Watergate was getting caught.

That lesson may soon have relevance in our own time. If the investigations into Trump produce concrete proof of grievous wrongdoing, a decision to leave him in office might cause far more harm than a decision to impeach.

Although upsetting to contemplate, it is possible that only 65 percent of the nation would believe a report which convincingly demonstrates "high Crimes and Misdemeanors." After all, Trump has worked hard to discredit investigators, and some Americans have been numbed to scandal by the endless parade of presidential misdeeds in plain sight. In the event of a public schism over proof of Trump's misdeeds, the Democrat-controlled House might well have the votes to impeach, but it may appear exceptionally doubtful that the Senate (with 53 Republicans) would be willing to convict.

Anticipating this possibility, several commentators have argued the House would be *obligated* to impeach. Steyer, for instance, asserts that "anything less would mean abandoning the Constitution."[54] And Cass Sunstein contends, "if the president has clearly committed an impeachable offense, the House has a constitutional duty to impeach him."[55]

As we explain in Chapter 3, that is incorrect. Even when legislators believe that the president has committed impeachable offenses, the law vests them with a nearly unbounded prerogative not to end his term in office. Within this sphere of discretion, the key judgment is whether impeaching the president would vindicate the Constitution and serve the greater interests of the nation.

In answering these questions, the House may account for a wide range of factors—including the odds of conviction in the Senate. To be sure, the House holds the "sole Power of Impeachment." It cannot properly abdicate that "sole Power" by giving the upper chamber an effective veto. But in assessing the risks of impeaching and not impeaching, as well as the adequacy of alternatives, the odds of conviction are a highly relevant factor. Indeed, it's commonplace for branches of government to exercise their unique constitutional powers with an eye on how the other branches will react. There's no good reason why impeachment should be an exception to that general rule. Just as the House is free to consider how the president has responded to impeachment hearings (and how he might respond to impeachment), so can the House consider how the Senate is likely to receive its arguments.

Further, to extend the analogy described in Chapter 3, nobody thinks a prosecutor with the sole power to file criminal charges is obliged to ignore how prospective jurors may be inclined to view the facts (or how reviewing judges may view the law). Here, unlike most prosecutors, the House knows in advance of bringing charges precisely who the individuals comprising the adjudicatory authority will be. As a matter of common sense and political wisdom, it would be exceedingly strange to require the House to treat that information as irrelevant to its deliberations.

In our view, there should be a strong presumption against impeachment in the House when it appears all but certain that the Senate will acquit. We appreciate the moral satisfaction of impeaching on principle. We realize that doing nothing might seem reckless or even immoral. And we agree that minds can be changed, especially if the House marshals a powerful case. But a failed impeachment would surely prove catastrophic to the very democratic principles and institutions it was initiated to save. As unsatisfactory as the alternatives might seem, activating the impeachment power is so traumatic for the nation—and so bruising for our political system—that it shouldn't be undertaken unless there is a serious likelihood of actually *removing* the president.

We thus agree with the standard offered by House Judiciary Committee Chairman Jerrold Nadler: "You have to be able to think at the beginning of the impeachment process that the evidence is so clear, of offenses so grave, that once you've laid out all the evidence, a good fraction of the opposition, the voters, will reluctantly admit to themselves 'They have to do it.'"[56] This approach is necessary, Nadler added, "because you don't want to tear the country apart."

* * *

In *Tyrant*, Stephen Greenblatt draws on his mastery of Shakespeare to explore the social breakdown that leads to tyranny: "The voice, even the very thought, of the opponent [becomes] almost unendurable. You are either with me or against me—and if you are not with me, I hate you and want to destroy you and all your adherents. Each party naturally seeks power, but seeking power becomes itself the expression of rage: I crave the power to crush you."[57] Slowly and then quickly, "it all begins to spiral out of control."

This dynamic is hauntingly familiar. If we are to arrest that spiral in our own time, we must find ways to overcome the forces of tribalism and partisanship that have overtaken so much of American life. We must also address the terrible harm to democracy that Trump has already inflicted and will continue to inflict. Impeachment may play a vital role in that process, or it may explode all that we're fighting to preserve. There are few easy answers here. We can but hope that this book has armed you with the right questions and the tools to help defend our democracy.

ACKNOWLEDGMENTS

Writing about impeachment is an exhilarating and maddening experience—especially in the Age of Trump. We could not have completed this book, or maintained perspective on its subject, without extraordinary support from our friends and families.

Where else to begin than with our partners? We thank Elizabeth Westling (Larry) and Hillel Smith (Joshua) for their love, insight, editorial guidance, and patience. Especially their patience. They stood by us through writer's block and blown deadlines, through fried hard drives and personal tragedies. When impeachment was all we could think, speak, or dream about, they did a valiant job of feigning interest. And when we worked around the clock, deep into caffeinated nights, they sacrificed with us to make this book possible. We are lucky, indeed, to have found such marvelous and talented partners in crime.

We must also thank our families. It's impossible to overstate how much their support has meant to us, both in writing this book and in so many other ways. We owe them more than we can express in words.

Just days before we completed this manuscript, Larry suddenly and unexpectedly lost his only sibling, Al Tribe (known to Larry and a few others as "Shurka"). Shurka was a constant source of strength and support. When he and Larry last spoke,

Shurka emphasized that he looked forward to reading this book. No one could ask for a better brother.

Of course, a book like this one required extensive research into law, history, and politics. In performing that work, we were aided by a stellar crew of undergraduates and law students. For their excellent work, we are grateful to Nicole Antoine, Hunter Fortney, Zeenia Framroze, Viviana Hanley, Andrew Jing, Andrew Sacks, Crispin Smith, Maile Yeats-Rowe, Ashim Vaish, and Andrew Yodis. We extend special thanks to Quent Fox, Daniel Ottaunick, Derek Reinbold, and Lark Turner, each of whom made particularly substantial contributions and helped us refine our view of impeachment. In addition, we received invaluable feedback on the manuscript from Travis Crum, Michael Dorf, Aaron Kotler, Leah Litman, Aaron Marcus, Erin Monju, Zachary Price, and Isaac Saidal-Goley. They made this book better. Needless to say, we take sole responsibility for any errors or omissions in the manuscript—though we hope they are few and insignificant!

As any author learns early on, writing a book is a team effort. We were privileged to work with a remarkable team at Basic Books. In particular, we had the good fortune of collaborating with a gifted editor, Brian Distelberg. Brian and his colleagues—including Lara Heimert, Betsy DeJesu, Isadora Johnson, Allie Finkel, Connie Capone, and Michelle Welsh-Horst—improved our prose and sharpened our vision. We also thank our agents, Ike Williams and Katherine Flynn of Kneerim & Williams, for their expert guidance.

Working on this book required much of our attention in late 2017. We are therefore grateful to our colleagues for their support, encouragement, and flexibility. Larry thanks Harvard Law School, and Joshua thanks Gupta Wessler PLLC and Kaplan & Company LLP. *To End a Presidency* reflects our views alone—not those of our institutions and employers—but we have learned much from our thoughtful, dedicated peers.

Finally, we thank each other. Writing a book—and doing so while based in different cities—could tax even the strongest of friendships. That's especially true when the authors don't see eye-to-eye on every issue. Instead, this process has been fun and collaborative. We've learned from each other, and we're grateful for that.

NOTES

PREFACE

1. Ezra Klein, "The Case for Normalizing Impeachment," *Vox*, November 30, 2017.

2. Cass Sunstein, *#Republic: Divided Democracy in the Age of Social Media* (Princeton: Princeton University Press, 2017), 78.

CHAPTER 1: WHY IMPEACHMENT?

1. Max Farrand, ed., "July 20," in *The Records of the Federal Convention of 1787*, rev. ed., vol. 2 (New Haven: Yale University Press, 1966), 65.

2. Raoul Berger, *Impeachment: The Constitutional Problems* (Cambridge: Harvard University Press, 1973), 1.

3. Peter Charles Hoffer and N. E. H. Hull, *Impeachment in America, 1635–1805* (New Haven: Yale University Press, 1984), 9.

4. Farrand, "July 20," in *The Records of the Federal Convention of 1787*, vol. 2, 61.

5. Farrand, "July 18," in *The Records of the Federal Convention of 1787*, vol. 2, 42.

6. Farrand, "July 20," in *The Records of the Federal Convention of 1787*, vol. 2, 65.

7. Ibid., 64.

8. Ibid., 65–66.

9. Ibid., 67.

10. Ibid., 65.

11. Ibid., 65–67.

12. Ibid., 67.

13. Ibid., 67–68.

14. Farrand, "June 2," in *The Records of the Federal Convention of 1787*, vol. 1, 86.

15. Alexander Hamilton, *Federalist* No. 69, in *The Federalist Papers*, ed. Clinton Rossiter (1961), 444–445.

16. Farrand, "July 20," in *The Records of the Federal Convention of 1787*, vol. 2, 68.

17. Farrand, "July 24," in *The Records of the Federal Convention of 1787*, vol. 2, 103.

18. Farrand, "July 20," in *The Records of the Federal Convention of 1787*, vol. 2, 66.

19. Michael J. Klarman, *The Framers' Coup: The Making of the United States Constitution* (New York: Oxford University Press, 2016), 237.

20. Farrand, "July 20," in *The Records of the Federal Convention of 1787*, vol. 2, 66.

21. *Free Enter. Club v. Pub. Co. Accounting Oversight Bd.*, 561 U.S. 477, 500 (2010).

22. Alexis de Tocqueville, *Democracy in America*, vol. 1 (Boston: John Allyn, 1882).

23. Ibid., 139.

24. Ibid., 136.

25. Michael Gerhardt, *The Federal Impeachment Process: A Constitutional and Historical Analysis*, 2nd ed. (Chicago: University of Chicago Press, 2000), 4.

26. de Tocqueville, *Democracy in America*, vol. 1, 135.

27. Joseph Story, *Commentaries on the Constitution of the United States*, § 785 (Boston: Little, Brown, and Company, 1873), 554.

28. "Letter from Joseph Story to Francis Lieber" (May 9, 1840), in *Life and Letters of Joseph Story, Associate Justice of the Supreme Court of the United States and Dane Professor of Law at Harvard University*, vol. 2, ed. William W. Story (London: J. Chapman, 1851), 330.

29. de Tocqueville, Democracy in America, vol. 1, 138.

30. Ibid., 139.

31. Ibid., 137.

32. Ibid., 136

33. Ibid., 137

34. Ibid., 139.

35. Ibid.

36. *Free Enterprise Fund,* 561 U.S. at 522 (Breyer, dissenting).

37. Stan Lee and Steve Ditko, "Spider-Man," in *Amazing Fantasy* 1, no. 15 (New York: Marvel Comics, 1962), 13.

38. "Letter from Henry Clay to J. J. Crittenden" (July 16, 1842), in *The Life of John J. Crittenden, with Selections from His Correspondence and Speeches*, vol. 1, ed. Chapman Coleman (Philadelphia: J. B. Lippincott & Co., 1873), 188–189.

39. "Letter from John Tyler to Robert McCandlish" (July 10, 1842), quoted in Gary May, *John Tyler* (New York: Henry Holt & Co., 2008), 80.

40. Michael Gerhardt, *The Forgotten Presidents: Their Untold Constitutional Legacy* (Oxford: Oxford University Press, 2013), 58.

41. William Shakespeare, *Julius Caesar*, act 3, sc. 2.

CHAPTER 2: IMPEACHABLE OFFENSES

1. Bruce Allen Murphy, *Wild Bill: The Legend and Life of William O. Douglas* (New York: Random House, 2003), 432.

2. Ibid., 433.

3. Stuart Taylor Jr., "The 'High Crimes' Riddle," *Washington Post*, September 21, 1998.

4. Ian Schwartz, "Maxine Waters: Impeachment Is Whatever Congress Says It Is, No Law That Dictates Impeachment," *Real Clear Politics,* September 21, 2017.

5. *Nixon v. United States*, 506 U.S. 224 (1993).

6. Ga. Const. art. III, § 7, para. 1.

7. Pa. Const. art. VI, § 6; N.J. Const. art. VII, § 3, para. 1; Mass. Const. pt. 2, ch. I, § 2, art. VIII.

8. *McCulloch v. Maryland*, 17 U.S. (4 Wheat.) 316, 407 (1819).

9. Klein, "The Case for Normalizing Impeachment."

10. Carlton F.W. Larson, "The Five Myths About Treason," *Washington Post*, February 17, 2017.

11. *McDonnell v. United States,* 136 S. Ct. 2355, 2372 (2016).

12. Max Farrand, ed., *The Records of the Federal Convention of 1787*, rev. ed., vol. 2 (New Haven: Yale University Press, 1966), 68.

13. Akhil Amar, *The Constitution Today: Timeless Lessons for the Issues of Our Era* (New York: Basic Books, 2016), 302.

14. Farrand, "July 26," in *The Records of the Federal Convention of 1787*, vol. 2, 121.

15. Farrand, *The Records of the Federal Convention of 1787*, 550.

16. 1 Annals of Cong. 498 (1789).

17. Antonin Scalia and Bryan A. Garner, *Reading Law: The Interpretation of Legal Texts* (St. Paul: Thomson/West, 2012), 199.

18. Quoted in Michael J. Graetz and Linda Greenhouse, *The Burger Court and the Rise of the Judicial Right* (New York: Simon & Schuster, 2017), 328.

19. Farrand, *The Records of the Federal Convention of 1787*, 550.

20. Charles L. Black Jr., *Impeachment: A Handbook* (New Haven: Yale University Press, 1998), 31–32.

21. Ibid., 32–33.

22. Ron Chernow, *Alexander Hamilton* (New York: Penguin Books, 2005), 710.

23. Charles Biddle, *Autobiography of Charles Biddle, Vice-President of the Supreme Executive Council of Pennsylvania* (Philadelphia: E. Claxton & Co., 1883), 308.

24. William H. Rehnquist, *Grand Inquests: The Historic Impeachments of Justice Samuel Chase and President Andrew Johnson* (New York: William Morrow & Co., 1992), 18.

25. Farrand, *The Records of the Federal Convention of 1787*, 550.

26. Quoted by Adam Cohen, "The Founders Had an Idea for Handling Alberto Gonzales," *New York Times*, August 19, 2007.

27. Alexander Hamilton, *Federalist* No. 65, in *The Federalist Papers*, ed. Clinton Rossiter (New York: Signet Classic, 1961), 396.

28. James Wilson, *Collected Works of James Wilson*, ed. Kermit L. Hall and Mark David Hall (Indianapolis: Liberty Fund, 2007), 736.

29. William J. Stuntz, *The Collapse of American Criminal Justice* (Cambridge: Harvard University Press, 2011), 99.

30. Ibid.

31. Joseph Story, *Commentaries on the Constitution of the United States*, 3rd ed. (Boston: Little, Brown and Company, 1858), 553.

32. Ibid., 553–554.

33. Black, *Impeachment*, 33.

34. Akhil Amar, *America's Constitution: A Biography* (New York: Random House, 2006), 200.

35. Black, *Impeachment*, 36.

36. *Lawrence v. Texas*, 539 U.S. 558 (2003); *Obergefell v. Hodges*, 135 S. Ct. 2584 (2015).

37. Jane Chong, "To Impeach a President: Applying the Authoritative Guide from Charles Black," *Lawfare*, July 20, 2017.

38. Annette Gordon-Reed, *Andrew Johnson: The American Presidents Series, the 17th President* (New York: Times Books, 2011), 12.

39. Michael Les Benedict, *The Impeachment and Trial of Andrew Johnson* (New York: W.W. Norton and Company, 1999), 39.

40. Orin S. Kerr, "The Mosaic Theory of the Fourth Amendment," *Michigan Law Review* 111 (2012): 311.

41. John Labovitz, *Presidential Impeachment* (New Haven: Yale University Press, 1978), 129–130.

42. Quoted in Lewis Deschler, *Deschler's Precedents of the United States House of Representatives,* vol. 3 (1974), 639.

43. Thurman Arnold, *The Symbols of Government* (New Haven: Yale University Press, 1935), 101, quoted in *Fisher v. Univ. of Tex. at Austin,* 133 S. Ct. 2411, 2433 n.2 (2013) (Ginsburg, J., dissenting).

44. Jane Chong, "Impeachment-Proof? The President's Unconstitutional Abuse of His Constitutional Powers," *Lawfare,* January 2, 2018.

45. Noah Feldman, "Arpaio Pardon Would Show Contempt for Constitution," *Bloomberg,* August 23, 2017.

46. David G. Savage, "Trump Could Pay a Price if He Hands Out Pardons in the Russia Probe as He Did for Joe Arpaio," *Los Angeles Times,* August 31, 2017.

47. Mike DeBonis, "House Votes to Kill Texas Lawmaker's Trump Impeachment Effort," *Washington Post,* December 6, 2017.

48. Zack Beauchamp, "How Donald Trump's Kleptocracy Is Undermining American Democracy," *Vox,* July 31, 2017.

49. David Robertson, *Debates and other Proceedings of the Convention of Virginia* (2nd ed. 1805) (1788), 345.

CHAPTER 3: TO IMPEACH OR *NOT* TO IMPEACH

1. 145 Cong. Rec. 2,569–2,571 (1999) (statement of Sen. Byrd).

2. Gerald M. Boyd, "Reagan Terms Nicaraguan Rebels 'Moral Equal of Founding Fathers,'" *New York Times,* March 2, 1985.

3. Anthony Lewis, "Abroad at Home; The Empty Chair," *New York Times,* February 27, 1987.

4. Editorial, "The Laws, Unfaithfully Executed," *New York Times,* November 19, 1987.

5. "Excerpts from Remarks by Panel Chairmen," *New York Times,* May 6, 1987.

6. Quoted in David E. Kyvig, *The Age of Impeachment* (Lawrence: University Press of Kansas, 2008), 253.

7. Ibid., 251.

8. David H. Gans, "Republicans Who Block Obama's Supreme Court Pick Are Violating the Constitution," *New Republic,* March 16, 2016.

9. Michael D. Ramsey, "Why the Senate Doesn't Have to Act on Merrick Garland's Nomination," *The Atlantic,* May 15, 2016.

10. 145 Cong. Rec. 2,569–2,571 (1999) (statement of Sen. Byrd).

11. Akhil Reed Amar, "On Impeaching Presidents," 28 *Hofstra Law Review* 291, 310 (1999).

12. 145 Cong. Rec. 579 (1999) (statement of Sen. Harkin); Lizette Alvarez, "The Trial of the President: The Senator; Harkin Wins Endorsement of Wider Role Than Jury," *New York Times,* January 16, 1999.

13. "Jan. 15: Sen. Harkin's Objection," The Impeachment Trial, *Washington Post,* January 15, 1999.

14. Lizette Alvarez, "The Trial of the President: The Senator; Harkin Wins Endorsement of Wider Role Than Jury," *New York Times,* January 16, 1999.

15. See Thomas E. Mann, *The Broken Branch: How Congress Is Failing America and How to Get It Back on Track* (New York: Oxford University Press, 2006).

16. See Norman Ornstein and Thomas E. Mann, *It's Even Worse Than It Looks: How the American Constitutional System Collided with the New Politics of Extremism* (New York: Basic Books, 2012).

17. See Eric A. Posner and Adrian Vermeule, *The Executive Unbound: After the Madisonian Republic* (New York: Oxford University Press, 2010), 4.

18. *Youngstown Sheet & Tube Co. v. Sawyer,* 343 U.S. 579, 635 (1952) (Jackson, J., concurring in the judgment and opinion of the Court).

19. Josh Chafetz, *Congress's Constitution: Legislative Authority and the Separation of Powers* (New Haven, CT, and London: Yale University Press, 2017), 24.

20. *Barenblatt v. United States,* 360 U.S. 109, 111 (1959).

21. Jack Goldsmith, *Power and Constraint: The Accountable Presidency after 9/11* (New York: W.W. Norton & Company, 2012), 209.

22. Lester J. Cappon, ed., *The Adams-Jefferson Letters: The Complete Correspondence between Thomas Jefferson and Abigail and John Adams* (Chapel Hill, NC, and London: University of North Carolina Press, 1988), 348.

23. Ezra Klein, "How to Stop an Autocracy," *Vox,* February 7, 2017.

24. Quoted in President Jackson's Message of Protest to the Senate, April 15, 1834.

25. Jon Meacham, *American Lion: Andrew Jackson in the White House* (New York: Random House, 2009), 279.

26. *President Jackson's Message of Protest to the Senate; April 15, 1834,* Avalon Project, http://avalon.law.yale.edu/19th_century/ajack006.asp.

27. Meacham, *American Lion,* 261.

28. Appendix to the Cong. Globe, 39th Cong., 1st Sess. 93 (1848).

29. Ibid., 157.

30. Bill Clinton, *My Life* (New York: Alfred A. Knopf, 2004), 486.

31. Benjamin Harrison, *This Country of Ours* (New York: C. Scribner, 1897), 320.

32. William H. Rehnquist, *Grand Inquests: The Historic Impeachments of Justice Samuel Chase and President Andrew Johnson* (New York: Morrow, 1992); William H. Rehnquist, "The Impeachment Clause: A Wild Card in the Constitution," *Northwestern University Law Review* 85 (1991): 903.

33. 145 Cong. Rec. 2,610–2,612 (1999) (statement of Rep. Hyde).

34. Keith E. Whittington, "What Is the Downside of Not Impeaching?" *Lawfare*, July 25, 2017.

35. Chong, "To Impeach a President."

36. James Buchanan, "Veto Message (March 28, 1860)," in *Veto Messages of the Presidents of the United States with the Action of Congress Thereon,* ed. Ben Perley Poore (Washington, DC: Government Printing Office, 1886), 276.

37. David Blumenthal and James Monroe, *The Heart of Power: Health and Politics in the Oval Office* (Berkeley: University of California Press, 2010), 222.

38. John A. Farrell, *Richard Nixon: The Life* (New York: Doubleday, 2017), 530–531.

39. Clinton, *My Life,* 494.

40. Cristiano Lima, "Roger Stone Predicts Violent 'Insurrection' if Trump Is Impeached," *Politico,* August 24, 2017.

41. William J. Jackman, et al., *The History and Government of the United States: A History of the American People,* vol. 5 (Chicago: L.W. Walter Company, 1911), 1364.

42. Heather Caygle, "Nadler Wins Top Democratic Post on Judiciary Committee," *Politico,* December 20, 2017.

43. 145 Cong. Rec. 2,569–2,571 (1999) (statement of Sen. Byrd).

CHAPTER 4: CONGRESS, THE DECIDER

1. *Bush v. Gore,* 531 U.S. 98 (2001) (per curiam).

2. Quoted in Joan Biskupic, *American Original* (New York: Sarah Crichton Books, Farrar, Straus and Giroux, 2009), 248.

3. *Bush,* 531 U.S. at 128 (Stevens, J., dissenting).

4. David Souter, "Commencement Address," *Harvard Law Review* 124 (2010): 429, 433.

5. James Madison, "Observations on the 'Draught of a Constitution for Virginia'" (October 15, 1788), in *Writings* (1999), 415–416.

6. James Madison, "Observations on Jefferson's Draft of a Constitution for Virginia," October 15, 1788, Papers 11: 285–293.

7. Max Farrand, ed., "May 29," in *The Records of the Federal Convention of 1787,* rev. ed., vol. 1 (New Haven: Yale University Press, 1966), 22.

8. Farrand, "The Pinckney Plan," in *The Records of the Federal Convention of 1787*, vol. 3, 596.

9. Farrand, "June 2," in *The Records of the Federal Convention of 1787*, vol. 1, 85.

10. Farrand "June 2," in *The Records of the Federal Convention of 1787*, vol. 1, 85.

11. Farrand, "June 13," in *The Records of the Federal Convention of 1787*, vol. 1, 223–224.

12. Farrand, "June 15," in *The Records of the Federal Convention of 1787*, vol. 1, 244.

13. Farrand, "Committee of Detail, III," in *The Records of the Federal Convention of 1787*, vol. 2, 136.

14. Farrand, "August 6," in *The Records of the Federal Convention of 1787*, vol. 2, 185–86.

15. Farrand, "September 4," in *The Records of the Federal Convention of 1787*, vol. 2, 493.

16. Farrand, "September 8," in *The Records of the Federal Convention of 1787*, vol. 2, 551.

17. Farrand, "August 9," in *The Records of the Federal Convention of 1787*, vol. 2, 227.

18. *The Debates in the Several State Conventions, on the Adoption of the Federal Constitution, as Recommended by the General Convention at Philadelphia in 1787*, 2nd ed., vol. 4, ed. Jonathan Elliot (Washington, DC: Self-Published, 1836), 113.

19. E. J. Dionne Jr., Norman J. Ornstein, and Thomas E. Mann, *One Nation after Trump* (New York: St. Martin's Press, 2017), 28–29.

20. Michael J. Klarman, *The Framers' Coup: The Making of the United States Constitution* (New York: Oxford University Press, 2016), 232.

21. Mason, September 4.

22. Farrand, "June 12," in *The Records of the Federal Convention of 1787*, vol. 1, 218.

23. Klarman, *The Framers' Coup*, 608.

24. N.Y. Const. art. VI, § 24.

25. Mo. Const. art. VII, § 2.

26. Neb. Const. art. III, § 17.

27. Farrand, "July 18," in *The Records of the Federal Convention of 1787*, vol. 2, 41–42; and "September 8," vol. 2, 551.

28. Gouverneur Morris raises this concern at "September 4," in Farrand, *The Records of the Federal Convention of 1787*, vol. 2, 500.

29. Farrand, "September 8," in *The Records of the Federal Convention of 1787*, vol. 2, 551.

30. Farrand, "July 18," in *The Records of the Federal Convention of 1787,* vol. 2, 42.

31. Farrand, "September 8," in *The Records of the Federal Convention of 1787,* vol. 2, 551.

32. Farrand, "September 8," in *The Records of the Federal Convention of 1787,* vol. 2, 551.

33. Farrand, "September 14," in *The Records of the Federal Convention of 1787,* vol. 2, 627.

34. Alexander Hamilton, *Federalist* No. 65, in *The Federalist Papers,* ed. Clinton Rossiter (New York: Signet Classic, 2003).

35. Farrand, "June 11," in *The Records of the Federal Convention of 1787,* vol. 1, 198.

36. Joseph Story, *Commentaries on the Constitution of the United States,* § 785 (Boston: Little, Brown, and Company, 1873), 551.

37. Woodrow Wilson, *Congressional Government: A Study in American Politics* (Boston: Houghton, Mifflin, and Company, 1901), 275–276.

38. Quoted in George Lardner Jr., "Nixon Case as Precedent Could Bode Well, Ill for Clinton," *Washington Post,* September 27, 1998.

39. Gerhardt, *The Federal Impeachment Process,* 40.

40. Richard Re, "Promising the Constitution," *Northwestern University Law Review* 110 (2016): 299, 304.

41. Quoted in Linda Greenhouse, "William H. Rehnquist, Architect of Conservative Court, Dies at 80," *New York Times,* September 5, 2005.

42. "Arlen Specter: Snarlin' No More," *The Economist,* October 20, 2012.

43. Russell Spivak, "A Premature Primer: How Do Impeachment Proceeding Actually Work?" *Lawfare,* June 5, 2017.

44. Clinton, *My Life,* 845.

45. Richard Posner, *An Affair of State: The Investigation, Impeachment, and Trial of President Clinton* (Cambridge: Harvard University Press, 1999), 127.

46. Ibid., 128.

47. Black, *Impeachment,* 17.

48. Charlie Savage, "How the Impeachment Process Works," *New York Times,* May 17, 2017.

49. Keith E. Whittington, "An Impeachment Should Not Be a Partisan Affair," *Lawfare,* May 16, 2017.

50. Sarah E. Igo, *The Averaged American* (Cambridge: Harvard University Press, 2007), 3.

51. Andrew Kohut, *How the Watergate Crisis Eroded Public Support for Richard Nixon,* Pew Research Center, August 8, 2014.

52. Jack Brewster, "Why You Should Be Skeptical about Polls on Impeaching Trump," *Time,* June 7, 2017.

53. CNN/ORC Poll 7, July 25, 2014, at 4, https://i2.cdn.turner.com/cnn/2014/images/07/24/rel7e.pdf.

54. John F. Harris, *The Survivor: Bill Clinton in the White House* (New York: Random House, 2005), 357.

55. Nate Silver, "Will Donald Trump Be Impeached?" *FiveThirty-Eight,* May 22, 2017.

56. Clinton, *My Life,* 835.

57. John A. Farrell, "What Today's Democrats Can Learn from Tip O'Neill's Reagan Strategy," *Politico,* November 24, 2016.

58. Thomas P. O'Neill, "Frenemies: A Love Story," *New York Times,* October 5, 2012.

59. Quoted in William B. Perkins, "The Political Nature of Impeachment in the United States," in *Checking Executive Power: Presidential Impeachment in Comparative Perspective,* ed. Jody C. Baumgartner and Naoko Kada (Westport: Praeger, 2003), 22.

60. Bob Woodward and Carl Bernstein, *The Final Days* (New York: Simon and Schuster, 2013), 415.

61. Ibid., 391.

62. David O. Stewart, *Impeached: The Trial of President Andrew Johnson and the Fight for Lincoln's Legacy* (New York, Simon and Schuster, 2009), 317.

63. Evan Thomas, *Being Nixon: A Man Divided* (New York: Random House, 2015), 241.

64. Ibid., 469.

CHAPTER 5: IMPEACHMENT TALK

1. 19 Annals of Cong. 1174 (1809).

2. Letter from Josiah Quincy to John Adams (December 15, 1808).

3. Edmund Quincy, *Life of Josiah Quincy* (1874), 88.

4. Henry Adams, *History of the United States,* vol. 4 (New York: Scribner, 1909), 422.

5. 19 Annals of Cong. 1176 (1809).

6. Ibid.

7. Ibid., 1182.

8. Quincy, *Life of Josiah Quincy,* 183.

9. Kyvig, *The Age of Impeachment,* 1.

10. George Washington's Letter to Catherine Macaulay Graham, January 9, 1790.

11. Letter from Casca in *Petersburg Intelligencer,* printed in the Aurora General Advertiser, October 16, 1795.

12. Letter from Pittachus, To the Editor of the Aurora, *Aurora General Advertiser,* November 26, 1795.

13. Letter from Thomas Jefferson to Thomas Ritchie (December 25, 1820).

14. 10 Reg. Deb. 1510 (1834).

15. Cong. Globe, 30th Cong., 1st Sess. app. at 157 (1848).

16. Ron Chernow, *Grant* (New York: Penguin Press, 2017), 825.

17. Ulysses S. Grant, "Message to the House of Representatives (May 4, 1876)," in *A Compilation of the Messages and Papers of the Presidents, 1789–1897,* vol. 7, ed. James D. Richardson (Washington, DC: Bureau of National Literature and Art, 1897), 362.

18. Milford W. Howard, *The American Plutocracy* (New York: Holland Pub. Co., 1895), 101.

19. "A Week of the World," *The Illustrated American,* June 6, 1896, at 7524.

20. Woodrow Wilson, "Address at Auditorium, Omaha, Nebraska (September 8, 1919)," in *Messages and Papers of Woodrow Wilson,* vol. 2, ed. Albert Shaw (New York: Review of Reviews Corporation, 1924), 810.

21. George C. Herring, *From Colony to Superpower: U.S. Foreign Relations Since 1776* (Oxford and New York: Oxford University Press, 2008), 430.

22. Letter from Henry Cabot Lodge to Theodore Roosevelt, March 1, 1915.

23. "Chicago Cheers Senate Radicals," *New York Times,* September 11, 1919, at 8.

24. "'Impeach Wilson,' Shout Kansas City Anti-League Crown," *San Diego Union,* September 14, 1919, at 1.

25. "Chicago Cheers Senate Radicals," at 1.

26. "Seek Men Who Want Wilson Impeached," *New York Times,* July 19, 1919, at 20.

27. "House Tables Move to Impeach Hoover," *Washington Post,* December 14, 1932, at 1, 3.

28. "House Rebukes Bill to Impeach Hoover, 361–8," *New York Herald Tribune,* December 14, 1932, at 6.

29. "Colleagues Plan to Put M'Fadden in Silent Limbo," *New York Herald Tribune,* December 18, 1932, at 11.

30. "Just a National Nuisance," *Philadelphia Inquirer,* December 15, 1932, at 1.

31. Kathy Gilsinan, "Thanksgiving in a Foxhole, 1950," *The Atlantic,* November 26, 2014.

32. Memorandum from Joint Chiefs of Staff to Commander in Chief, European Command, December 6, 1950.

33. Harry S. Truman, *Memoirs by Harry S. Truman: 1946–52, Years of Trial and Hope* (New York: Doubleday, 1956), 441–442.

34. *Military Situation in the Far East: Hearing Before the Select Committee on Armed Services and Foreign Relations*, 82nd Cong. 732 (1951) (statement of Gen. Omar Bradley).

35. Radio Report to the American People on Korea and U.S. Policy in the Far East, 1951 Pub. Papers (April 11, 1951), 226.

36. David McCullough, *Truman* (New York: Simon and Schuster, 1992), 844.

37. Editorial, "Impeach Truman," *Chicago Tribune*, April 12, 1951, at 1.

38. McCullough, *Truman*, 842.

39. William White, "G.O.P. Hits Ouster," *New York Times*, April 12, 1951, at 3.

40. Ibid.

41. McCullough, *Truman*, 896–897.

42. 98 Cong. Rec. 4156 (April 21, 1952).

43. 98 Cong. Rec. 4418 (April 24, 1952); 98 Cong. Rec. 4396 (April 24, 1952).

44. "Transcript of Truman's News Conference Explaining His Powers," *New York Times*, April 25, 1952, at 4.

45. Transcript of Oral Argument, *Youngstown Sheet & Tube Co. v. Sawyer*, Civil Action Nos. 1550-52, 1655-52, 1539-52, 1647-52, 1732-52, 1700-52, 1549-52 (D.D.C. April 24, 1952), in Transcript of Record, *Youngstown Sheet & Tube Co. v. Sawyer*, at 371 (1952).

46. Ibid.

47. See, e.g., *United States v. Stuart*, 489 U.S. 353, 374–375 (1989); *Nixon v. Fitzgerald*, 457 U.S. 731, 757 (1982); *Ex parte Grossman*, 267 U.S. 87, 121 (1925).

48. Larry Blomstedt, *Truman, Congress, and Korea: The Politics of America's First Undeclared War* (Lexington: University Press of Kentucky, 2015), 173.

49. *Youngstown*, 343 U.S. at 640 (Jackson, J., concurring in the judgment and opinion of the Court).

50. The leading account of this theory is Kyvig, *The Age of Impeachment*.

51. H.R. Res. 370, 98th Cong. (1983).

52. James Dao, "Rep. Ted Weiss, 64, Dies; Liberal Stalwart in House," *New York Times*, September 15, 1992.

53. 129 Cong. Rec. 32130 (November 10, 1983).

54. John Meacham, *Destiny and Power: The American Odyssey of George Herbert Walker Bush* (New York: Random House, 2015), 452.

55. Ibid., 453.

56. Ibid., 455.

57. Martin Weil, "Henry Gonzales, 37-Year Texas Representative, Dies," *Washington Post*, November 29, 2000.

58. H.R. Res. 34, 102nd Cong. (January 16, 1991).

59. H.R. Res. 86, 102nd Cong. (February 21, 1991).

60. Hugh Heclo, "Campaigning and Governing: A Conspectus," in *The Permanent Campaign and Its Future*, ed. Norman J. Ornstein and Thomas E. Mann (Washington, DC: American Enterprise Institute and Brookings Institution, 2000), 1, 30.

61. Norman Ornstein, "Ending the Permanent Campaign," *The Nation*, August 12, 2010.

62. Michelle Goldberg, "Democrats Should Embrace Impeachment," *New York Times*, October 23, 2017.

63. "32% Favor Bush Impeachment," *Rasmussen Reports*, December 15, 2005.

64. *USA Today*, "As You May Know, Impeachment Is the First Step . . .?" Gallup/*USA Today* Poll Question 14 of 85, July 6, 2007. Ithaca, NY: Cornell University, Roper Center for Public Opinion Research, iPOLL.

65. David D. Kirkpatrick, "Call for Censure Is Rallying Cry to Bush's Base," *New York Times*, March 16, 2006.

66. Editorial, "The Impeachment Agenda," *Wall Street Journal*, March 15, 2006.

67. Kirkpatrick, "Call for Censure."

68. Kirkpatrick, "Call for Censure."

69. Charles Babington, "Democrats Won't Try to Impeach President," *Washington Post*, May 12, 2006.

70. Susan Ferrechio, "Pelosi: Bush Impeachment 'Off the Table'," *New York Times*, November 8, 2006.

71. Susan Milligan, "Democrats Scuttle Proposal to Impeach Bush," *Boston Globe*, June 12, 2008.

72. Carl Hulse, "The Why-Haven't-You-Impeached-the-President-Tour," *New York Times*, August 15, 2008.

73. Jon Greenberg, "It's True: Donald Trump Once Supported Impeaching George W. Bush," *Politifact*, February 16, 2016.

74. Catalina Camia, "Sen. Coburn: Obama 'Perilously Close' to Impeachment," *USA Today*, August 23, 2013.

75. Ruth Tam, "Rep. Farenthold Say House Could Impeach Obama," *Washington Post*, August 12, 2013.

76. "Chaffetz Doesn't Rule Out Impeachment for Obama," *CNN*, May 14, 2013.

77. Mollie Reilly, "GOP Congressman Suggests Obama Could Be Impeached over Health Care Delays, Immigration," *Huffington Post*, March 12, 2014.

78. Rachel Weiner, "Rep. Steve Stockman Threatens to Impeach Obama over Guns," *Washington Post*, January 15, 2013.

79. Aaron Blake, "GOP Congressman: Impeaching Obama Would Be a 'Dream Come True'," *Washington Post*, August 21, 2013.

80. Jonathan Easley, "Bachmann: House Could Impeach 'Dictator' Obama for His Offenses," *The Hill*, October 9, 2013.

81. "Judge Jeanine to Obama: 'You Have Defrauded the American People'," *Fox News*, May 4, 2014.

82. Sarah Palin, "Exclusive—Sarah Palin: 'It's Time to Impeach' President Obama," *Breitbart*, July 8, 2014.

83. Andrew McCarthy, *Faithless Execution: Building the Political Case for Obama's Impeachment* (New York: Encounter Books, 2014), 6.

84. Peter Moore, "One Third of Americans Want to Impeach Obama," *YouGov*, July 14, 2014; Paul Steinhauser, "CNN/ORC Poll: Majority Say No to Impeachment and Lawsuit," *CNN*, July 25, 2014; Philip Bump, "One-Third of Americans Support Impeaching Obama; One-fifth Don't understand "Impeachment'," *Washington Post*, July 25, 2014.

85. Nick Corasaniti, "Impeachment, on GOP Lips, Animates Democrats' Base," *New York Times*, July 29, 2014.

86. Lauren Carroll and Steve Contorno, "Republicans Are Trying to Impeach Obama, Civil Rights Group Says," *Politifact*, October 30, 2014.

87. David A. Graham, "21 Emails From the Democratic Party About Impeachment," *The Atlantic*, July 30, 2014.

88. Neil Irwin, "Impeachment Julep," *New York Times*, August 1, 2014.

89. Darren Samuelsohn, "Could Trump Be Impeached Shortly After He Takes Office?," *Politico*, April 16, 2016.

90. Mike DeBonis, "Republicans Are Discussing Their Plans for President Clinton—Starting with Impeachment," *Washington Post*, November 3, 2016.

91. Ed Kilgore, "If Clinton Wins, Get Ready for Another Impeachment," *New York Times*, November 3, 2016; Editorial, "Donald Trump's Impeachment Threat," *New York Times*, November 3, 2016.

92. DeBonis, "Republicans Are Discussing Their Plans for President Clinton."

93. Laurence H. Tribe, "Donald Trump Will Violate the US Constitution on Inauguration Day," *The Guardian*, December 19, 2016.

94. See, e.g., Emily Jane Fox, "The Evidence to Impeach Donald Trump May Already Be Here," *Vanity Fair*, December 20, 2016; Robert Kuttner, "Impeaching Trump," *Huffington Post*, January 1, 2017.

95. Jay Willis, "How to Impeach a U.S. President (Say, Donald Trump), Explained," *GQ*, January 20, 2017.

96. Ricki Harris, "If You're Going to Bet on Trump's Impeachment, Now Is a Good Time to Do It," *Esquire*, January 20, 2017.

97. Carrie Dann, "Poll: Just 35% of Americans Indicate They Would Vote for Trump in 2020," NBC News, December 20, 2017.

98. Celeste Katz, "Donald Trump Is an 'Idiot' and a 'Liar,' Americans Say in New Poll," *Newsweek,* December 12, 2017.

99. Jessica Kwong, "Will Trump Be Impeached in 2018? Here's What the Odds Say," *Newsweek,* December 22, 2017.

100. Masha Gessen, "One Year After Trump's Election, Revisiting 'Autocracy: Rules for Survival,'" *New Yorker,* November 8, 2017.

101. "GOP Tax Plan Benefits Rich, U.S. Voters Say Almost 3–1, Quinnipiac University National Poll Finds; Trump Job Approval Stuck at 35 Percent," Quinnipac University Poll, December 5, 2017.

102. Donald Trump (@realDonaldTrump), *Twitter* (Jan. 2, 2018, 7:49 PM).

103. Tim Marcin, "Trump Eats McDonald's Because He's Afraid of Being Poisoned Elsewhere," *Newsweek,* January 3, 2018.

104. Klein, "The Case for Normalizing Impeachment."

105. Laura Koran et al., "US Science Envoy Steps Down, Spells Out "Impeach" In Resignation Letter," *CNN,* August 24, 2017.

106. Donald Trump (@realDonaldTrump), *Twitter* (Oct. 27, 2017, 6:58 AM).

107. Niall Stanage, "The Memo: Impeachment Fervor Fuels Dem Tensions," *The Hill,* December 22, 2017.

108. Abigail Tracy, "Will Impeachment Mania Doom the Democrats?," *Vanity Fair,* November 1, 2017.

109. Heather Caygle, "Pelosi Moves to Muzzle Trump Impeachment Talk," *Politico,* November 1, 2017.

110. Sam Stein, "Chuck Schumer to Dems: Chill out with the Donald Trump Impeachment Talk," *The Daily Beast,* November 10, 2017.

CHAPTER 6: IMPEACHMENT, INCAPACITY, AND BROKEN POLITICS

1. Pew Research Center, *The Partisan Divide on Political Values Grows Even Wider*, Pew Research Center, October 5, 2017.

2. Pew Research Center, *Partisanship and Political Animosity in 2016*, Pew Research Center, June 22, 2017.

3. Bill Bishop, *The Big Sort: Why the Clustering of Like-Minded America Is Tearing Us Apart* (Boston: Mariner Books, 2009), 5.

4. Sunstein, *#Republic*, 10.

5. Ross Douthat, "The Swine of Conservatism," *New York Times*, November 11, 2017.

6. Paul Harris, "One in Four Americans Think Obama May Be the Antichrist, Survey Says," *The Guardian*, April 2, 2013.

7. Charles J. Sykes, "Charlie Sykes on Where the Right Went Wrong," *New York Times*, December 15, 2016.

8. Lee Drutman, "We Need Political Parties. But Their Rabid Partisanship Could Destroy American Democracy," *Vox*, September 5, 2017.

9. Charles E. Cook Jr., "The Urgent Need to Repair Our Broken Politics," *Cook Political. Report*, September 15, 2017.

10. Sunstein, *#Republic*, 122–124.

11. Maeve Duggan and Aaron Smith, *The Political Environment on Social Media*, Pew Research Center, October 25, 2016.

12. Craig Silverman, "This Analysis Shows How Viral Fake Election News Stories Outperformed Real News on Facebook," *BuzzFeed*, November 16, 2016.

13. Sunstein, *#Republic*, 3.

14. Jonathan Haidt and Sam Abrams, "The Top 10 Reasons American Politics Are So Broken," *Washington Post*, January 7, 2015.

15. Tim Dickinson, "How Roger Ailes Built the Fox News Fear Factory," *Rolling Stone*, May 25, 2011.

16. Thomas E. Mann and Norman J. Ornstein, *It's Even Worse Than It Looks: How the American Constitutional System Collided with the New Politics of Extremism* (New York: Basic Books, 2012), 44.

17. See, e.g., Jordan Ellenberg, "How Computers Turned Gerrymandering into a Science," *New York Times*, October 6, 2017.

18. Pew Research Center, *Political Polarization in the American Public: Political Engagement and Activism*, Pew Research Center, June 12, 2014.

19. Darrell M. West, "Broken Politics," *Issues in Governance Studies*, no. 33, Brookings Institution, March 2010.

20. Mann and Ornstein, *It's Even Worse Than It Looks*, 50.

21. David Fontana, "The Geography of Campaign Finance Law," 90 *Southern California Law Review* 90 1247, 1249 (2017).

22. Jonathan Rauch, "How American Politics Went Insane," *Atlantic Monthly*, July/August 2016.

23. Heather K. Gerken, "The Real Problem with Citizens United: Campaign Finance, Dark Money, and Shadow Parties," *Marquette Lawyer*, Summer 2014.

24. Glenn Kessler, "When Did McConnell Say He Wanted to Make Obama a 'One-Term President'?" *Washington Post*, September 25, 2012.

25. Drutman, "We Need Political Parties. But Their Rabid Partisanship Could Destroy American Democracy."

26. Roberto Foa and Yascha Mounk, "Are Americans Losing Faith in Democracy?" *Vox*, December 18, 2015.

27. Nathaniel Persily and Jon Cohen, "Americans Are Losing Faith in Democracy—and in Each Other," *Washington Post,* October 14, 2016.

28. Hannah Fingerhut, *Deep Racial, Partisan Divisions in Americans' Views of Police Officers,* Pew Research Center, September 15, 2017; Rich Morin and Renee Stepler, *The Racial Confidence Gap in Police Performance*, Pew Research Center, September 29, 2016.

29. Art Swift, "Americans' Trust in Mass Media Sinks to New Low," *Gallup News,* September 14, 2016.

30. Art Swift, "Democrats' Confidence in Mass Media Rises Sharply from 2016," *Gallup News,* September 21, 2017.

31. Daniel T. Rodgers, *Age of Fracture* (Cambridge: Belknap Press of Harvard University Press, 2012).

32. Kurt Andersen, *Fantasyland: How America Went Haywire: A 500-Year History* (New York: Random House, 2017), 5.

33. Ibid., 11.

34. Ibid., 425.

35. Sykes, "Charlie Sykes on Where the Right Went Wrong."

36. David Roberts, "Donald Trump Is the Sole Reliable Source of Truth, Says Chair of House Science Committee," *Vox,* January 27, 2017.

37. Masha Gessen, "The Putin Paradigm," *New York Review of Books,* December 13, 2016.

38. Alexander Hamilton, *Enclosure: Objections and Answers Respecting the Administration* (August 18, 1792).

39. Timothy Snyder, *On Tyranny: Twenty Lessons from the Twentieth Century* (New York: Tim Duggan Books, 2017), 65.

40. Hannah Arendt, *The Origins of Totalitarianism* (New York: Harcourt Brace Jovanovich, 1973), 382.

41. Angel Au-Yeung, "Billionaire 'Doubling Down': Commits $20 Million to Trump Impeachment Campaign," *Forbes,* November 9, 2017.

42. Abby Ohlheiser, "The Creator of Godwin's Law Explains Why Some Nazi Comparisons Don't Break His Famous Internet Rule," *Washington Post,* August 14, 2017.

43. "Full Text of John McCain's Senate Floor Speech: 'Let's Return to Regular Order,'" *USA Today,* July 25, 2017.

44. Norm Ornstein, "Let's Be Realistic: The Senate Is Almost as Broken as the House," *Atlantic Monthly,* June 27, 2013.

45. Michael M. Grynbaum, "Trump Calls the News Media the 'Enemy of the American People'," *New York Times,* February 17, 2017; Amy B. Wang, "Trump

Lashes Out at 'So-called Judge' Who Temporarily Blocked Travel Ban," *Washington Post,* February 4, 2017.

46. David Frum, "How to Build an Autocracy," *Atlantic Monthly,* March 2017. See also David Frum, Trumpocracy (New York: Harper Collins 2015), 235.

47. Dexter Filkins, "Rex Tillerson at the Breaking Point," *The New Yorker,* October 16, 2017.

48. Tina Nguyen, "An 'Idiot' and a 'Dope': McMaster Reportedly Unloads on Trump During a Private Dinner," *Vanity Fair,* November 20, 2017.

49. Philip Rucker and Karoun Demirjian, "Corker Calls White House 'An Adult Day Care Center' in Response to Latest Trump Tirade," *Washington Post,* October 8, 2017.

50. Leinz Vales, "James Clapper Calls Trump Speech 'Downright Scary and Disturbing,'" *CNN,* August 24, 2017.

51. Ross Douthat, "The 25th Amendment Solution for Removing Trump," *New York Times,* May 16, 2017.

52. Joe Scarborough, "Trump's Mental Meltdown," *Washington Post,* December 7, 2017.

53. Joseph Frankel, "Joe Scarborough Claims Sources Say Trump Has 'Early Signs of Dementia.' What Does That Mean?," *Newsweek,* January 8, 2018.

54. Bandy Lee, *The Dangerous Case of Donald Trump* (New York: St. Martin's Press, 2017).

55. Tweet from @realDonald Trump, January 6, 2018 at 4:25 a.m.

56. Bandy X. Lee and Norman Eisen, "On Trump's Mental Fitness, the Experts Are Silenced and the Public's in the Dark," *USA Today,* January 19, 2018.

57. Douthat, "The 25th Amendment Solution."

58. David Brooks, "When the World Is Led by a Child," *New York Times,* May 15, 2017.

59. Quoted in John D. Feerick, *The Twenty-Fifth Amendment: It's Complete History and Applications,* 3rd ed. (New York: Fordham University Press, 2014), 115.

60. Ibid.

61. Ibid., 117.

62. Ezra Klein, "The Case for Normalizing Impeachment," *Vox,* December 6, 2017.

63. Keith Whittington, "Will the 25th Amendment Save Us? Lessons from the Nation's First Impeachment Trial," *Vox,* May 18, 2017.

64. Jennifer Rubin, "Let's Be Clear About What the 25th Amendment Does and Doesn't Do," *Washington Post,* May 17, 2017.

65. Jeannie Suk Gersen, "Will Trump Be the Death of the Goldwater Rule?," *New Yorker,* August 23, 2017.

66. Cass R. Sunstein, *Impeachment: A Citizen's Guide* (Cambridge: Harvard University Press, 2017), 145.

67. Brian Kalt, "The Case Against Using the 25th Amendment to Get Rid of Trump," *New York Times*, October 14, 2017.

68. Michael Grunwald, "Trump Is a Consequential President. Just Not in the Ways You Think," *Politico*, December 30, 2017.

69. Sam Friedlander (Publisher), "Impeachara," *YouTube*, March 9, 2017.

70. Dahlia Lithwick, "Is It Too Late for Robert Mueller To Save Us?," *Slate*, December 1, 2017.

71. Andrés Miguel Rondón, "To Beat President Trump, You Have to Learn to Think Like His Supporters," *Washington Post*, December 26, 2017.

72. W.B. Yeats, *The Second Coming* (1919).

73. Abraham Lincoln, First Inaugural Address (March 4, 1861).

EPILOGUE TO THE PAPERBACK EDITION

1. Philip Rucker et al., "'Winter Is coming': Allies Fear Trump Isn't Prepared for Gathering Legal Storm," *Washington Post*, August 29, 2018.

2. Aaron Blake, "Rudy Giuliani Keeps Admitting That He's Just Saying Stuff," *Washington Post*, July 31, 2018.

3. Ibid.

4. Kate Sullivan, "Trump Tells Supporters It'll be 'Your Fault' if He Gets Impeached," CNN, September 7, 2018.

5. John Bowden, "Trump: I Don't Think Democrats Can Impeach Me Since 'I'm Doing a Great Job,'" *The Hill*, August 30, 2018.

6. Deanna Paul, "Trump Says 'The People Would Revolt' if He Were Impeached," *Washington Post*, December 11, 2018.

7. Perry Bacon Jr., "Republicans Are Talking About Impeachment Way More Than Democrats," *FiveThirtyEight*, August 23, 2018.

8. Jacqueline Alemany, "Power Up: Only 21 Percent of New House Democrats Ready to Impeach Trump," *Washington Post*, November 13, 2018.

9. Allan J. Lichtman, *The Case for Impeachment* (Dey St., 2017), 111, 123, 228.

10. Jessica Kwong, "Trump Impeachment Process Gains Support as 66 Democrats Vote to Debate Removing President in Defeated Effort," *Newsweek*, January 19, 2018.

11. Elizabeth Holtzman, *The Case for Impeaching Trump* (New York: Hot Books, 2018), 2–5.

12. "Donald Trump's 9 Impeachable Offenses," *Need to Impeach,* https://www.needtoimpeach.com/impeachable-offenses/ (accessed December 15, 2018).

13. Bob Bauer, "A President's Words Matter, Part II: Impeachment Standards and the Case of the Demagogue," *Lawfare,* October 11, 2017.

14. Gillian Metzger, "Impeachment: Partisan Warfare or Defending the Constitutional Order?" *Take Care,* June 19, 2018.

15. Michiko Kakutani, *The Death of Truth* (New York: Tim Duggan Books, 2018), 94.

16. Jack Goldsmith, "Our Non-Unitary Executive," *Lawfare,* July 30, 2017.

17. Bob Bauer, "Standards for Impeachment: Trump's Defense of Putin in the Face of Russia's Electoral Attacks," *Lawfare,* July 17, 2018.

18. See Chapter 2, n. 34.

19. See Chapter 2, n. 33.

20. Holtzman, *Impeaching Trump,* at 54.

21. *United States of America v. Michael Cohen,* No. 18-cr-602 (S.D.N.Y.), Dkt. 27 at 25.

22. Richard L. Hasen, "Trump's 'Obama Did It Too' Legal Defense Does Not Hold an Ounce of Water," *Slate,* December 10, 2018.

23. Charles L. Black Jr. and Philip Bobbitt, *Impeachment: A Handbook,* new ed. (New Haven and London: Yale University Press, 2018), 93.

24. Black and Bobbitt, *Impeachment,* 95–144; Jeffrey A. Engel et al., *Impeachment: An American History* (New York: Modern Library, 2018), 3–46; Michael J. Gerhardt, *Impeachment: What Everyone Needs to Know* (Oxford University Press, 2018), 6–23, 41-72; Holtzman, *Impeaching Trump,* 1–28; Sunstein, *Impeachment,* 34–53, 117–124.

25. Alan Dershowitz, *The Case Against Impeaching Trump* (New York: Hot Books, 2018), 8–28.

26. Ibid., 9.

27. Ibid., 10.

28. Ibid., 17.

29. Ibid., 10.

30. Ibid., 10.

31. Ibid., 26.

32. *King v. Burwell,* 135 S. Ct. 2480, 2501 (2015) (Scalia, J., dissenting).

33. Dershowitz, *Against Impeaching Trump,* 24.

34. Ibid., 24.

35. *Bradley v. Fisher,* 80 U.S. 335, 350 (1871).

36. See generally Robert A. Katzmann, *Judging Statutes* (Oxford University Press, 2016).

37. See, e.g., *United States v. Traficant*, 368 F.3d 646, 649 (6th Cir. 2004); see also Robert W. Greene, *The Sting Man: Inside Abscam* (Penguin Books, 2013).

38. See generally Cynthia Brown and Todd Garvey, "Expulsion of Members of Congress: Legal Authority and Historical Practice," *Congressional Research Service,* January 11, 2018.

39. Quoted in Holtzman, *Impeaching Trump,* 146–147.

40. *Cramer v. United States,* 325 U.S. 1, 30-31 (1945)

41. *United States v. Sun-Diamond Growers of California,* 526 U.S. 398, 404–405 (1999).

42. *Elonis v. United States,* 135 S. Ct. 2001, 2009 (2015) (citations and quotation marks omitted).

43. Dershowitz, *Against Impeaching Trump,* 26.

44. Ibid., 24

45. Ibid., 22.

46. Engel et al., *Impeachment,* xiv.

47. Ibid., 222–223.

48. Ibid., 223

49. Jane Chong, "The Mystification of Impeachment," *Los Angeles Review of Books,* December 3, 2018.

50. Engel et al., *Impeachment,* 195.

51. Ibid., 175.

52. Holtzman, *Impeaching Trump,* 2.

53. Ibid., 2.

54. Tom Steyer, "Why Democrats Must Impeach the President," *New York Times,* November 8, 2018.

55. Cass R. Sunstein, "When Impeachment Is Mandatory," *Bloomberg,* December 12, 2018.

56. Caitlin Oprysko, "House Dem: Impeaching Trump on Party Lines Would 'Tear the Country Apart,'" *Politico,* November 26, 2018.

57. Stephen Greenblatt, *Tyrant* (New York & London: W.W. Norton & Company, 2018), 28.

SELECTED FURTHER READING

The Trump presidency has prompted a flood of writing about impeachment. As is evident from our endnotes, we've benefited in many ways from topical insights offered since the 2016 election. But we've also learned a great deal from scholarly works on the history and theory of impeachment. Here we identify some of the books and articles that most heavily influenced our approach. We recommend them to those brave readers who are eager to fall deeper down this rabbit hole.

BOOKS

Amar, Akhil Reed. *America's Constitution: A Biography*. New York: Random House, 2006.

Baumgartner, Jody C., and Naoko Kada, eds. *Checking Executive Power: Presidential Impeachment in Comparative Perspective*. Westport: Praeger, 2003.

Berger, Raoul. *Impeachment: The Constitutional Problems*. Cambridge: Harvard University Press, 1973.

Black, Charles L. *Impeachment: A Handbook*. New Haven: Yale University Press, 1998.

Chafetz, Josh. *Congress's Constitution: Legislative Authority and the Separation of Powers*. New Haven: Yale University Press, 2017.

Gerhardt, Michael J. *The Federal Impeachment Process: A Constitutional and Historical Analysis*, 2nd ed. Chicago: University of Chicago Press, 2000.

Hoffer, Peter Charles, and N. E. H. Hull. *Impeachment in America, 1635–1805*. New Haven: Yale University Press, 1984.

Klarman, Michael. *The Framers' Coup: The Making of the United States Constitution*. New York: Oxford University Press, 2016.

Kyvig, David E. *The Age of Impeachment: American Constitutional Culture since 1960*. Lawrence: University Press of Kansas, 2008.

Labovitz, John. *Presidential Impeachment*. New Haven: Yale University Press, 1978.

Posner, Richard A. *An Affair of State: The Investigation, Impeachment, and Trial of President Clinton*. Cambridge: Harvard University Press, 1999.

Sunstein, Cass R. *Impeachment: A Citizens' Guide*. Princeton: Princeton University Press, 2017.

Whittington, Keith E. *Constitutional Construction: Divided Powers and Constitutional Meaning*. Cambridge: Harvard University Press, 1995.

SCHOLARLY ARTICLES

Amar, Akhil Reed. "On Impeaching Presidents." *Hofstra Law Review* 28, no. 2 (1999): 291–341.

Chafetz, Josh. "Impeachment and Assassination." *Minnesota Law Review* 95 (2010): 347–423.

Gerhardt, Michael J. "The Lessons of Impeachment History." *George Washington Law Review* 67 (1999): 603–625.

———. "The Special Constitutional Structure of the Federal Impeachment Process." *Law and Contemporary Problems* 63 (Winter/Spring 2000): 245–256.

Katyal, Neal Kumar. "Impeachment as Congressional Constitutional Interpretation." *Law and Contemporary Problems* 63 (Winter/Spring 2000): 169–192.

Klarman, Michael J. "Constitutional Fetishism and the Clinton Impeachment Debate." *Virginia Law Review* 85, no. 4 (May 1999): 631–659.

O'Sullivan, Julie R. "The Interaction between Impeachment and the Independent Counsel Statute." *Georgetown Law Journal* 86, no. 6 (1998): 2193–2266.

Rakove, Jack N. "Statement on the Background and History of Impeachment." *George Washington Law Review* 67 (1999): 682–692.

In addition, Larry's treatise—*American Constitutional Law*, 3rd ed., University Treatise Series (Foundation Press), 2000—contains a substantial discussion of impeachment at pages 152 to 202.

INDEX

Laurence Tribe is the Carl M. Loeb University Professor and a professor of constitutional law at Harvard University. One of America's foremost constitutional scholars, he is the coauthor of *Uncertain Justice* (with Joshua Matz) and numerous other books and articles. He lives in Brookline, Massachusetts.

Joshua Matz, a graduate of Harvard Law School and a constitutional lawyer, is the publisher of *Take Care*, which provides legal analysis of the Trump presidency. He lives in Washington, DC.